The Welfare State in Europe

The Welfare State in Europe

Economic and Social Perspectives

Second Edition

Pierre Pestieau and Mathieu Lefebvre

OXFORD
UNIVERSITY PRESS

OXFORD
UNIVERSITY PRESS

Great Clarendon Street, Oxford, OX2 6DP,
United Kingdom

Oxford University Press is a department of the University of Oxford.
It furthers the University's objective of excellence in research, scholarship,
and education by publishing worldwide. Oxford is a registered trade mark of
Oxford University Press in the UK and in certain other countries

© P. Pestieau and M. Lefebvre 2018

The moral rights of the authors have been asserted

First Edition published in 2005

Second Edition published in 2018

Impression: 1

All rights reserved. No part of this publication may be reproduced, stored in
a retrieval system, or transmitted, in any form or by any means, without the
prior permission in writing of Oxford University Press, or as expressly permitted
by law, by licence or under terms agreed with the appropriate reprographics
rights organization. Enquiries concerning reproduction outside the scope of the
above should be sent to the Rights Department, Oxford University Press, at the
address above

You must not circulate this work in any other form
and you must impose this same condition on any acquirer

Published in the United States of America by Oxford University Press
198 Madison Avenue, New York, NY 10016, United States of America

British Library Cataloguing in Publication Data
Data available

Library of Congress Control Number: 2018938835

ISBN 978-0-19-881705-5

Printed in Great Britain by
Ashford Colour Press Ltd, Gosport, Hampshire

Preface to the Second Edition

More than a decade ago, the first author published *The Welfare State in the European Union. Economic and Social Perspectives*. The motivation for writing that book was the urgency of defending the welfare state, which was under continuous attack from conservative circles, and at the same time, essential in a world of increasing socio-economic disparities. Twelve years later, the need for an active and performing welfare state is more than ever acute, as the social divide has intensified in Europe with the onset of the global financial crisis. High and rising inequality hampers social cohesion and fuels distrusts in institutions, which have yet been responsible for the prosperity Europe has enjoyed over the last century. For this reason, the author thought it was about time to update this book and expand it to analyse how the welfare state should address these new challenges. He asked his colleague, Mathieu Lefebvre, to join him in this new endeavour. Together, both authors have slightly changed the title of the book by dropping the direct reference to the European Union, since they now encompass all Europe. The basic structure of the book has not changed, however. Besides the updating of the statistical material, some new material concerning long-term care and recent developments in employment policies and health care have been added. This edition also addresses the new challenge facing modern welfare states, namely how to cope with the rising socio-economic divides that plague our societies and lead us to populism, as well as what we can expect from the digital revolution.

Contents

List of Figures	xi
List of Tables	xiii
About the Authors	xv

1. Introduction	1
1.1 Questioning the Welfare State	1
1.2 Definitions and Objectives	4
1.3 Equity Versus Efficiency	5
1.4 Why the Welfare State?	7
1.5 The Social Divide and the Populist Vote	9
2. Poverty and inequality	11
2.1 Introduction	11
2.2 Comparing Poverty	12
2.3 Comparing Inequality	15
2.4 Redistributive Effect of Social Protection	17
2.4.1 Effect on the Poverty of Households	17
2.4.2 Aggregate Effect on Poverty and Inequality	18
2.4.3 Permanent Inequality and Poverty across European Countries	21
2.5 Social Divide and Populism	23
2.6 Conclusion	25
3. Social Spending	26
3.1 Introduction	26
3.2 Level and Profile	26
3.3 Evolution	30
3.4 Problems of Comparison	33
3.5 The Entitlement Problem	36
3.6 Conclusion	37
4. Revenue Sources	38
4.1 Introduction	38
4.2 Financing the Welfare State	38

Contents

4.3 Alternative Sources	40
4.3.1 Regressive Taxation	40
4.3.2 Adverse Effect on Competition	41
4.3.3 A Shrinking Tax Base	43
4.4 Social Insurance Contributions	45
4.5 Conclusion	46
5. Types of Social Protection	**47**
5.1 Introduction	47
5.2 Taxonomy of Social Protection	48
5.3 Implications of Alternative Regimes	51
5.3.1 Redistribution	51
5.3.2 Incentives	51
5.3.3 Political Support	52
5.4 Styles of Welfare State	55
5.5 The Active versus Passive Welfare State	57
5.6 Alternative Approaches	59
5.7 Conclusion	60
6. Social Protection and Globalization	**61**
6.1 Introduction	61
6.2 Benefits of Globalization	62
6.3 Tax Competition and Race to the Bottom	64
6.4 Some Evidence	67
6.5 Incidence of Redistribution	69
6.6 The Open Method of Coordination	73
6.7 Another View	75
6.8 Conclusion	75
7. Welfare State and Economic Efficiency	**78**
7.1 Introduction	78
7.2 Individual Behaviour	79
7.3 A Numerical Example	82
7.4 Aggregate Evidence	85
7.5 An Historical View	87
7.6 Conclusion	88
8. Performance and Efficiency of the Welfare State	**89**
8.1 Introduction	89
8.2 The Matthew Effect	91
8.3 Administrative Costs	93
8.4 Doing Better with Less	94
8.5 The Performance of the Welfare State	98
8.6 Conclusion	102

Contents

9. Social versus Private Insurance	105
9.1 Introduction	105
9.2 Social Insurance	106
9.2.1 The State, the Market, and the Family	106
9.2.2 The Specificity of Social Insurance	106
9.2.3 Expenditure for Insurance, Private, and Public	108
9.2.4 Charity	110
9.3 Standard Cases for Social Insurance	111
9.3.1 Market Failures	111
9.3.2 Social Insurance as a Redistributive Device	112
9.4 New Arguments Pro and Con	113
9.4.1 Increasing Demand and Evolving Labour Market	113
9.4.2 Payroll Taxation, Fiscal Competition, and Social Dumping	114
9.4.3 Credibility and Commitment	115
9.5 The Limits of Redistributive Policy	116
9.6 Implications and Conclusion	117
10. Old Age Pensions	123
10.1 Introduction	123
10.2 The Pension Systems	124
10.3 Old-Age Poverty	126
10.4 The Challenges of Pension Systems	128
10.4.1 Population Ageing	128
10.4.2 Employment of the Elderly	129
10.5 The Future of Pensions	133
10.6 Conclusion	135
11. Health Care	137
11.1 Introduction	137
11.2 Expenditure on Health Care	138
11.3 Cost Containment	142
11.4 Inequality in Health and Health Care	144
11.5 Conclusion	148
12. Long-Term Care	150
12.1 Introduction	150
12.2 Informal Care and LTC Private Insurance	152
12.3 Public Spending Projections	153
12.4 The Design of LTC Social Insurance	154
12.5 Conclusion	156
13. Unemployment and Poverty	157
13.1 Introduction	157
13.2 Unemployment and Employment	158

Contents

13.3 Unemployment Insurance	161
13.4 Flexibility and Protection	163
13.5 The Changing Nature of Employment	167
13.5.1 Posted Workers	167
13.5.2 Uberization and Automation	168
13.5.3 The Universal Basic Income	169
13.6 In-Work Poverty	171
13.7 Conclusion	173
14. Family Policy	**174**
14.1 Introduction	174
14.2 Evolution and Structure of Child Benefits	174
14.3 Child Poverty	177
14.4 Early Child Development Policies	179
14.5 Types of Child Care Policies	181
14.6 Conclusion	182
15. Conclusion	**184**
15.1 Two Views	184
15.2 The Acquired Rights Issue	185
15.3 Towards a European Social Protection	186
15.4 Looking Ahead: Two Challenges	187
15.4.1 Digital Revolution	187
15.4.2 The Social Divide	188
15.5 Wrapping Up	189
Glossary	193
Bibliography	201
Name Index	211
Subject Index	213

List of Figures

1.1.	Welfare state and social protection	5
1.2.	Equity and efficiency	6
2.1.	Evolution of poverty in five countries	14
2.2.	Lorenz curves	15
2.3.	Evolution of inequality in five countries	16
2.4.	Social expenditure and poverty, 2015	19
2.5.	Social expenditure and income inequality, 2015	20
3.1.	Social spending and GDP per head, (a) 1980, (b) 2015	28
3.2.	Social spending as a share of GDP, 1980–2014	31
3.3.	Real growth of social spending by functions at the EC level (1980 = 100)	33
3.4.	Gross and net social spending as a percentage of GDP, 2011	35
3.5.	Convergence of gross and net social spending	36
4.1.	Time trend in implicit tax rate on labour	42
4.2.	Average tax on labour and tax wedges: EU28	43
5.1.	Percentage of people who agree or strongly agree that government should reduce differences in income levels	55
6.1.	Race to the bottom	65
6.2.	Implicit tax rate on capital	68
6.3.	Social spending and openness	70
6.4.	Redistribution and openness	71
6.5.	Poverty alleviation, and openness	71
7.1.	Excess burden of wage taxation	79
7.2.	Disincentive for workers	83
7.3.	Disincentive for beneficiaries	84
7.4.	Social spending in 2015 and per capita GDP growth rate over 2000–2015	85
8.1.	Productive inefficiency	95
8.2.	Evolution of SPI performance indicators, EU15 1995–2014	101

List of Figures

8.3.	Convergence of DEA performance indicators, EU15 1995–2014	102
9.1.	Social spending and private insurance % GDP, 2014	108
9.2.	Private to social insurance ratio	109
10.1.	Old-age dependency ratio	129
10.2.	Change in gross public pension expenditure between 2013 and 2060 (in percentage points of GDP)	134
11.1.	Public health spending (a) high spending (b) low spending	140
11.2.	Persons reporting an unmet need for a medical examination because of problems of access (%)	147
11.3.	Persons reporting an unmet need for a dental examination because of problems of access (%)	147

List of Tables

2.1.	Income, poverty and inequality in the EU28, 2015	13
2.2.	Poverty alleviation (1995–2015)	18
2.3.	Impact of social spending on poverty and income inequality (2015)	19
2.4.	Life-cycle income	21
3.1.	Total expenditure for social protection as a percentage of GDP, 1995, 2005, and 2015	27
3.2.	Social protection benefits by function, 2014	29
3.3.	Convergence of social spending (1995–2014), EU 28	32
3.4.	Gross to net social spending as a percentage of GDP, 2011	35
4.1.	Financing of social protection (in %)	39
4.2.	Average tax on labour and tax wedges in 2015	43
5.1.	Taxonomy of social transfers	48
5.2.	The rank role of welfare state. Decommodification scores	49
5.3.	Generosity versus redistribution	50
5.4.	Two views on the welfare state	54
6.1.	Prisoner's dilemma	66
6.2.	Tax game: capital income taxation	67
6.3.	Inclusion indicators (2014)	74
A.6.1.	Openness and redistribution	76
A.6.2.	Normalized indicators: 2014	77
8.1.	Administrative costs as a percentage of social security benefit expenditures in Europe	93
8.2	Efficiency studies	97
8.3	Performance indicators EU 28: 2014	100
A.8.1.	Normalized Partial Indicators EU 28: 2014	104
9.1.	Resources of elderly people	107
9.2.	Social protection and private insurance in Europe, 2014 (% GDP)	109
9.3.	Comparative advantage of social over private insurance	117
10.1.	Expenditure on old-age pension: 2000–2014	125
10.2.	Poverty and inequality at old-age (65+): 2015	127

List of Tables

10.3.	Employment and activity rate of the elderly: 2016	130
11.1.	Total spending on health and the relative part of public spending, 2000–2015	139
11.2.	Public health care coverage and out-of-pocket payment	144
11.3	Persons reporting an unmet need for medical acts because of problems of access: 2015 (%)	146
11.4.	Redistributive indices for the financing source of health care	148
11.5.	Comparative advantages of private versus public health care insurance	149
12.1.	Total Public Spending on LTC as % of GDP	154
13.1.	Employment, activity and unemployment rates. Persons aged 15–64 (%): EU28 2016	159
13.2.	Labour market policy in the EU: 2015	162
13.3.	Minimum wage and employment protection: 2014	164
13.4.	Basic income estimations	170
13.5.	In-work poverty in the EU: 2015	172
14.1.	Family allowances and tax breaks in 2014	176
14.2.	Family allowances and poverty: 2014	178
14.3.	Family allowances and poverty among children: 2014	179
14.4.	Index of family-related policies	182

About the Authors

Pierre Pestieau received his Ph.D. from Yale. He has taught economics at Cornell University and then at the University of Liege till 2008. He is now member of CORE, Louvain-la-Neuve and Professor Emeritus at the University of Liege. He is also associate member of PSE, Paris, IZA and a CESIfo Fellow. His major interests are pension economics, social insurance, inheritance taxation, and redistributive policies. He has published many articles in leading economic journals. He has also written books devoted to the performance of public enterprises, inheritance taxation, the underground economy, social security and the welfare state.

Mathieu Lefebvre holds a Ph.D. from the University of Liège. He is an associate professor at the University of Strasbourg where he is a member of the BETA (Bureau d'Economie Théorique et Appliquée). Previously, he has held positions at the University of Lyon and the University of Montpellier. His research is in the areas of public economics, labour economics, and behavioural economics and includes, among other topics, the evaluation of labour market policies towards the elderly, the performance of social protection, and the measurement of poverty at old age.

1

Introduction

> **KEY CONCEPTS**
>
> altruism
> constitutional approach
> efficiency or Pareto efficiency
> equity
> equity-efficiency trade-off
> leaky bucket
> market failure
> merit good
> political economy
> social divide
> veil of ignorance

1.1. Questioning the Welfare State

Unquestionably, the welfare state is a fundamental and distinguishing feature of the European social model. A major achievement of post-war Europe, it has enabled societies to cope with tremendous economic and social upheavals and adaptations. Social cohesion, which is the basis and the outcome of the welfare state, is an objective of European states as much now as it was in 1945, when the welfare state began. Yet, in recent years the welfare state has come under increasing attack. Although in Europe there continues to be a large degree of consensus that it is the responsibility of government to insure that nobody who is poor, sick, disabled, unemployed, or old is left deprived, there are mounting calls to roll back spending on the welfare state. Two main charges are raised: that it fails to achieve some of its main objectives, and that it is responsible for a decline in economic performance.

Although we believe that these charges are to be taken seriously, one needs to remember past achievements to know how much we would lose were the welfare state to disappear. We believe that saving the welfare state is a top priority, one that is as important as saving the Parthenon or the Mona Lisa.

In this book we intend to provide a balanced and informed account of the current functioning and performance of the welfare state in Europe,[1] as well as some thoughts regarding its prospects in an increasingly integrated world. Written by two economists whose concern is both equity and efficiency, this book gives a set of answers to a number of important questions regarding the current social situation of Europe. These questions concern the actual working and expected evolution of its welfare states, and are the subject of academic research among economists, political scientists, and sociologists. More importantly, they are the daily concern of European policymakers and citizens.

The following questions correspond to the fifteen chapters of this book:

1. What is the welfare state? What are its functions? How can it be distinguished from concepts such as social protection and social insurance?
2. What is the current state of poverty, deprivation, and social inequality in the European Union? Can we say that the welfare state contributes to their reduction? What can be expected in the near future?
3. What is the size and the structure of the welfare state? Does it vary across countries, over time? Can we, in particular, speak of a decline in social spending in the recent past?
4. How is the welfare state financed in different countries? Does it rely on payroll taxes or on general taxation?
5. What types of social protection exist in Europe? More precisely, are benefits linked to contributions, attached to means testing, or are they universalist?
6. One often hears that factor mobility and economic integration make it difficult to redistribute income, thus leading to what is called social dumping. How serious is such a threat?

---

[1] This book is about Europe. However, most data come from the European Union, namely EUROSTAT. We will consider different sets of member countries. First, we have the EU15 that includes the first fifteen members. Then we have the EU28 that includes the members that progressively joined the EU with its extension towards the countries from Eastern Europe. These countries are, by year of entry: (1958) Belgium, France, Germany, Italy, Luxembourg, Netherlands; (1973) Denmark, Ireland, United Kingdom; (1981) Greece; (1986) Portugal, Spain; (1995) Austria, Finland, Sweden; (2004) Cyprus, Czechia, Estonia, Hungary, Latvia, Lithuania, Malta, Poland, Slovakia, Slovenia; (2007) Bulgaria, Romania; (2013) Croatia. We also use EU27, thus excluding Croatia, the last comer, because of data availability. After the completion of Brexit, the EU membership will also include 27 countries. But at the time this book is written, the UK is still a member of the EU.

Introduction

7. Is the welfare state a real obstacle to economic efficiency and economic growth because of distorted incentives and large deficits?
8. Can we say that, compared to market activities, the welfare state's activities are costly and inefficient? What is the performance of the welfare state with regard to fighting poverty and reducing inequalities?
9. What are the comparative advantages of social and private insurance in reducing uncertainty for the individual?
10. Social security in Europe is mainly unfunded and publicly managed. How can it meet the challenge of demographic ageing and economic stagnation?
11. Health care in Europe is public, and it faces huge financial problems. How can one maintain its financial soundness and universal accessibility?
12. How do European governments stand regarding the rapid increase of needs for long-term care?
13. Can we really assert that there is an unavoidable trade-off between poverty and unemployment, and that most European countries, except Germany, the UK, and Ireland, have chosen the latter?
14. Most European countries have programs of family allowances that pursue certain objectives: to foster fertility, avoid child poverty, and achieve horizontal equity. What is the performance of the welfare state regarding these objectives?
15. Finally, how seriously can we consider privatization as a partial way of solving some of the problems of the European welfare state? More generally, should the welfare state in Europe be saved at all costs? If so, how?

To pre-empt the answer to the last question, it is our conviction that the welfare state must be saved, and quickly. Its main functions cannot be fulfilled by either the market or the family. The fulfilment of those functions is an essential part of what can be considered a modern and democratic society. Reforming it is of utmost urgency because its present operation cannot resist the challenges that lie ahead. Saving the welfare state is possible, but it requires some fundamental changes in the institutions. Above all, it requires changes in the behaviour of European citizens who all too often, as the saying goes, 'want to have their cake and eat it too'.

Over the last few decades, demographic, economic, and social changes have occurred across Europe with profound implications for the welfare states. The ageing of the population, the decreasing employment rate, the change in the gender balance, the increase in the demand for support services are typical of these changes. Yet most important are the phenomenon of vanishing compliance and the increasing opportunism of all the economic players. We are talking about ageing but healthy workers who use disability insurance to get a well-paid early retirement. We are talking about employers who use the unemployment insurance to get rid of workers they find too costly; or farmers who insist on keeping subsidies that no longer have any economic justification. We are talking about the practice on the part of the national governments of tax competition and social dumping to attract foreign investors and employment. Changing such opportunistic behaviour and rediscovering some sense of solidarity are surely big challenges facing our welfare states.

The rest of this introduction is devoted to the definition of the concepts of the welfare state, social protection, and social insurance, and to their rationale, as well as to the trade-off between equity and efficiency. It ends with what can be viewed as the main challenge of European welfare states, namely the mounting socio-economic divide.

1.2. Definitions and Objectives

It is tempting not to define the welfare state. As Barr (1992)[2] puts it, 'defining the welfare state continues to baffle writers and much high-grade effort has been vested in the search'.[3] Indeed, let us just indicate what it comprises and what its functions are. The welfare state consists of a number of programs through which the government pursues the goal of social protection on behalf of citizens against certain categories of risk, of social assistance for the needy, and of encouraging the consumption of certain services such as education, housing,, and child care. This is depicted in Figure 1.1.

These programs were introduced to meet certain objectives, the two most important being to relieve poverty and to provide a sense of security to all. When assessing the performance of the welfare state, it is important to do so with respect to these goals. Assistance and insurance are not the only objectives of the welfare state. Some of its programs also have effects on macroeconomic stabilization and growth. Conversely, some assistance and some insurance can be achieved by institutions other than the government. Insurance can be provided by the market, and both insurance and assistance can be provided by the family and more broadly by the non-profit sector. As

---

[2] Compared to Barr (1998), this book focuses more on the redistribution issue and less on the insurance mission of the welfare state.

[3] One could use Sandmo's (1995) definition: 'The welfare state is a subsection of the public sector, concerned with redistribution (via social security and social assistance) and the provision of those social goods which have a strong redistributive element, like health care and education.' See also Sandmo (1991).

Introduction

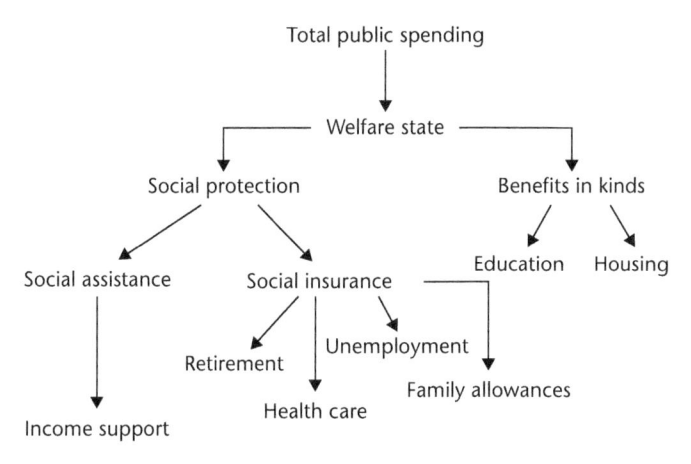

```
                    Total public spending
                            │
                            ▼
              ┌────── Welfare state ──────┐
              ▼                            ▼
       Social protection            Benefits in kinds
        ╱         ╲                   ╱         ╲
       ▼           ▼            Education     Housing
  Social      Social ──────────────┐
  assistance  insurance            │
     │        ╱   │  ╲             │
     │  Retirement │ Unemployment  │
     │            │                │
     │            ▼       Family allowances
     ▼         Health care
  Income support
```

Figure 1.1. Welfare state and social protection

will be shown, neither the market nor the family can have the negative impact on the working of the economy that is attributed to the welfare state. Yet, the scope of the family and the non-profit sector is much narrower than that of the welfare state; further, the market achieves little, if any, redistribution.

1.3. Equity Versus Efficiency

Throughout this book, we shall be concerned with the equity-efficiency quandary, which is at the heart of modern public economics. To illustrate this quandary, consider a simple economy with two individuals, whom we shall refer to as Robinson Crusoe and Tintin. Assume, initially, that Robinson Crusoe has eight oranges, while Tintin has only two. This seems inequitable. Assume that we play the role of government and attempt to transfer three oranges from Robinson to Tintin, but in the process one orange gets lost. This refers to Okun's (1974) notion that money transferred from rich to poor is carried in a *leaky bucket*: 'The money must be carried from the rich to the poor in a leaky bucket. Some of it will simply disappear in transit, so the poor will not receive all the money that is taken from the rich.' Hence Robinson ends up with five oranges, and Tintin with four. We have eliminated most of the inequity, but the total number of oranges available has been diminished. Thus we see a trade-off between efficiency, the total number of oranges available, and equity, the way they are divided.

This trade-off between equity and efficiency is at the heart of many discussions of public policy. It is often represented as in Figure 1.2 by the AB curve.

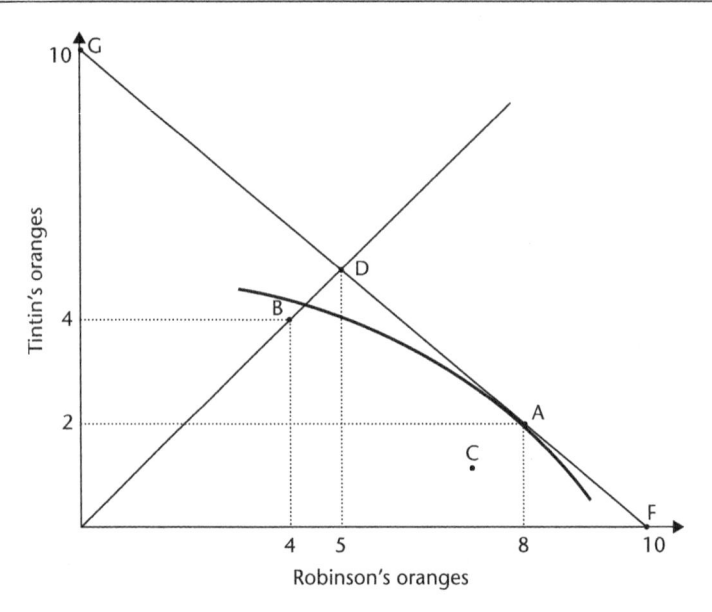

Figure 1.2. Equity and efficiency

A is the initial endowment, B is the equal-sharing allocation which involves a loss of more than one orange.

To get more equity, some amount of efficiency must be sacrificed. Two questions are debated. First, there is disagreement about the nature of the trade-off. In order to reduce inequality, how much efficiency do we have to give up? Will one or two oranges be lost in the process of transferring three oranges from Robinson to Tintin? For instance, the attempt to reduce inequality by progressive taxation is commonly regarded as giving rise to work disincentives, thereby reducing efficiency. How big are these disincentives? This is the question to which we will return.

Secondly, there is disagreement about how much value should be assigned to a decrease in inequality, and how much to a decrease in efficiency. Some people claim that inequality is the central problem of society, and that society should simply minimize the extent of inequality, regardless of the efficiency consequences. Others claim that efficiency is the central issue. Still others maintain that in the long run the best way to help the poor is not to worry about how the pie is to be divided, but rather to 'increase' the size of the pie, by growing as rapidly as possible so that there is more for everyone. This is the famous and controversial trickle-down theory.

Maximizing efficiency is frequently equated with maximizing the value of national income. A program is said to be inefficient, if it reduces national income, for example, through discouraging work or investment. By contrast, a program is said to promote equality, if it transfers resources from someone richer to someone poorer.

Although this would provide a first approximation, economists have devoted considerable attention to assessing the circumstances in which using such measures might be misleading or inapplicable. Suppose the government increased taxes and squandered the proceeds, while, in order to maintain the same standard of living, individuals worked harder and longer than they had previously. National income as conventionally measured would go up, but 'efficiency'—as we normally think of it—would decrease.

To assess efficiency gains, one uses the concept of Pareto improvement instead of national income. To characterize an efficient allocation, one speaks of Pareto optimality or efficiency. In Figure 1.2, going from C to A implies a Pareto improving move such that everyone is better off (or at least not worse off). Both A and D are Pareto optimal, since from these points one cannot make someone better off without making someone else worse off.

If one had to choose the most important proposition in modern economic theory, one would very likely pick Adam Smith's 'invisible hand': a laissez-faire economy resulting in a Pareto-efficient allocation. In other words, the competitive market leads to a point on the line FG in Figure 1.2. The allocations F, A, D, G are all Pareto-optimal, which does not mean that from an equity viewpoint they are equally desirable. Thus, even if the market is Pareto-optimal, there are grounds for government action if the resulting distribution of income, or consumption, is socially undesirable or even repugnant.

There are other reasons for government activity and these are the so-called market failures. Imperfect competition, externalities, public goods, imperfect information are sources of such failures. To illustrate: the market outcome can be an allocation such as C in Figure 1.2.

Note, however, that the presence of market failures is not a sufficient condition for government intervention. One has to make sure that the correction itself is not going to cost more than the slack it intends to correct. Indeed, we have seen that redistribution implies some efficiency cost. This is also true of other programs, even those aimed at restoring efficiency. Modern public economics is very much concerned with the right balance between market and state failures. It is noteworthy that from 1945 to about 1980, the pendulum first swung towards market failures; most recently, over the last two decades, it has swung towards state failures. Now it seems to be swinging back towards market failures.

1.4. Why the Welfare State?

There are a number of theories that explain the birth and the development of the welfare state. Such an explanation is, indeed, needed when starting from a market or a laissez-faire economy that leads to an efficient outcome at best, but does not have any prior concern for equity.

Without being exhaustive, we suggest several explanations for this: market failures, social contract, ethical norms, paternalistic altruism, class interest, political economy. These different explanations can be combined as we will show throughout this book.

1. Market failure. As just seen, there are several areas where the market forces are not able to achieve efficiency. When individual decisions have a positive, or a negative, effect on the welfare or the behaviour of other agents, the price system is often unable to reflect what is called an 'externality'. For example, if investing in education has a benefit not only for me, but also for society as a whole, my market choice will be guided exclusively by my individual return, and not by the social benefit it implies. Here is a clear case for public intervention in the name of efficiency.

2. The social contract behind the 'veil of ignorance'. One can imagine that in adopting a given welfare state, people are guided by some degree of impersonality. They are in a situation such that they don't know their ability, their health status, their life expectancy just as if they were at time zero of their own existence and that of their offspring. Behind such a 'veil of ignorance', people rationally favour social protection, redistributive transfers, and progressive taxation as insurance against bad luck. But this argument has recently been challenged by the assumption that individuals know more and more about their future even at the start of their lives. Based on the social, economic, and medical status of one's parents, a large part of future uncertainty can be controlled. As a consequence, this 'behind the veil' argument is no longer viewed as a good foundation for the welfare state. Or, to put it differently, it explains why the welfare state could eventually shrink and become less and less redistributive.[4]

3. Ethical norm. According to Kant and other philosophers, self-interested individuals could follow a number of ethical norms that are contrary to, or independent of, their immediate interests, and which constrain them in their daily lives. Accordingly, people have two distinct personalities, their self-interested selves being essentially out of joint with their ethical selves. Self-interested preferences guide their day-to-day participation in the market economy, while ethical ones apply to their participation in collective decision-making, including support to the welfare state.[5]

---

[4] This is at the heart of the 'new social question', developed by Rosenvallon (1995).
[5] This leads to the so-called merit goods.

Introduction

4. Class interest. This is the Marxist view, according to which the welfare state serves the interest of the capitalist class in two ways: by increasing the quantity and quality of the labour force (the reproduction of labour power) and by maintaining social harmony (the reproduction of the relations of production). For example, public health can improve the productivity of the labour force as well as defuse a potential source of tensions.

5. Altruism. Altruism is a hypothesis used by economists to explain why taxpayers are prepared to vote and to pay for some kind of redistribution to the poor. It is better to talk of paternalistic altruism, as it often takes the form of providing the less well-off with specific services or aid, such as health care or food stamps. Implicit in this view is the idea that the tax payers do not trust the poor to spend any transfer in cash wisely.

6. Political economy. Most of the above hypotheses are of a normative nature. They do not really explain why the welfare state is what it is, and whether or not its size and structure are appropriate. To do so, we have to focus on the setting within which political decisions are made. One development within this framework has been the constitutional approach. Accordingly, the desired type of social protection is chosen at a constitutional stage of choice. At this point people are to a considerable extent uncertain about their own position and about the implications of different types of social protection for their own interests. Therefore they may be guided by the kind of consideration that underlines the ethical view just considered, and adopt a criterion of social welfare such as the Rawlsian maximin (maximizing the utility of the worst-off individuals) or the utilitarian sum of individuals' utilities. In the second stage of choice, actual tax rates and benefit levels are governed by the political process, direct or representative democracy, with possible bureaucratic pitfalls.

1.5. The Social Divide and the Populist Vote. A Challenge for the Welfare State

The social divide has been on the rise in Europe over the past decades. High and rising inequality harms our societies and hampers social cohesion. It can explain the populist revolt illustrated by the election of Donald Trump, the victory of Brexit, and the electoral success of the French Front National. As expressed by Michael Sandel (2017), this revolt resulted from the failure of elites to grasp the discontent roiling politics in democracies around the world. (It) marked the rejection of a technocratic approach to politics incapable of understanding the resentments of voters who feel the economy and the culture have left them behind.

The socio-economic divide is not only about juxtaposing 'the rich' and 'the poor' in terms of wages or incomes. The phenomenon is a complex web involving accumulated wealth or debts, but it also has to do with health status, quality of jobs, education, and perception of social mobility, and migration threat. This complexity constitutes a huge test for the welfare state whose toolbox is not prepared to cope with these problems. Adapting our policy instruments to deal with the social divide is one of the most serious challenges faced by modern welfare states.

2

Poverty and Inequality

KEY CONCEPTS

equivalence scale
Gini coefficient
Lorenz curve
populism
poverty line
poverty rate
regression

2.1. Introduction

The failure of the market system to satisfactorily achieve the objectives that our society has set itself is at the heart of the welfare state. This failure is of two types: the 'traditional' market failure that comes from the inability to produce an efficient allocation of resources, and the rather 'normal'[1] failure to provide an equitable outcome. To measure the performance of the market and of the welfare state in terms of equity, we focus on two standard concepts: poverty and inequality.

Poverty and inequality are indeed two ways of characterizing the equity of income distribution. But a number of economists[2] do not want to consider distributional issues at all. According to them, any ideas about the right income distribution are value judgments, and there is no scientific way to resolve differences in matters of ethics. The problem with this view is that

---

[1] Normal as long as altruism is assumed away.
[2] The best advocate of this view is undoubtedly Robert Lucas (2005) when he writes: 'Of the tendencies that are harmful to sound economics, the most seductive, and in my opinion the most poisonous, is to focus on questions of distribution... The potential for improving the lives of poor people by finding different ways of distributing current production is nothing compared to the apparently limitless potential of increasing production'.

decision-makers care about the distributional implications of policy. Yet if economists ignore distribution, policymakers may end up paying no attention at all to efficiency, focusing only on distributional issues.

In this chapter, we approach the issue of income distribution from the viewpoint of poverty and inequality. Then we look at the effect of social protection on each one and we conclude with the question of populism and social divide.

2.2. Comparing Poverty

In measuring poverty and income inequality, we will focus on the household as the reference unit, and on disposable income as the source of well-being for the household. To standardize the disposable income of heterogeneous households we use an equivalence scale. This is a rather arbitrary choice and it can have implications. The scale recommended by the OECD is used most often in the figures presented here. It assigns a weight of 1.0 to the first adult in a household, 0.5 to each additional adult, and 0.3 to each child. The equivalent (or standardized) income of a household is obtained by dividing its disposable income by the equivalence scale value, e.g. 2.1 for a couple with two children.

Income distribution can be considered in terms of its dispersion. Thus one looks at the entire distribution of income. Alternatively, it can be studied by focusing on the bottom of the distribution, namely on the extent of poverty. To measure the level of poverty one traditionally computes the number of households below the 'poverty line', a fixed level of real income considered enough to provide a minimally adequate standard of living. Not surprisingly, there is no agreement on how to determine what is adequate. The poverty lines can be based on basic needs (the cost of minimum food requirements) or on some percentage of mean or median income. The latter approach is based on the idea that poverty is a situation of relative deprivation, and that the poverty line should, therefore, be linked to some indicator of the standard of living in society. We will use this approach, which is objective, financial, and relative. It is particularly fit for international comparisons. Unless mentioned otherwise, our poverty line will be 50 per cent of median income.

Table 2.1 shows the proportion of people below the poverty line (50 per cent of median income) in EU28 plus the US. In 2015, poverty rates range from 5.3 in Czechia[3] and in Finland to 19.8 in Spain. One can distinguish countries with relatively low rates (below 7 per cent): Czechia, Finland, the Netherlands and France; and those with high rates (above 15 per cent): Bulgaria, Romania, Spain and Greece. This can be contrasted with a rate of 17.5 per cent in the US.

---

[3] The alternative, and less formal name, recently introduced, for the Czech Republic.

Table 2.1. Income, poverty and inequality in the EU28, 2015

Country	GDP per head (2010 dollars and prices)	Poverty rate (50%)	Persistent poverty rate (50%)	Gini coefficient (%)	Social spending (% of GDP)*
Austria	42 750	8.3	4.7	27.2	30.0
Belgium	39 944	7.8	3.4	26.2	30.3
Bulgaria	–	15.5	10.9	37.0	18.5
Croatia	–	13.5	7.7	30.4	21.6
Cyprus	–	9.0	2.5	33.6	23.0
Czechia	28 729	5.3	1.3	25.0	19.7
Denmark	42 198	7.1	1.8	27.4	32.9
Estonia	25 587	12.5	6.7	34.8	15.1
Finland	37 582	5.3	2.4	25.2	31.9
France	36 789	6.5	2.8	29.2	34.3
Germany	42 850	10.2	5.3	30.1	29.1
Greece	24 306	15.0	8.6	34.2	26.0
Hungary	23 854	9.0	3.6	28.2	19.9
Ireland	50 217	8.8	2.8	29.8	20.6
Italy	32 677	13.4	8.2	32.4	29.9
Latvia	22 098	14.7	5.7	35.4	14.5
Lithuania	25 609	14.4	7.9	37.9	14.7
Luxembourg	87 313	8.2	5.6	28.5	22.7
Malta	–	8.5	6.2	28.1	18.2
Netherlands	45 305	5.8	2.3	26.7	30.9
Poland	23 884	10.7	5.5	30.6	19.1
Portugal	26 243	13.8	7.8	34.0	26.9
Romania	–	19.8	13.6	37.4	14.8
Slovakia	27 417	8.4	5.0	23.7	18.5
Slovenia	28 151	8.4	3.9	24.5	24.1
Spain	32 209	15.9	10.5	34.6	25.4
Sweden	44 090	8.0	2.7	25.2	29.6
United Kingdom	38 378	9.7	2.6	32.4	27.4
United States	51 450	17.5*	n.a.	39.4*	19.2

Note: * stands for the year 2014
Sources: Eurostat (2017a, 2017b), OECD (2016a, 2016b, 2016c)

If one were to look in more detail, one would observe the types of individuals who are particularly subject to poverty: young households and female-headed households in which no husband is present. Low educational level and persistent unemployment are also factors of poverty. The size of the family, particularly when no economies of scale are accounted for, also leads to poverty. This pattern of poverty according to household types applies to most European countries. As we see below, the observed poverty levels are the result of two main sources: the market outcome and the presence and effectiveness of social protection.

Admittedly our approach to poverty is a bit simple. It can only be explained by our concern for international comparisons. Clearly, sociologists tend to go deeper and look for causes. For example, one might wonder what the long-term unemployed, young people looking for work and on training schemes, single mothers, young couples crippled by the impossibility of paying bills and rent, all have in common? In an interesting paper, Castel (2003) puts forward the hypothesis that they express a particular mode of dissociation from the social bond: a disaffiliation. This is a condition of misery different from that of poverty in the strict sense. The latter can perhaps be read as a state, whose forms can be listed in terms of lack (lack of earnings, of housing, of medical care, of education, lack of power or of respect). By contrast, situations of destitution constitute an effect at the place where two vectors meet: one, the axis of integration/non-integration through work; the other, an axis of integration/non-integration into a social and family network. Present-day insecurity largely results from the growing fragility of protective regulations which were implemented from the nineteenth century onwards in order to create a stable situation for workers: the right to work, extended social protection, coverage of social risks set up by the welfare state. Castel describes the specific nature of present-day insecurity as relating to the structure of wage society, its crisis or its disintegration since the mid-1970s. This analysis although very relevant cannot lend itself to straightforward comparisons. We come back to this in the section on the social divide.

Over the last two decades, poverty has increased in several countries. Figure 2.1 provides the evolution of poverty in five European countries. The UK is the only country that has experienced a decline in poverty over the period 1995–2015. Spain, Sweden, and Germany have gone through an increase of poverty though at different levels.

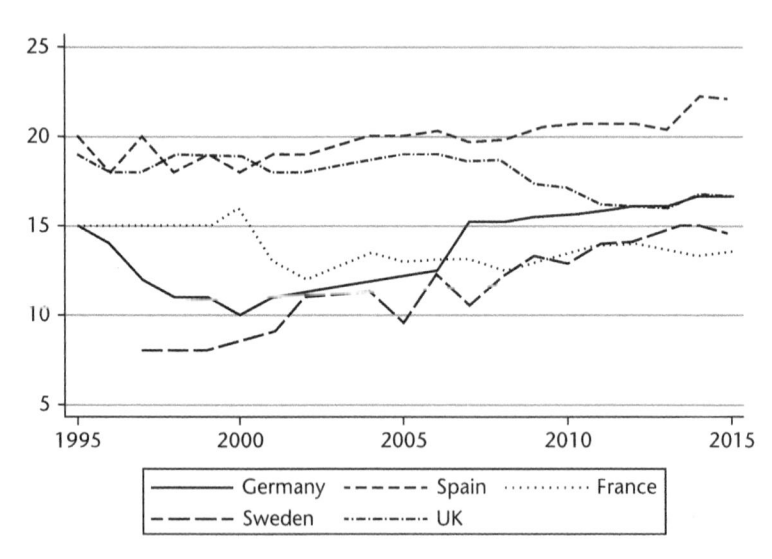

Figure 2.1. Evolution of poverty in five countries

Note: Poverty is defined as the % of people in the population with a disposable income below 60% of the median income

Source: Eurostat (2017a)

2.3. Comparing Inequality

The headcount poverty rate used here, as well as alternative measures of poverty, focus on a particular population. It is often argued that poverty alleviation is not the sole redistributive objective of social policy, and that insuring that income is more equitably distributed is just as important. There exist a number of summary statistics aimed at compressing a vast amount of information concerning differences in income distributions. These statistics, which measure in particular the degree of dispersion or of inequality of peoples' incomes, quite often convey value judgments. For example, under some assumptions, and keeping aggregate income constant, more inequality is shown to imply less social welfare.

In this chapter we will use the Gini coefficient as a measure of inequality. To obtain this coefficient, one first compares the cumulative distribution of income to the cumulated distribution of households in the population concerned. This is the Lorenz curve, which plots the percentage of income received by the bottom 20, 30, etc. per cent of the population. If there were full equality, x per cent of the population would receive x per cent of the aggregate income, and then the Lorenz curve would lay along the diagonal of the diagram in Figure 2.2. The further the curve is away from the diagonal, the further the distribution from full equality, and therefore the greater the inequality.

The Gini coefficient is calculated by dividing the area between the Lorenz curve and the diagonal, by the area of the triangle formed by the diagonal and the axes. In Figure 2.2, there are two hypothetical Lorenz curves corresponding to two countries: b, for Borduria and s, for Syldavia. The Gini coefficient of

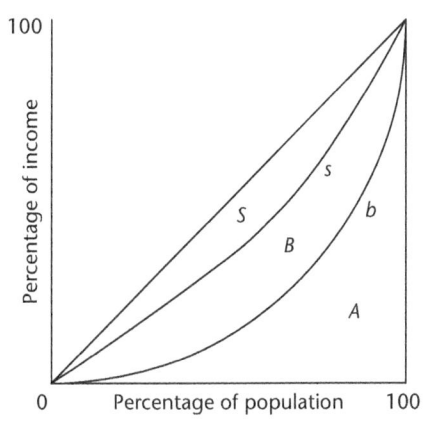

Figure 2.2. Lorenz curves

Syldavia is equal to the area S divided by the area $S + B + A$ and that of Borduria is equal to $S + B$ divided by $S + B + A$. Clearly, income is more unequally distributed in Borduria than in Syldavia.

Table 2.1 presents the Gini coefficient of EU28 countries plus the United States. As in the case of poverty, one can distinguish two groups of European countries. The Nordic countries, Belgium, Czechia, Slovenia, and the Netherlands have the lowest coefficients. In contrast Romania, Bulgaria, and Lithuania have the highest coefficients, closer to that of the USA. This clustering is quite similar to that obtained in other studies. As we show in the next section, the ranking of countries by either the Gini coefficient or the head count poverty rate can be explained in part by the differing form and extent of social protection, as well as by the role of redistributive income taxation.

Figure 2.3 gives the changes in inequality from mid-1990 to mid-2010 for a number of European countries. It appears that during that period, the Gini coefficient increased steadily in Sweden. It also increased in Spain and in Germany after a sharp decline in the latter. In France, it remained broadly stable. In spite of these contrasting trends, the overall pattern has not changed much: low inequality in the Nordic countries, Czechia, Slovenia, and the Netherlands and higher inequality in the Anglo-Saxon, the Southern European countries, and most East European countries. Increasing inequalities after 2008 were largely driven by growing unemployment in many countries

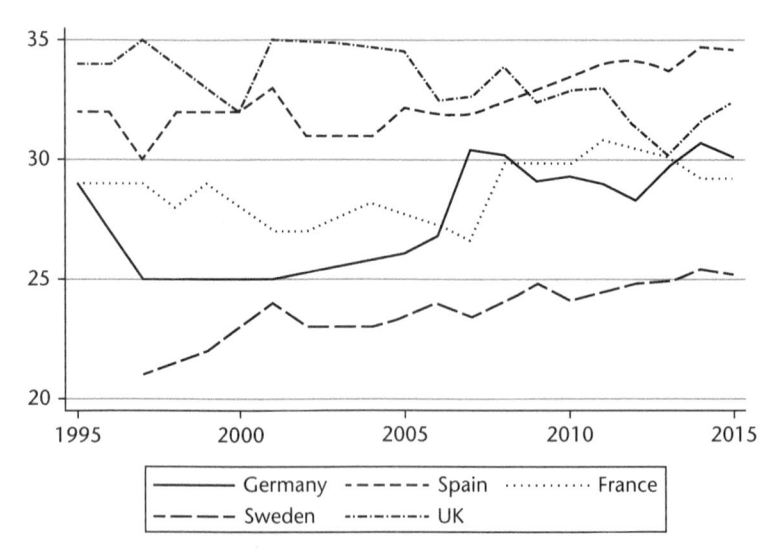

Figure 2.3. Evolution of inequality in five countries
Note: Inequality is the Gini index
Source: Eurostat (2017a)

following the great recession. A number of studies signalled widening wage differentials as the main reason behind this evolution[4].

It should be noted that the Gini coefficient does not account for what is happening at the extremes of the income distribution. It particularly forgoes the concentration of income in the top percentile of the distribution. The share of the richest 1 per cent in total pre-tax income has increased in most European countries in the past three decades, particularly in some English-speaking countries but also in some Nordic (from lower levels) and Southern European countries[5]. Today, these shares range between 7 per cent in Denmark and the Netherlands up to almost 15 per cent in the UK (20 per cent in the United States). This increase is the result of the top 1 per cent capturing a disproportionate share of overall income-growth dividend over the past three decades. This explains why the majority of the population cannot reconcile the aggregate income-growth figures with the performance of their incomes.

2.4. Redistributive Effect of Social Protection

The extent of poverty and inequality studied thus far concerns incomes that are net of direct taxes and which include social protection transfers. We now want to look at the impact of such transfers on poverty and inequality. To do so we proceed in two stages: at the aggregate level and at the level of households.

2.4.1. Effect on the Poverty of Households

To measure the impact of social protection, we simply compare poverty rates before and after transfers. The practical advantage of this method is that it does not require data on gross income, just on disposable income and on transfers. One major disadvantage of this method is that it overestimates the impact of transfers on poverty. The extent of the bias depends on the level of taxation that low-income households pay. Another and more serious pitfall of this approach is that it assumes a constant behaviour. Indeed it is clear that without some social benefits individuals would change their behaviour regarding retirement, work, health treatment, and so on.

As it appears in Table 2.2, for the most recent year (2015), poverty alleviation (APO) defined as the difference between poverty rates before and after transfers ranges from 33.3 in Hungary to 21.3 in the Latvia. For the year 2005, the range goes from 36.1 for Hungary to 14.1 for Cyprus. These figures are quite high. They reflect the generosity of the transfer systems but also the level

---

[4] Eurofound (2017). [5] OECD (2014), Stiglitz (2015).

The Welfare State in Europe

Table 2.2. Poverty alleviation (1995–2015)

	POV	APO	DAP	POV	APO	DAP
Austria	5.8	29.6	2.6	8.3	30.2	0.6
Belgium	7.7	29.5	1.5	7.8	31.1	1.6
Bulgaria	12.5	27.0	–	15.5	21.4	–
Croatia	–	–	–	13.5	25.8	–
Cyprus	9.0	14.1	–	9.0	23.5	9.4
Czechia	5.5	27.5	–	5.3	26.4	–1.1
Denmark	5.7	28.0	–	7.1	29.5	1.5
Estonia	11.3	22.8	–	12.5	21.7	–1.1
Finland	5.0	30.2	–	5.3	32.3	2.1
France	6.4	32.3	4.3	6.5	32.4	0.1
Germany	6.7	31.7	8.7	10.2	28.9	–2.8
Greece	12.6	20.8	4.8	15.0	31.6	10.8
Hungary	7.5	36.1	–	9.0	33.3	–2.8
Ireland	11.2	24.1	–6.9	8.8	32.3	8.2
Italy	12.4	23.8	4.8	13.4	26.2	2.4
Latvia	12.7	22.9	–	14.7	21.3	–1.6
Lithuania	14.3	23.2	–	14.4	23.2	0,0
Luxembourg	7.3	26.3	0.3	8.2	29.1	2.8
Malta	7.2	18.2	–	8.5	23.4	5.2
Netherlands	6.2	25.4	–0.6	5.8	27.8	2.4
Poland	14.5	30.3	–	10.7	26.9	–3.4
Portugal	12.5	22.1	7.1	13.8	29.1	7.0
Romania	–	–	–	19.8	24,0	–
Slovakia	8.2	26.2	–	8.4	23.3	–2.9
Slovenia	7,0	28.2	–	8.4	27.4	–0.8
Spain	13.1	19.5	–4.5	15.9	25.8	6.3
Sweden	5.0	30.3	–	8.0	28.7	–1.6
United Kingdom	11.8	26.4	2.4	9.7	29.9	3.5
Period	2005	2005	1995–2005	2015	2015	2005–2015

Notes: POV: Poverty rate (50% median income), APO: Poverty alleviation: poverty before minus poverty after transfers, DAP: Increase in poverty alleviation
Source: Eurostat (2017a)

of gross income poverty. What is may be more interesting is the change in poverty alleviation over the two subperiods (1995–2005 and 2005–2015). For the first subperiod, it increased for most countries except for Ireland, the Netherlands, and Spain. For the more recent subperiod, for which we have more observations, the outcome is mixed. In the chapter on globalization, we will try to relate these changes in poverty alleviation (DAP) to economic integration and factor mobility.

2.4.2. Aggregate Effect on Poverty and Inequality

Another approach to the same issue is to consider the aggregate relationship between social spending, and either the poverty rate or the inequality measure. To do that we use the data from Table 2.1. Figure 2.4 provides the line of regression of the poverty rate against social spending. We see clearly that

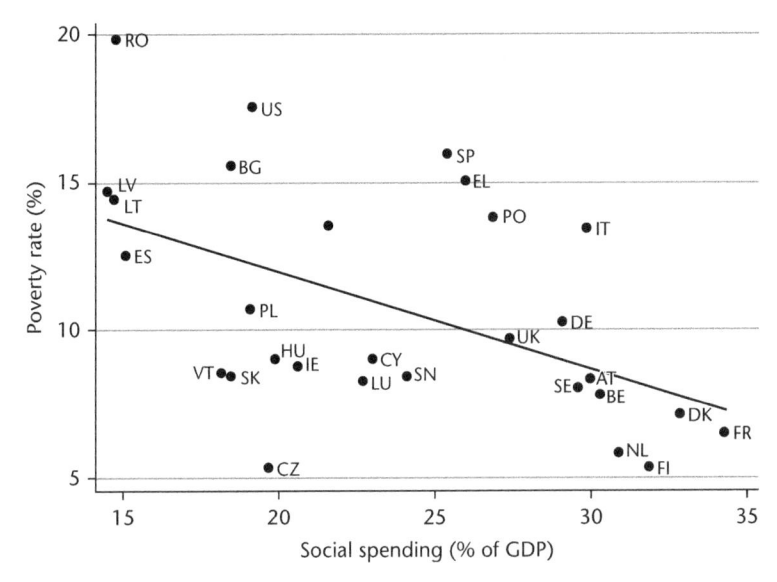

Figure 2.4. Social expenditure and poverty, 2015
Source: Table 2.1

Table 2.3. Impact of social spending on poverty and income inequality (2015)

Dependent variable	Constant	Social spending	R^2
Poverty rate	18.51	−0.328	0.261
	(7.12)	(−3.09)	
Gini coefficient	38.91	−0.347	0.219
	(12.58)	(−2.75)	

Note: t-value between brackets
Source: Table 2.1

social transfers exert a clear-cut effect on poverty and that there is a negative correlation between the two variables.

The results presented in Table 2.3 confirm that larger social expenditure corresponds to lower poverty levels. Tests on the time stability of the estimated coefficients suggest that the impact of social transfers on poverty rates has not changed over time.

We should, however, be cautious in interpreting these relations. Indeed they can indicate that social protection 'works'. Yet at the same time, this can simply mean that countries with low poverty rates have a strong preference for social protection. Furthermore, part of the redistribution can be prior to social protection spending. For example, it has been shown that the distribution of wages tends to be more equal in countries with a corporatist setting

The Welfare State in Europe

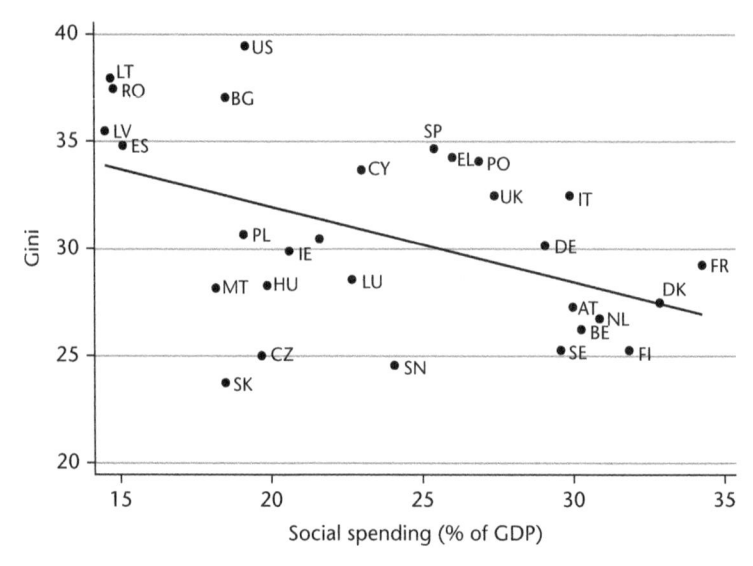

Figure 2.5. Social expenditure and income inequality, 2015
Source: Table 2.1

than in countries where wage is exclusively set by the market. Moreover, we know that corporatist countries tend to have rather generous welfare states. This points to something to which we return in Chapter 5. Even though this book focuses on the spending side of the welfare state, one should remember that social protection can influence resource allocation and income distribution by other means such as social legislation.

The relation between social protection and an inequality indicator such as the Gini coefficient is not so clear. But it is clearly negative, as shown by Figure 2.5 and the correlation coefficient is equal to about 22 per cent. Table 2.3 gives the regression of the Gini coefficient against social spending. The estimators are quite significant. However, the same reservation made for the poverty rate holds for the indicator of inequality. A society with incomes that are more or less equal can have a strong preference for social protection. Thus the causality link would be reversed. The truth is very likely to be somewhere in between. During the great recession, the role of welfare state redistribution in reducing inequality was important. This was especially true in countries hardest hit by the crisis in the European periphery, where welfare states largely cushioned growing market income inequalities[6].

[6] Eurofound (2017).

2.4.3. *Permanent Inequality and Poverty across European Countries*

The comparison presented so far can be criticized because it relies on single-year incomes or earnings. It has long been recognized that there could be high annual-income inequality even if the inequality of lifetime (also called permanent) income is very low. The more households move up and down the income ladder throughout their life-cycle, the more single-year inequality will deviate from the inequality of income measured over a longer period of time. As a consequence, if there are differences in income mobility across countries, single-year inequality ranking may yield a misleading picture. Naturally, the same remark applies to poverty measures. In comparison to poverty over time or across countries, instantaneous poverty does not necessarily evolve as persistent poverty. Table 2.1 provides, besides the standard rate of poverty, a rate of persistent poverty that shows the percentage of the population living in poverty in the current year and at least two out of the preceding three years.

To illustrate this point, consider two countries in which individuals live for three periods of equal length. Population is constant. In country *A*, each individual earns very little in the first period, but makes up for it in the two following periods. A cross-sectional view of country *A* shows that one third of the population is poor (the young generation) and two thirds (the middle aged and the old generations) have a reasonable income. As a consequence, one has a poverty rate of 33 per cent. Yet, in life-cycle terms, everyone is alike and there is no poverty. In country *B*, 20 per cent of the population is persistently poor through the three periods. The others have a constant income. Cross-sectional poverty is thus 20 per cent. This rate is also the rate of persistent poverty.

This example is presented in Table 2.4. One can easily check that the same conclusion applies for inequality measures.

It is thus widely agreed that lifetime income, if available, should be used to assess inequality and poverty measures. It could bring a different view,

Table 2.4. Life-cycle income

Periods	Society A Generations t	$t+1$	$t+2$	Society B (20%/80%) Generations t	$t+1$	$t+2$
1	10	10	10	10/35	10/35	10/35
2	40	40	40	10/35	10/35	10/35
3	40	40	40	10/35	10/35	10/35
Average cross-sectional income		30			30	
Average life-time income		30			30	
Cross-sectional poverty		1/3			1/5	
Persistent poverty		0			1/5	

supplementing that obtained with income obtained in a given period. Unfortunately, to compare income inequality and poverty across countries on longer time periods than one year requires data that are rarely available. We now examine the existing scanty evidence.

Using longitudinal data sets from four countries, Denmark, Norway, Sweden, and the United States, Aaberge et al. (2002) look at how the ordering of these countries with respect to income inequality changes when the accounting period is extended from one to several years. They show that the ordering by and large remains unchanged when the period is extended by up to eleven years (1980–90). The United States is consistently the most unequal country in spite of a rather high income mobility. They conclude that extending the accounting period and taking account of income mobility have only minor effects on intercountry differences in income inequality.[7] This conclusion is similar to that obtained by Burkhauser and Poupore (1997) and Burkhauser et al. (1997) in their comparison of Germany and the United States. It is also the same as that of OECD (1996a) that looks at a larger set of countries.

There is indeed a belief that higher inequalities do go hand-in-hand with greater mobility over the working life with the consequence that mobility being an equalizer of long-term earnings would imply a lower degree of persistent inequality. This belief does not seem to be supported by the facts. Using a consistent comparative dataset for fourteen countries—the European Community Household Panel—Sologon and O'Donoghue (2012) show that the country ranking in long-term earnings inequality is similar to the country ranking in annual inequality, which is a sign of limited long-term equalizing mobility within countries with higher levels of annual inequality. Garnero et al. (2016) reach the same conclusion using a larger sample of industrialized countries.

With respect to poverty measurement, research has increasingly focused on persistent income poverty. Using the first three waves of the European Community Household Panel, Whelan et al. (2003) compare for 1995 cross-sectional income poverty at 60 per cent of median income with persistent poverty at 70 per cent of median income. The first ranges from 10.7 per cent in the Netherlands to 21.7 per cent in Portugal and the second from 6.3 per cent in Denmark to 19 per cent in Portugal. Here again the rank correlation between these two indicators is high. Breen and Moisis (2003) use the first four waves of the European Panel. A comparison between poverty rate in wave 4 and the percentage of households being poor in the four waves shows again a rather high correlation. Their main conclusion is that mobility in poverty is highly overestimated if measurement error is ignored. More recently,

---

[7] See also Bjorklund et al. (2002).

Vaalavuo (2015) has analysed long-term poverty in Europe. The idea is that fighting persistent poverty should be a priority for governments. Poverty is never pleasant but the longer one spends in poverty, the harder and the more insidious it becomes. She finds that the duration of poverty varies greatly between countries: on average 37 per cent of the poor are poor only for one year (out of four possible years). In the UK and Austria it is around half of the poor and in Romania only a fifth of the poor. The likelihood of long-term poverty varies across age groups and countries: in Slovenia, Finland and Cyprus, elderly people are more at risk of long-term poverty; in the Netherlands, Belgium, Portugal and Romania children face a higher risk. Finally, she finds that instantaneous poverty and persistent poverty are highly correlated.

To conclude, there is no doubt that looking at lifetime income inequality and persistent poverty is important; it brings an alternative viewpoint to the issue of inequality and exclusion. To date, mainly for statistical reasons, there are few studies comparing lifetime income inequality and lifetime income poverty in the European Union countries. Moreover, the existing studies show that the ranking based on yearly income is not much different from that based on lifetime income.

2.5. Social Divide and Populism

Traditionally, the study of social polarization focuses on income inequality and poverty, which both call for corrective tax and social policies. This narrow approach is increasingly questioned, as the phenomenon is complex and involves health status, quality of jobs, education, migration background, and digital connections. A large fraction of the population feels destitute because of low life expectancy, miserable dwellings, poorly paid and unstable jobs, feelings of discrimination on the part of the native-born children of immigration, distance from the city centres, etc. Besides this complexity, another key feature of the social divide is that it rests not only on the realities just mentioned but also on perceptions and fears that might not be well founded but yet generate resentment. A typical example of that is the perception that outsourcing and capital mobility are the causes of many problems even when this is proved wrong. Another example is the fear that foreigners will take your job even in areas where there is no immigration. A third feature of the widespread social divide is dynamic. A major source of social anger is downward social mobility that people perceived as not being taken care of by distant policymakers.

This increasing social divide is often viewed as the source of the populist revolt observed in a number of countries as well as the electoral failure of progressive parties that have been unable to rethink their mission and their purpose. It is about time that they realized that the grievances expressed by their traditional constituency are about social esteem, not only about wages and incomes.

The link between the social divide and extremism is now well documented. In that respect, the experience of the twenties and the thirties is quite interesting. Three economists, O'Rourke et al. (2012), have carefully studied the determinants of 171 elections held between 1919 and 1939 in a number of countries. Their analysis suggests that the danger of political polarization and extremism is greater in some national circumstances than others. It is greatest in countries with relatively recent histories of democracy, with existing right-wing extremist parties, and with electoral systems that create low hurdles to parliamentary representation of new parties. Above all, it is greatest where depressed economic conditions are allowed to persist.

Two other researchers, Geishecker and Siedler (2012), using seventeen years of the German Socio-Economic Panel, examine whether job-loss fears impact on individuals' party identification. They find strong and robust evidence that subjective job-loss fears foster affinity for parties at the far right-wing of the political spectrum. The importance of subjective fears has an interesting parallel in history: recent studies on the elections in the Weimar Republic have presented evidence that it was mainly those who feared a loss of work or economic status who supported the Nazi party.

Becker et al. (2017) analyse the determinants of the Brexit vote. They find that the 2016 Brexit referendum result is strongly correlated with various fundamental characteristics of the voters across the 380 local authority areas. Having few or no qualifications is a strong predictor of the Brexit vote. Furthermore, areas with a strong tradition of manufacturing employment were more likely to vote Leave, and also those areas with relatively low pay and high unemployment. They finally also find evidence that the growth rate of migrants from the twelve EU accession countries played a role in the vote to Leave.

Autor et al. (2016) study the populist vote in the 2016 American presidential elections. Growing import competition from China has contributed to the disappearance of moderate legislators in Congress, a shift in congressional voting toward ideological extremes, and net gains in the number of conservative Republican representatives, including those affiliated with the Tea Party movement. Also areas with larger housing-price declines embrace ideologically more-extreme legislators.

A recent study by Algan et al. (2017) tries to explain the Front National (FN) vote during the recent French presidential election. According to this research, a sense of deteriorating wellbeing is one of the main explanations for rising support for the FN, cutting across most boundaries of age, education, or economic status. The researchers explain this link between well-being and

FN as a 'crisis of hope', saying that after almost ten years of financial crisis, many people—well beyond the working and middle class—have lost hope of a better future. They have the feeling of being left behind. Age, income, employment status, and level of education do remain relevant but are less important to voting intentions than how gloomy one is about one's future.

To sum up this evidence, we indeed see that the concept of social divide is more complex than the traditional polarization in terms of wages and incomes. The question is then of how to fight problems such as loss of hope for a better future, the prevalence of medical and internet deserts, gender gaps, racial discrimination, and social immobility. What is clear is that the traditional recipes of our welfare states are not working. It does not mean that they have to be abandoned but that they have to be reformed in such a way that the focus is not just on income but other factors that explain the feeling of being left behind. Among the policy measures one might have in mind, one can list: improve public schools with a concern for true equal opportunity; give workers a voice in their companies; fight the rural digital divide and the medical deserts; enhance public transport; erase residential ghettos; dismantle no-go zones; foster participative democracy and active citizenship. Clearly some of these policies are beyond the scope of this book.

2.6. Conclusion

We can now wrap up this chapter on inequality and poverty in the EU, and restate our main findings. First, there are important differences in poverty rates and Gini coefficients across European countries. At the one extreme, there are the Benelux and Nordic countries with little poverty and small inequalities. At the other extreme, there is a mixed group consisting of Southern, Eastern, and Anglo-Saxon countries. Secondly, a part of these differences is attributable to differences in social spending. Thirdly, changes in poverty and inequality over time, have been rather small. Keeping in mind that the most recent figures available are a few years old, there are a number of reliable signals pointing to an increase in the near future of poverty and inequality. The main factors leading to this conjecture are unfavourable social and demographic trends, as well as increasingly restrictive public finance. Finally, we have shown that beyond the traditional social polarization based on income and wealth, there is a deeper and multicausal divide that represents the most serious challenge to our welfare states. Unfortunately the extent of that social divide is not easy to measure and even less to compare across countries.

3

Social Spending

> **KEY CONCEPTS**
> entitlement principle
> entitlement programs
> net social spending
> social burden
> convergence
> mandatory schemes
> out-of-pocket spending

3.1. Introduction

There is a great diversity among welfare states in the EU. As different systems have developed within the national context, mostly after 1945, it is difficult to generalize about a 'European model' of the welfare state. This diversity—which is at the heart of this book—is reflected in the scale of expenditures for social protection systems, the division of expenditures among programs, the structure and design of benefits, the organization and the sources of financing. This chapter deals with the first two points. We first look at the level and structure of expenditures for the last year for which data is available. Then, we turn to the evolution of social expenditure over time. The financing issue is dealt with in Chapter 4. We discuss the issue of comparison of social expenditures across countries and consider the problem of entitlement that explains why dismantling programs that have lost their relevancy is so difficult.

3.2. Level and Profile

The level of expenditure on welfare states in Europe for the year 2015 varies between 34.3 per cent of GDP in France and 14.5 per cent in Latvia, as shown

Social Spending

Table 3.1. Total expenditure for social protection as a percentage of GDP, 1995, 2005, and 2015

	1995	2005	2015
Austria	28.9	28.1	30.0
Belgium	26.9	26.8	30.3
Bulgaria	–	14.6	18.5
Croatia	–	–	21.6
Cyprus	–	16.7	23.0
Czechia	16.2	18.0	19.7
Denmark	31.4	29.5	32.9
Estonia	–	12.5	15.1
Finland	30.6	25.6	31.9
France	29.9	30.5	34.3
Germany	27.5	28.9	29.1
Greece	19.1	24.1	26.0
Hungary	–	21.5	19.9
Ireland	18.2	16.7	20.6
Italy	23.3	25.3	29.9
Latvia	–	12.1	14.5
Lithuania	–	13.2	14.7
Luxembourg	–	22.1	22.7
Malta	15.8	17.1	18.2
Netherlands	28.8	25.8	30.9
Poland	–	20.0	19.1
Portugal	20.1	23.8	26.9
Romania	–	13.4	14.8
Slovakia	18.2	16.2	18.5
Slovenia	–	22.6	24.1
Spain	21.0	20.1	25.4
Sweden	32.4	29.5	29.6
United Kingdom	25.9	26.2	27.4
United States	15	15.5	19.2

Source: Eurostat (2017a), OECD (2016c)

in Table 3.1. This lower bound is quite below the 19.2 per cent in the US. Besides France, the figures for Austria, Belgium, the Netherlands, and the Nordic countries are above 30 per cent. By contrast, expenditures in the East European countries, with the exception of Slovenia and Croatia, are below 20 per cent. It is tempting to check whether there is a relation between social protection and GDP per head. For decades there was a tendency for the richer countries to have the largest welfare states. Lately, this relation has disappeared, as Figures 3.1(a) and (b) show. In 1980, there is a clear positive relation between per capita GDP and social spending per capita. In 2014, this relation has disappeared.

Countries with more or less the same GDP now show a wide range of behaviour. This new pattern is good news. When there was a clear relation between social spending and GDP, one was facing a 'chicken or egg' causality problem. At the same time one could argue that higher spending leads to

The Welfare State in Europe

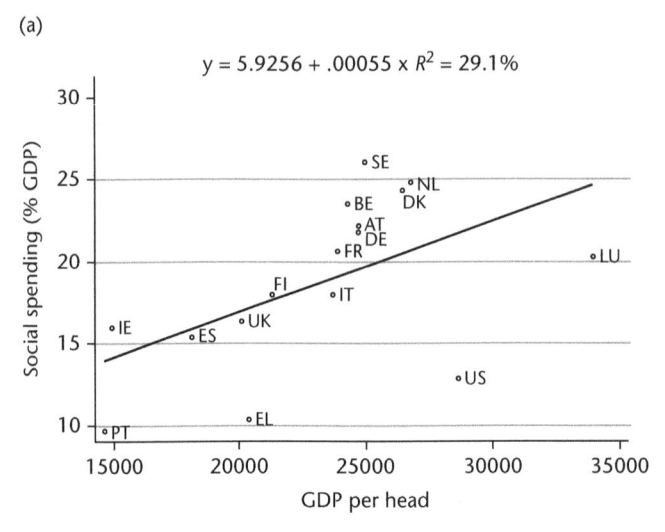

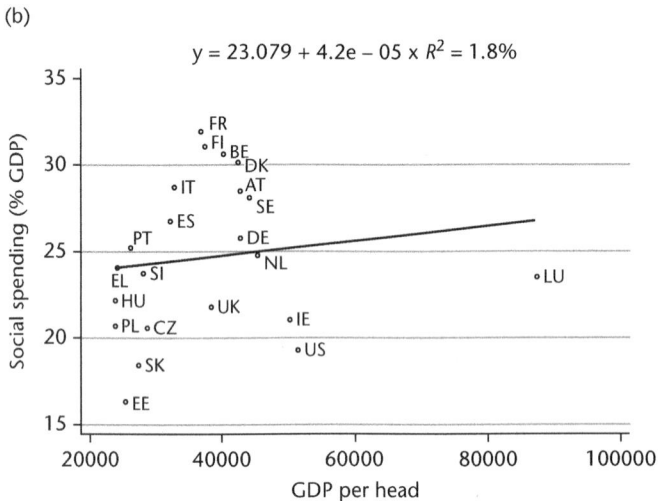

(a)

$y = 5.9256 + .00055 \times x \quad R^2 = 29.1\%$

(b)

$y = 23.079 + 4.2e - 05 \times x \quad R^2 = 1.8\%$

Figure 3.1. Social spending and GDP per head, (a) 1980, (b) 2015
Sources: Eurostat (2017a), OECD (2016c)

higher national income, and conversely that successful countries with high income per head can afford generous social protection. We shall come back to this question, as it has some bearing on the alleged depressive effect of social protection on economic performance. At this point we will simply note that today there is no such relation between social protection and GDP. When there was one, one could have hypothesized that the industrialization of the economy and the ensuing social changes led to both higher levels of income

Social Spending

Table 3.2. Social protection benefits by function, 2014

Country	Health	Old-age	Family /housing	Labour market	Others	Total
Austria	32.94	50.22	10.25	5.14	1.45	100
Belgium	36.61	39.65	8.34	12.54	2.86	100
Bulgaria	34.05	50.29	10.57	3.57	1.51	100
Croatia	52.16	38.04	7.38	2.21	0.2	100
Cyprus	25.23	52.32	9.92	6.75	5.77	100
Czechia	37.35	48.01	9.79	3.23	1.63	100
Denmark	34.56	41.04	14.25	6.17	3.99	100
Estonia	39.95	44.46	11.74	3.06	0.79	100
Finland	36.81	40.67	12.82	6.94	2.76	100
France	35.35	45.72	10.47	6.04	2.42	100
Germany	41.74	40.22	13.31	4.17	0.57	100
Greece	25.91	59.31	6.31	6.33	2.14	100
Hungary	31.11	51.91	13.89	2.63	0.46	100
Ireland	38.25	29.31	15.83	15.43	1.19	100
Italy	29.62	59.76	4.28	5.68	0.67	100
Latvia	30.57	56.17	8.18	3.69	1.4	100
Lithuania	37.06	46.75	8.78	2.72	4.7	100
Luxembourg	36.59	37.89	17.46	5.8	2.26	100
Malta	33.5	55.37	6.67	2.99	1.48	100
Netherlands	43.91	41.69	4.82	4.75	4.84	100
Poland	32.37	60.08	5.12	1.66	0.77	100
Portugal	32.39	54.77	4.9	6.81	1.14	100
Romania	34.71	54.26	8.72	1.13	1.18	100
Slovakia	39.4	44.06	10.16	4.02	2.36	100
Slovenia	38.61	47.14	8.55	3.07	2.62	100
Spain	33.49	45.62	6.01	14.03	0.84	100
Sweden	38.08	43.34	12.14	4.12	2.32	100
United Kingdom	36.51	42.11	16.1	2.36	2.92	100

Source: Eurostat (2017b)

and to the need for more social protection. Industrialization made life uncertain; at the same time, it forced out traditional insurance mechanisms such as the family at large.

The breakdown of total social expenditures into individual programs reveals interesting similarities and specificities, as presented in Table 3.2.

Pension benefits account for the largest share of social expenditures in welfare states, this level being particularly high in Italy and Greece, and particularly low in Ireland. The second largest component is health care: above 40 per cent in Ireland, Luxembourg, the Netherlands, Sweden, the UK, and Portugal, and equal or below 30 per cent in Greece and Austria. Together social security and health care account for over 75 per cent of social spending in all European countries. For the other functions, there is a large diversity that can be explained by social policy objectives. Unemployment benefits make over 10 per cent in Belgium, Slovenia, and Ireland, but are negligible in Portugal. Maternity and housing benefits represent more than 15 per cent of social spending in Ireland and Lithuania.

3.3. Evolution

A number of articles and books published over recent decades talk of the dismantlement (Pierson 1997),[1] the rolling back (Atkinson 2000), the end (Taylor-Gooby and Svallfors 1999) of the welfare state. In this section, we try to determine to what extent this scenario has been borne out.

Real social expenditures increase in all countries. But this upward movement proves to be far from homogeneous across time and countries. In any case, the most relevant comparison must concern social spending as a percentage of GDP, sometimes labelled 'social burden' for short.

Globally, the social burden goes up in all countries over the period 1995–2015, except in Sweden. But time trends are not linear. In the decade 1995–2005, it declines in a number of countries, particularly in the Netherlands, Ireland, and the Nordic countries, but in the decade 2005–2015, it only decreases in Poland and Hungary. In the US, the social burden increases from 15 to 19.2 per cent during those two decades.

Beyond a number of national differences, it is nevertheless possible to statistically identify three rather homogeneous subgroups[2] in Europe. Homogeneity is measured in terms of level of and change in social burden. The period is 1980–2015. Figure 3.2 represent the evolution of social spending in these countries. In each case, the thick line represents their average.

- High spending countries (Austria, Belgium, Denmark, Finland, France, Germany, the Netherlands and Sweden) display both the largest social spending rates and per capita incomes of the Union. We observe an important increase till the mid-nineties. Then a decline and again an increase in 2007, the start of the financial crisis.
- Medium spending countries (Spain, Italy, Luxembourg, Hungary, Poland, and the Netherlands) lie halfway between those of the other two subgroups. The Netherlands experiences a decline till 2007. The other countries have a slowly increasing pace.
- Low spending countries (Greece, Portugal, Czechia, Estonia, Slovakia, and the United Kingdom) remaining 'laggards' in terms of social protection while experiencing the highest growth rates (particularly Greece and Portugal).

---

[1] Pierson (2001) is one of the political scientists in favor of the so-called 'new politics' of the welfare states. His view focuses on two factors limiting the decline of welfare states: the popularity of the welfare state and the existence of formal and informal institutional veto forces. As a consequence, he finds evidence supporting the effects of partisan politics. In contrast, there is another school of thought adopting the 'amended' power resources approach for which partisan politics plays a decisive role in the decline of modern welfare states. Korpi and Palme (2003) adopt this view in their analysis of the British case.

[2] The F-test indicates that subgroup mean values are significantly different from each other for each year and for the entire period.

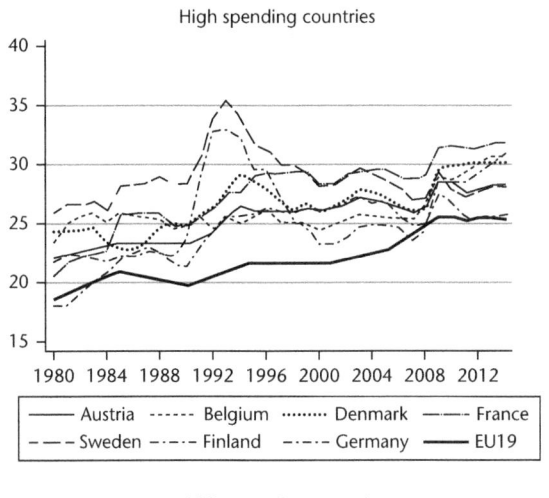

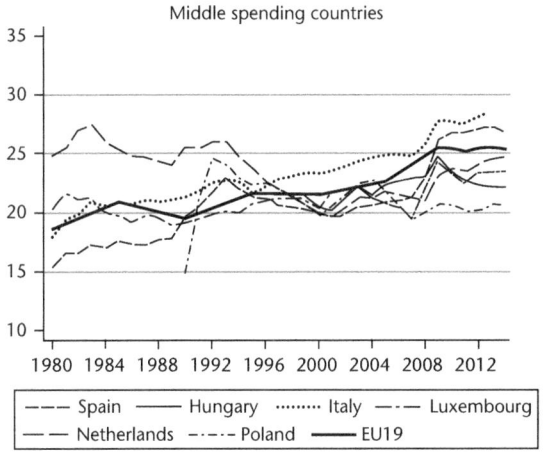

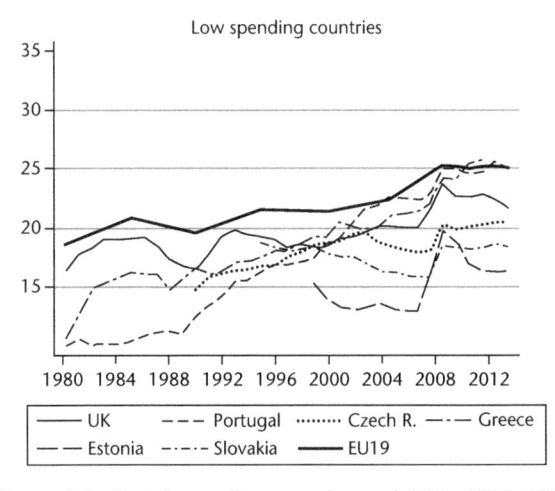

Figure 3.2. Social spending as a share of GDP, 1980–2014
Source: Eurostat (2017b)

Table 3.3. Convergence of social spending (1995–2014), EU 28

Year	Min/Max ratio	Coefficient of variation
1995	47.30	22.48
1996	47.32	21.94
1997	47.88	21.13
1998	48.19	20.59
1999	47.52	21.06
2000	46.29	20.92
2001	45.88	20.54
2002	43.81	20.29
2003	43.37	20.66
2004	45.34	20.37
2005	44.14	20.29
2006	43.72	19.92
2007	44.09	19.30
2008	53.82	17.13
2009	58.81	15.25
2010	57.93	15.50
2011	53.50	16.47
2012	51.53	17.23
2013	50.48	17.82
2014	51.01	17.94

	Initial social spending and subsequent annual growth rate	
EU15		
Correlation coefficient	−0.53	
Regression		
Constant	24.5	(20.73)
Slope	−0.16	(−2.73)
EU28		
Correlation coefficient	−0.8	
Regression		
Constant	23.5	(21.22)
Slope	−0.1	(−5.64)

Note: t-statistics between brackets

What have been the implications of those contrasted evolutions for existing international differences? The usual statistics and econometric tests show that they have markedly declined over time (see Table 3.3). On the one hand, the 25 per cent increase in the minimum to maximum ratio indicates that the gap between extreme social expenditure rates has fallen somewhat over the twenty-year period. It reached a peak in 2009 as a result of the financial crisis to which different countries reacted differently. On the other hand, there has been a certain reduction in the overall range of the European social burden, as illustrated by the fall in the coefficient of variation (from 22 to 17).

This reduction in dispersion results mainly from the fact that less generous social systems (Greece, Portugal, Spain and Italy) in the early eighties experienced globally higher growth rates than more thriving systems (northern states). The existence of such a converging scheme is widely supported by the strong negative correlation between the initial social burden and the

Social Spending

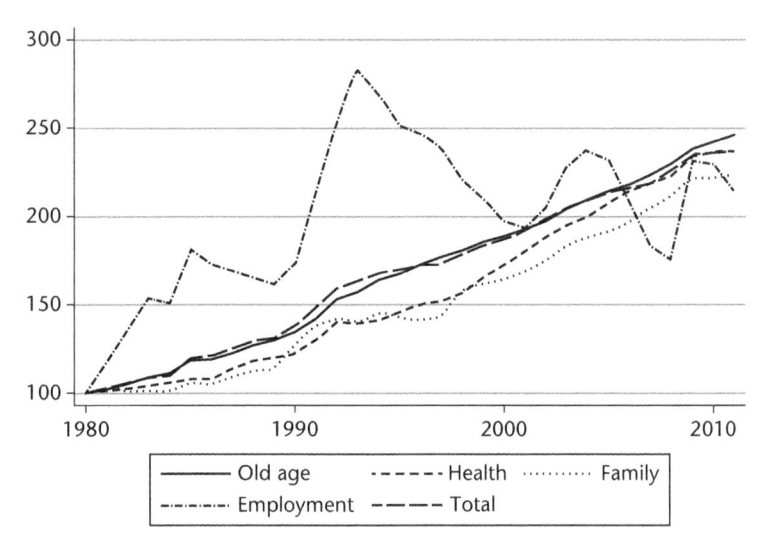

Figure 3.3. Real growth of social spending by functions at the EC level (1980 = 100)
Source: Eurostat (2017b)

subsequent growth rate as well as by the regression presented in Table 3.3. As one observes, the convergence is sharper in EU15 than in EU28.

To sum up, social burdens in Europe have been following a converging and globally increasing path since 1980, with some stagnation between 1993 and 2007. In the chapters devoted to specific social spending, we shall see whether these evolutions can be explained in part by an increase in the risk related to that particular spending. For example, one would expect the evolution in unemployment benefits to be linked to the rate of unemployment, and the evolution in social security spending to the increase in the dependency ratio. Figure 3.3 indicates that all functions except unemployment insurance have increased quite smoothly.

3.4. Problems of Comparison

Throughout this book we use social expenditure data made comparable over time and across countries by both OECD and Eurostat. Yet, this data may fail to reflect the true effort of a country in providing social support during a given year. Account should be taken of the role of taxes of benefits and of the transfers, which, although mandatory, are not paid by government. In other words, ideally, we should use a net rather than a gross concept of social expenditure. To do so, various delicate adjustments to raw data are needed. As it will appear, after correcting for differences in tax and institutional arrangements, some international disparities are less sharp than they appear at first sight.

Following Adema et al. (2011) and Adema (1999, 2001), we look at four examples where adjustments are needed. To do so we consider two fictitious countries: Borduria and Syldavia.

- Borduria and Syldavia have a sickness benefit program involving contributions by employers to a social insurance fund as well as payments from that fund to qualified individuals. Borduria decides to abolish this program and by law to force employers to make payments to qualified individuals. As a consequence, social spending falls in Borduria relatively to Syldavia.
- Borduria and Syldavia do not tax social security benefits. Borduria decides to impose the regular income tax to retirees, but to increase their benefits so as to keep their net income unchanged. Social spending increases in Borduria.
- Borduria's social security system consists of a meagre flat benefit, but it gives large tax advantages on contributions to private pension plans. As a consequence, social security spending is much lower in Borduria than in Syldavia even though the total flow of public money is the same in the two countries.
- Borduria and Syldavia are identical economies in all respect, except that Borduria experiences a great deal of volatility in GDP. As a consequence, social spending is much higher in Borduria in a period of cyclical bust, than in Syldavia, because of a higher demand for unemployment benefits.

Table 3.4 gives some results of these adjustments for a number of European countries plus the US for the year 2011. It can be seen that the magnitude and the sign of the adjustments of social spending vary quite a lot across countries. However, one should note that if two countries provide the same amount of social spending in net terms, this does not mean that the two systems have the same allocative and distributive effects. Take the case of the US and of Belgium. Based on gross figures, Belgium has clearly a more generous social protection system than the US. After the adjustments we have the opposite result. The reason is that in the US there are mandatory private schemes in the health care and the pension areas and that in Belgium most social benefits are subject to taxation. To the extent that private schemes are earnings related, one would expect the 'net' US social protection to be less redistributive than that of Belgium.

This type of adjustment has led some people to think that the US is after all not that different from many European countries. Focusing on health care, Kirkegaard (2009) notes that the share of total medical expenses that Americans pay out-of-pocket is lower than in the vast majority of European countries. He concludes that Americans are *more* likely to ask someone else to pay for their health care than people in many other countries and hence that their system is more 'socialized' than in most European countries. At the same time, we should keep in mind how inequitable is the American health care system.

Social Spending

Table 3.4. Gross to net social spending as a percentage of GDP, 2011

Country	Gross	Net
Austria	27.7	24.3
Belgium	29.4	27.4
Czechia	20.1	19.3
Denmark	30.1	26.1
Finland	28.3	23.4
France	31.4	31.3
Germany	25.5	25.3
Greece	25.7	23.7
Hungary	22.6	20.6
Ireland	22.3	21.9
Italy	27.5	25.4
Luxembourg	22.5	19.1
Netherlands	23.5	25.8
Portugal	24.8	24.0
Slovenia	24.0	21.6
Spain	26.8	24.8
Sweden	27.2	24.6
United Kingdom	22.7	26.1
United States	19.0	28.8

Source: Adema et al. (2011)

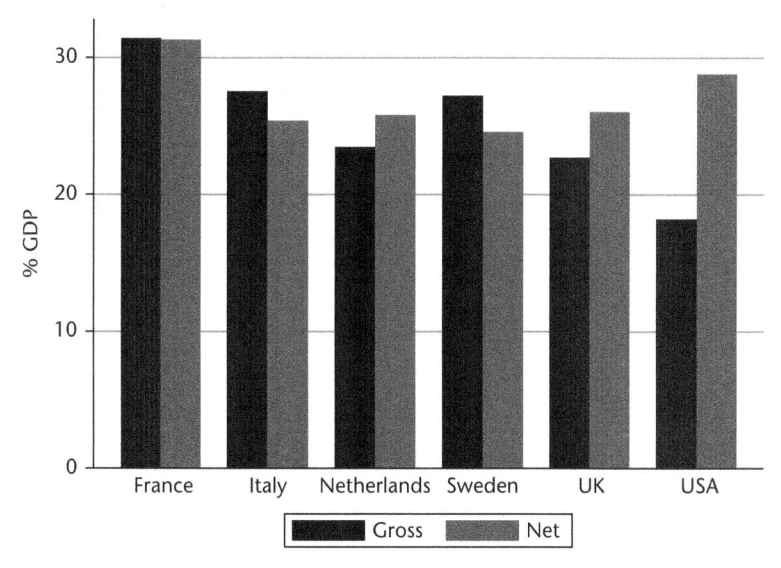

Figure 3.4. Gross and net social spending as a percentage of GDP, 2011
Source: Adema *et al.* (2011)

In Figure 3.4, we illustrate more clearly the difference between net and gross social spending in six countries. It is interesting to observe that gross social spending seems to converge more than net social spending. This is illustrated on Figure 3.5. To a certain extent, net social spending seems to correspond to a

35

The Welfare State in Europe

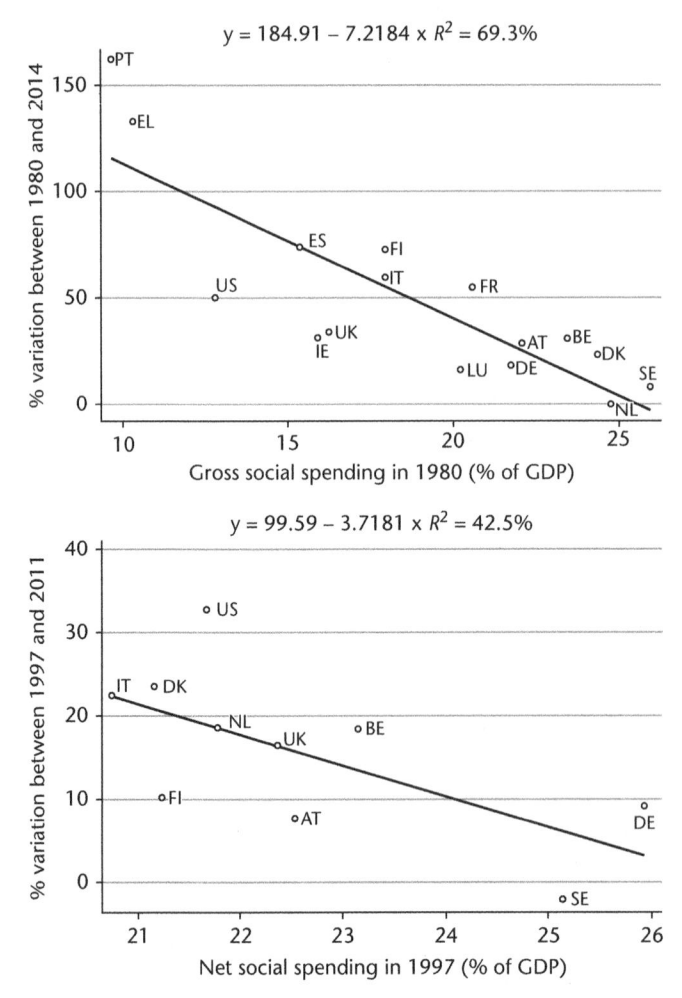

Figure 3.5. Convergence of gross and net social spending
Source: Adema *et al.* (2011)

stationary equilibrium, an equilibrium balance between the public and the private (mandatory) sectors.

3.5. The Entitlement Problem

It is somehow surprising to observe that in almost all EU countries, even the high spenders, social spending as a percentage of GDP is increasing. As we see below, there are a number of factors acting against such an evolution. The main reason for the continuous increase of the social burden is the growth of entitlements.

Entitlements are government programs providing funds to those who qualify, rather than appropriating a fixed amount of money for a program. For example, unemployment compensation is paid to those unemployed individuals who qualify; there is no set budget for the program (although there is an estimate of how much the program will cost). Entitlement spending is sometimes referred to as uncontrollable, because once the program is in effect, the level of expenditures depends upon external conditions. As a matter of routine, recent entitlement expenditures have exceeded estimates in all sectors of social protection, except family allowances. But this has not always been the case. In the beginning of social protection, programs made surpluses that were accumulated in funds.

The fact is that entitlement program spending is really not uncontrollable. At any time, public authorities can raise the eligibility requirements for any program, modify it, or cancel it altogether. But in order to do that, they face powerful lobbies. Cutting back entitlement programs when costs can be displaced onto future generations is particularly harsh in terms of political feasibility.

We shall come back to this difficulty, which is at the centre of the crisis of the welfare state, and specifically of the social security systems.

3.6. Conclusion

This chapter has provided an overview of the level, pattern, and evolution of social spending in Europe. Even though one observes some convergence, social spending is increasing in almost all countries. One of the reasons for this is the development of entitlements that make it difficult to dismantle programs that have lost most of their *raison d'être*. Another issue that has been discussed concerns the international comparison of programs that are public in some countries and private, but heavily subsidized, in others.

4
Revenue Sources

> **KEY CONCEPTS**
> fiscalization
> marginal tax rate
> payroll tax
> regressive
> tax expenditure
> tax shifting
> tax wedge

4.1. Introduction

In this chapter we look at the alternative sources of financing social protection in Europe. The main source is payroll taxation. Two issues are often raised: that of the regressivity of payroll taxation and that of enlarging a tax base that is increasingly restricted to salaried work.

4.2. Financing the Welfare State

There are a number of sources of financing for the welfare state in European countries. These include:

- General tax revenue—direct and indirect taxes
- Employer/employee social insurance contributions—either earmarked for individual programs or put in a general fund to finance the social protection system as a whole
- Special taxes—e.g. energy tax or income tax surcharges forming a 'solidarity contribution' towards financing social protection systems

- Direct charges and fees for public goods and services
- Tax expenditures—e.g. tax breaks towards private education, health insurance and pension schemes.

Table 4.1 presents the structure and the evolution of social protection financing in eighteen European countries. Together, employer and employee social insurance contributions form the largest source of finance in European countries. In 1990, employers' and employees' contributions accounted for more than 60 per cent of total receipts of social protection in the majority of countries. This percentage has decreased over the period 1990–2013. A notable exception is Denmark where general tax revenue forms a large share of finance and where payroll taxes have increased during that period. One should note that this prevailing financing structure is at the heart of a social protection program based on the labour market and co-managed by unions and employers. Thus it is not surprising to see Ireland and the UK as outliers in this respect as in many others. It is more surprising to see Denmark, and to a lesser degree Portugal, adopt a different financing structure relative to the other European states.

In the case of social spending, we have spoken of convergence. We can also speak of converging trends in the financing of social protection: an increase in the tax-financed component, and a reduction in employer contributions, particularly for certain categories of workers (young, unskilled). The share of

Table 4.1. Financing of social protection (in %)

	Social contributions			General government contributions			Other		
	1990	2000	2013	1990	2000	2013	1990	2000	2013
BE	67	67.6	59.8	23.8	29.4	38	9.2	3.0	2.2
CZ	–	73.8	70	–	25.0	28.5	–	1.2	1.5
DK	13.2	29.4	19.4	80.1	63.9	75.6	6.8	6.7	5
DE	–	65.9	64.9	–	31.7	33.4	–	2.3	1.7
EE	–	79.2	81.7	–	20.6	18.1	–	0.2	0.2
IE	40.3	35	36.1	59.4	64.8	60.5	0.3	0.3	3.5
EL	59	60.8	55.3	33.0	29.2	39.8	8.0	10.0	4.8
ES	71.3	67.5	53.4	26.2	29.9	44	2.5	2.7	2.6
FR	78.7	65	61.9	17.6	32.0	34.7	3.7	3.1	3.4
IT	68.9	56.9	50.3	28.9	40.8	47.8	2.2	2.4	2
LT	–	60	70.9	–	38.5	28.3	–	1.5	0.8
LU	50.5	48.5	46.3	41.5	46.9	41.9	8.1	4.6	11.8
NL	59.0	72.6	67.3	25.0	11.8	19.1	15.9	15.6	13.6
PL	–	66.2	62.7	–	21.6	21.8	–	12.2	15.5
PT	61.7	53	45.3	26.1	39.1	46.1	12.3	7.9	8.6
SK	–	66.8	64.1	–	31.0	31.7	–	2.2	4.2
FI	52.1	49.9	47.7	40.6	42.9	47.2	7.3	7.2	5.1
UK	55	52.4	41.7	42.6	46.4	51.1	2.4	1.2	7.2

Source: Eurostat (2017e)

government funds, as opposed to wage-related contributions, is increasing regularly in the majority of countries. This trend, known as one of 'fiscalization' is particularly evident in the Southern European countries, France and Belgium. Along the same lines, some countries have introduced a new 'solidarity tax' in an attempt to make up deficits in social protection programs. The creation of the CSG (Contribution Sociale Généralisée) in France, and of the Solidarity Payroll Tax in Belgium, is an attempt to widen the tax base upon which social protection schemes are traditionally funded. These new taxes are supposed to reach capital income and replacement income, in particular.

The share of employer contributions has fallen a lot, particularly in countries where that share was important. The pressure for further reduction is mounting. Reforms have focused on selective cuts. Problems of unemployment have prompted reductions in contributions for low-income earners and young workers. These cuts are observed in France, Belgium, Ireland, and the UK. Paradoxically, the trend towards fiscalization is sometimes coupled with a trend towards developing actuarial schemes, whereby contributions and benefits are closely linked, as in private insurance. This is particularly true in the area of pensions and health care. We will come back to this evolution towards a two-tier system of social protection: social assistance financed by general revenue and ensuring a flat benefit to all and actuarially fair schemes that are often, but not necessarily, private.

4.3. Alternative Sources

The various effects of labour-specific employer and employee social insurance contributions are the subject of various debates and of a large number of studies. Labour-specific taxes are often deemed to be regressive and to hurt competitiveness and employment. As a consequence, governments are increasingly searching for alternative sources of finance, notably through the fiscalization of social systems. Their hope is to have a financing structure that is less regressive, that implies fewer disincentives, and that rests on a wider base than the current one.

4.3.1. Regressive Taxation

From a purely public finance viewpoint, a payroll tax is just a flat tax on labour income. In some countries there are ceilings: that is, earnings levels beyond which the marginal tax rate falls to zero. Compared to a progressive personal income tax, for example, such a payroll tax is less redistributive. Not only is the relative tax burden the same for low and average wage earners, but also it may decrease for high wage earners when there is a ceiling. Given that the share of wage earnings that comprises the income of a household decreases as income increases, one sees that payroll taxation is as regressive as consumption taxation.

4.3.2. *Adverse Effect on Competition*

It is also argued that financing social protection from labour-specific taxes has an adverse effect on a nation's competitiveness. Payroll taxes add to a firm's wage costs and costs of production. The higher this burden, the less competitive that firm will be relative to firms from countries with lower tax burdens. This argument is linked to the notions of fiscal competition and social dumping (to which we will come back in Chapter 6) and whereby investment decisions are heavily influenced by the cost of labour input. This argument holds in particular with unskilled, low-wage labour that suffers from competition with countries having lower levels of social protection and lower labour costs. It has led a number of EU countries to introduce payroll tax cuts for unskilled labour.

At this point two remarks are in order. They pertain to the concept of tax shifting and to the benefit side of taxation. In theory, any increase in labour-specific taxes in perfectly competitive labour and product markets would have no impact on unemployment and wage costs. Any attempt by workers to compensate for higher taxes through higher wage demands would push up unemployment levels, driving wages back down again. In the real world, however, product and labour markets are not perfectly competitive. Higher wage demands may be passed on to consumers, wages do not clear automatically; and the final result of the wage-bargaining process depends on the relative strength of the position of employers and employees. Unemployment is not a simple function of wage costs; it has a number of other causes and influences. This is particularly true for unskilled labour, where real wages cannot adjust downwards because of the minimum wage prevailing in a number of countries.

Once again, in theory and in a Robinson Crusoe economy, one would expect that for each Euro of contribution there would be a Euro of benefit, and that such a one-to-one relation would neutralize any adverse effect of social insurance contribution. We will see that for a number of reasons this one-to-one relation does not really hold. But rather in some cases, it turns out to be a one-to-nothing relation.

To measure the burden of the taxes on labour we use the concept of implicit tax that approximates an average effective tax burden on labour income in the economy. To measure the distortive effect of these taxes, we use the concept of tax wedge. The tax wedge is defined as the ratio between the amount of taxes paid by an average single worker (for example, a single person at 67 per cent of

The Welfare State in Europe

Figure 4.1. Time trend in implicit tax rate on labour

Note: The average implicit tax rate on labour based on ESA79 system of national accounts is weighted by the total compensation of employees in the economy, whereas, for ESA95, the GDP-weighted average is used. Data based on ESA79 are only available for the EU-9 and EU-15 Member States (1970–79 and 1980–97, respectively). EU9 = EU6 + UK, Ireland and Denmark. EU19 is the Eurozone

Sources: European Commission (2000, 2009, and 2016)

average earnings) without children and the corresponding total labour cost for the employer. The tax wedge measures the extent to which the tax on labour income discourages employment and competition.

In Figure 4.1, we represent the average tax on labour for the period 1973–2015. It comes from different sources but definitively shows an increasing trend till 2000. After that, the tax reaches a sort of fluctuating ceiling at a quite high level. Figure 4.2 gives both the tax wedge and the average tax on labour for EU28 over the period 2003–2015. The two variables fluctuate quite a lot. The average implicit tax has been decreasing since 2009 and the tax wedge since 2012. This recent evolution reflects the desire of most European governments to increase their level of employment and to foster competitiveness.

Table 4.2 show important differences across European countries and also the fact that average tax and tax wedge are not correlated. For example, Sweden has the highest average tax on labour but not the highest tax wedge. The UK and Ireland have a quite low tax wedge as opposed to Belgium, Germany, and France.

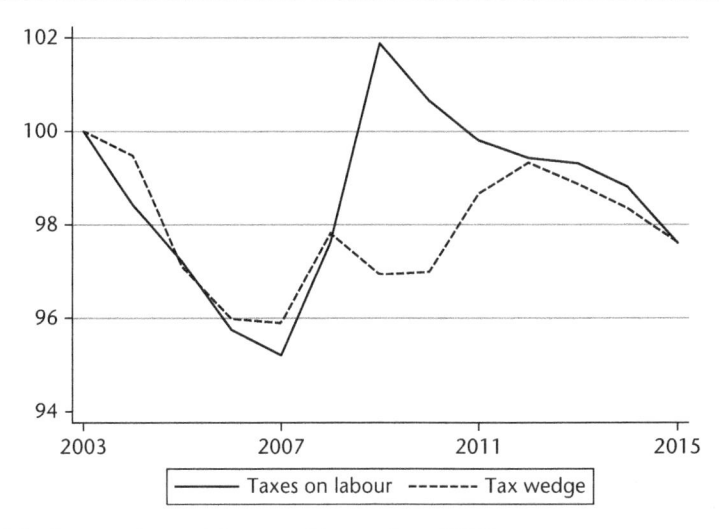

Figure 4.2. Average tax on labour and tax wedges: EU28

Note: Taxes on labour as % of total taxation and tax wedges for a single worker with 67% of average earnings, no children

Source: European Commission (2016)

Table 4.2. Average tax on labour and tax wedges in 2015

	Belgium	Germany	Ireland	France	Spain	Sweden	UK
Average tax	53.2	56.6	43.0	52.1	47.8	57.6	37.8
Tax wedges	49.5	45.3	21.6	43.7	36.0	40.7	26.0

Note: Taxes on labour as % of total taxation and tax wedges for a single worker with 67% of average earnings, no children

Source: European Commission (2016)

4.3.3. A Shrinking Tax Base

There is another reason why governments have become increasingly concerned about the growing share of tax on labour as a way to finance social protection, and more generally public expenditure. The share of regular, steady salaried labour is declining in a large number of countries, and thus the share of payroll tax base in the GDP is shrinking. As a result, governments are searching for alternative sources of finances. At the risk of being overly simplistic in our view of national accounts, we could say that on the expenditure side there are two main components: consumption, C, and savings, S. On the income side there are: wage earnings, W, other sources of earnings (self-employed, informal work), E, and capital income, K, to which one adds social benefits, B, and subtracts direct taxes, T. We write national income, Y, net of tax:

$$Y - T = C + S = W + E + K + B - T$$

As just mentioned, the share of wage earnings in national income (W/Y) is decreasing. At the same time, social protection caters to individuals who have no direct relationship to the regular wage market: non-working spouses, children, informal workers, unemployed, and so on. These individuals benefit from social protection without contributing to it, at least directly or sufficiently.

Over the period 1980–2000, labour-specific taxes, that is, social insurance contributions and personal income taxation applied to earnings, have increased as a source of government revenue in most European countries. This trend stopped and since 2000, the European labour-specific taxes have fluctuated as it appears on Figure 4.1, but they are set at high levels. One is thus faced with the simple question: why can't we find serious alternative sources of finance for public and social spending?

Let us briefly consider some potential alternative taxes.

- Consumption taxes.

These are surely the most serious alternative. By increasing taxes such as VAT, the tax burden falls on consumers rather than on workers and producers. People who receive an income from capital are also contributing to tax revenue. The disadvantages are that flat rate consumption taxes are already widely used in Europe, and that they tend to be regressive, slightly more and differently from payroll taxes.

- Taxes on capital.

Capital income and profits are subject to rather low taxes in the EU. There are two main reasons for this. First, as we shall see, tax competition is particularly strong for this type of tax. The second reason is that taxation of financial capital, as opposed to real estate, can easily be avoided, if not evaded.

- Tax on self-employment.

The issue of compliance also explains why effective taxation on self-employment, and on informal activities is low.

- Tax on replacement incomes.

Social protection benefits are less and less tax exempted at least beyond a minimum level. In an ageing society where elderly people benefit from incomes as high as those of other age groups, imposing taxes at least partially is increasingly accepted. This is an indirect way to tax income from occupational pensions, life insurance and other forms of savings.

To sum up, there is not much of an alternative to payroll taxation. The only tax base that seems to resist erosion is either the wage bill or final consumption. Both concern the same people. As a consequence, the alternative seems to be something between a regressive payroll tax and another, but differently, regressive value added tax. It is important to note that the choice of a source of finance has implications, not only in terms of efficiency and equity, but also in terms of organization. Countries, which move away from wage-related contributions, also move towards a more centralized state-managed organization from a 'corporatist' conception of social protection, that is, a set of programs jointly managed by employees and employers.

4.4. Social Insurance Contributions

In a large number of countries, social insurance contributions have long been considered as distinct from other sources of finance. In the beginning they were sufficient to finance social insurance. Indeed, it was possible to create funds to be used in case of bad times. Social insurance contributions were sometimes, and still are, divided according to function: family allowances, retirement, and unemployment, to generate distinct funds. Today most funds are depleted and these distinctions are at best formal.

The specificity of social insurance contributions can be explained in two ways. First, social insurance was co-managed by employee unions and employer organizations; together they decide the amount of benefits, contribution rates and investment in funds. Secondly, social contributions were viewed as totally different from taxes. Because they were earmarked and because the amount of contributions paid by a worker determined the amount of his/her benefits, contributions (also called payroll taxes) were considered as quasi-premiums, quasi-prices rather than taxes.

There are few empirical studies that try to assess the perception workers and employers have of these payroll taxes. Conventionally, OECD treats contributions to social insurance as pure taxes, for example, in calculations of the tax wedges. But this approach ignores any future rights to benefits perceived as such by contributors. In fact, social benefits contain both an actuarial and a redistributive component, the relative importance of which depends on whether the system is more or less contributive.[1] Recently all this has changed, which may be due to the idea that payroll taxes are less and less viewed as premiums even when benefits are related to payments. The share of contributions decreases consistently; (central) governments are taking over the organization and the management of social protection. As a consequence, more and more contributions are viewed as taxes. We will come back to this important issue. Indeed, if payroll contributions are considered to be taxes, that is, if they have the same distortionary effects as any other income tax, even when benefits are totally linked to these contributions, then the case for social insurance weakens.

---

[1] See Section 5.2.1 on this point.

4.5. Conclusion

Payroll taxation is still today the main source of financing social protection in the European Union. Ireland and Denmark are the only exceptions. In most countries, payroll taxation is an integral part of the social insurance compact, which involves unions and management. Payroll taxes are often presented as contributions or premiums paid for an insurance service. However whether it is so perceived by workers is an open question.

5

Types of Social Protection

> **KEY CONCEPTS**
>
> Beveridgean
> Bismarckian
> categorical benefits
> decommodification
> earnings-related benefits
> EITC, earned income tax credit
> individualization
> means-tested benefits
> paradox of redistribution
> poverty trap
> workfare

5.1. Introduction

There does not exist a single model for the welfare state in Europe. Each country has its own model that is the result of its political and social culture and of its economic evolution. There exist a number of taxonomies of welfare states, which focus on specific features of their functioning. We often favour a taxonomy based on two characteristics: the generosity and the redistributiveness of programs. The main interest of distinguishing among types of social protection programs is the different implications they have in terms of efficiency, equity and political sustainability.

5.2. Taxonomy of Social Protection

Most social protection systems include a mixture of transfers that differ by being either in cash or in kind, and by a type of benefit formula. One distinguishes three basic formulas: means-tested benefits, flat-rate benefits, and earnings-related benefits, to which one could add public subsidies for the purchase of private goods or services.

To receive a means-tested benefit, a family has to show that its income—its means—falls below a certain level. Welfare compensations such as the RMI (Revenu Minimum d'Insertion) in France or Income Support in the UK are typical means-tested transfers paid to those with low incomes and not working.

There are two non-means-tested formulas, also called categorical. Categorical benefits are paid to all those who fall within a particular category (the elderly, families with children, the unemployed, and so on). The first categorical benefits are those that are uniform, that is, unrelated to past contributions. One also speaks of 'universalistic' programs as providing equal benefits: equal access to health care to all, or child allowances that go to all families with children regardless of income.

The second type of categorical benefits are the earnings-related benefits. There are indeed a number of programs that pay benefits that depend on past income or contributions. Table 5.1 presents those different types of programs. Even though all European countries employ policies of all types, the mixture can differ dramatically.

To cite one example, the US government spends as much as most European governments on health care. However, there is a large difference in the design of health care policies. In most European countries, health care is a universalistic equal benefit program of care for all. By contrast, in the US, health care public expenditures are divided into a universalistic program for the elderly (medicare), a means-tested program for the poor (medicaid), and tax subsidies for private health care for private sector employees.

In 'The Three Worlds of Welfare Capitalism', Esping-Andersen (1990) distinguishes between three different types of welfare state, which he calls 'welfare

Table 5.1. Taxonomy of social transfers

	Means-tested	Categorical	
		Flat benefits (universalistic, Beveridgean)	Earnings-related benefits (social insurance, Bismarkian)
In cash	Welfare compensation	Family allowances	Unemployment compensation
In kind	Food stamps	Health services	–

Types of Social Protection

Table 5.2. The rank role of welfare state. Decommodification scores

Country	Esping/Andersen (1990)	Bambra (2006)
United States	13.8	14.0
Ireland	23.3	22.1
United Kingdom	23.4	15.4
Italy	24.1	27.6
France	27.5	31.5
Germany	27.7	27.7
Finland	29.2	34.6
Austria	31.1	31.1
Belgium	32.4	31.9
Netherlands	32.4	28.0
Denmark	38.1	29.0
Sweden	39.1	34.7

Source: Esping-Andersen (1990) and Bambra (2006)

state regimes', and which correspond to three different mixtures of benefit formula and generosity in spending.[1]

First, there is the 'liberal' welfare state where means-tested assistance predominates. Benefits accrue mainly to a clientele of low-income households. In countries that adopt this welfare state regime, entitlement rules are strict and often associated with stigma, while benefits are typically modest. The archetypal examples of this model are the UK, the USA, Canada, and Australia. The second welfare state regime clusters nations such as Austria, France, Germany, and Italy. They are strongly 'corporatist', above market forces, and attached to class and status. Their welfare states leave little room for private insurance and are hardly redistributive. The third welfare state regime caters to 'social democratic' countries, such as the Scandinavian ones, in which the principle of universalism of social rights prevails. It tends to be rather generous and redistributive, and committed to a heavy social-service burden.

Esping-Andersen (1990) uses the concept of 'decommodification' of social protection, meaning that services are rendered and transfers made as a matter of right, without reliance on the market. Using a number of indicators, he builds a scale of decommodification and rates his sample of welfare states accordingly. Table 5.2 ranks twelve nations according to their decommodification score.[2] This allows him to distinguish between three welfare state regimes: the Anglo-Saxon nations are all concentrated at the bottom of his index; the Scandinavian countries are at the top; in between, we find the continental

---

[1] See also Svallfors (1997), who analyses attitudes to redistribution and income differences in eight Western nations and on that basis develops his own taxonomy of welfare states: the social democratic (Sweden/Norway), the conservative (German/Austria), the liberal (US/Canada) and the radical (Australia/New Zealand).

[2] Esping-Andersen in fact ranks eighteen countries. Table 5.2 considers only European countries and the United States.

European countries, some of which, like Belgium and the Netherlands, fall close to the Nordic cluster. Table 5.2 provides also the ranking of Bramba (2006)[3], which is more recent and slightly differs from that of Esping-Andersen.

Note that the ranking of countries is likely to vary according to the programs at hand. Furthermore, Esping-Andersen's is not the only type of clustering. Another distinction often made is between Bismarckian and Beveridgean systems (Purton 1996). In the first, contributions through employment generate entitlement to benefits, and benefits are closely linked to occupations and income. The Beveridgean system, on the other hand, ensures that all individuals belonging to some category are entitled to a basic level of income at a flat rate and independent of income. This distinction, widely used, is a bit surprising. Beveridge had originally argued that everyone should pay the same contribution and receive the same benefit. Bismarck, on the other hand, was in favour of an earnings-related benefit scheme, but without assistance features. There is naturally some overlap between Esping-Andersen's three regimes, and the Beveridge-Bismarck dichotomy. Actually, the rate of decommodification increases with the generosity (size of spending) and the redistributiveness of the system (how Beveridgean it is).

But why are we concerned with such a taxonomy? There are at least three reasons. Depending on the welfare state regime, the implications for income inequality and poverty, for incentives and for political sustainability may vary a lot. Before looking at these three implications, it is important to note that a social protection system can be defined by its degree of redistributiveness and by its generosity. The first one is characterized by the level of flat benefit awarded to everyone, or by the parameters of means-testing. The second one can be proxied by the share of spending to GDP. This distinction is quite important when comparing countries. In the above distinction of welfare state regimes, the 'Nordic' and the 'Anglo-Saxon' regimes are both redistributive, but the former are by far more generous. Table 5.3 presents a classification of welfare states according to those two dimensions, generosity and redistributiveness.

Table 5.3. Generosity versus redistribution

	Redistributive	Not redistributive
Generous	Nordic countries	Bismarckian France, Germany
Not generous	Beveridgian Anglo-Saxon countries	

---

[3] Bambra (2007) provides a good overview of alternative welfare state regimes as well as his own country ranking.

5.3. Implications of Alternative Regimes

5.3.1. *Redistribution*

Consider a given amount of resources. How can it be best allocated if the main purpose is poverty relief? Clearly, a means-tested transfer program prevails over a flat benefit scheme, and surely over an earnings-related benefit scheme. Conversely, a pure earnings-related benefit scheme has no effect on poverty or even on income inequality. One way to assess the effect of alternative systems on poverty is to calculate what has been termed their 'vertical expenditure efficiency', that is, the proportion of the benefits that accrue to households that would have been poor in the absence of benefits.[4]

Paradoxically, it has been observed that a number of means-tested programs have poor vertical efficiency (Beckerman and Clark 1982). This explains why some egalitarian and social protection reformers argue for a 'Back to Beveridge' approach. In other words they favour universalistic rather than means-tested programs. They do so because of two major disadvantages of means-tests: their relative low take-up and their high administrative cost. People eligible for means-tested benefits often do not apply for them partly because of a lack of knowledge, partly because of a reluctance to accept what may be perceived as charity,[5] and partly because of the complex administrative procedures involved. Universalistic benefits often have 100 per cent take up. They also cost less, as they don't imply any control of admissibility, except for the category involved.

5.3.2. *Incentives*

The three benefits rules: means-tested, flat-rate, and earnings-related are also very different with respect to their effects on the incentive to work. All forms of social protection create some disincentive to work. On the revenue side, the payroll tax, or any other tax, implies some allocative distortion. On the benefit side, payments mean that their recipients have to work less hard to obtain a given standard of living. In the terminology of Chapter 7, increased resources (the income effect) discourage work. Means-tested benefits have a built in additional disincentive, for they always involve a reduction in benefit if the individual concerned works harder, and thus raises his or her means of support. The gains from substituting work for leisure are reduced. Put another way, individuals face a marginal tax on their earnings that can go above 100 per cent: for every Euro earned, more than one Euro is taken away in benefits (welfare payment, housing subsidy, school lunch, etc.). This situation is often

---

[4] This is close to the effect of social protection on poverty and inequality studied in Chapter 3.
[5] One speaks of stigmatization.

termed the 'poverty trap', that is to say, a situation where there is no net financial gain by working. This may explain part of the current unemployment in the Europe and has led to corrective measures in the spirit of the EITC (Earned Income Tax Credit) in the United States, namely an employment subsidy.

Note, however, that some categorical benefits are also subject to the same disincentive effects as means-tested benefits. When the category is somewhat manipulable, there can be an incentive to belong to it in order to get benefits. Disability and unemployment are typical of such categories. In the Netherlands, where disability compensations were relatively high and disability tests rather loose, the percentage of disabled workers just before retirement exceeded an astonishing 1/2 for several years.

Conversely, earnings-related benefits are expected to bring fewer disincentive effects than flat-rate benefits. The reason is simple. Assume a payroll tax of rate τ and an earnings related scheme that gives back k per cent of earnings ($k < \tau$) to the individual concerned. If this individual really understands the relation between contributions and benefits, his or her effective tax rate will drop to $\tau - k$, instead of τ that would be the tax rate of a universalistic program with the same generosity. On the other hand, the higher k, the lower the program redistributiveness. We thus come back to the equity-efficiency quandary.

In a Bismarckian system, even a partial one, the relevant question is whether or not contributors perceive that what they pay will be returned to them at least in part. As yet there has been little work on this. Disney (2004) has tried to split between the Beveridgean (tax) and the Bismarckian (premium) component in social security benefits across a range of OECD countries and time periods. He has found that the Beveridgean component has an adverse effect on the activity of women, but not of men.[6] In the French tradition, the concept of solidarity is widely used to characterize a welfare state of the Bismarckian type. One of the alleged properties of a solidarity-based welfare state is that it provides a lot of insurance but also some redistribution, but in a way that is widely accepted by everyone; hence there is little or no distortion. Unfortunately, empirical testing of the virtues of solidarity is extremely difficult.

5.3.3. Political Support

Another implication of these alternative welfare state regimes is the political support each of them is capable of attracting. There is a long-standing debate in Europe, as well as in the United States, regarding the relative advantages of alternative types of social policies. In the United States, the debate focuses on

---

[6] See also Ooghe et al. (2003).

the opposition between means-tested and universalistic programs, whereas in Europe it focuses on the opposition between a flat benefit and earnings-related benefit programs. Advocates of the universalistic program argue that programs that spread benefits widely garner greater political support than programs whose benefits go only to a minority of the population. On the other side, advocates of means-testing argue that universalistic programs are unnecessarily expensive for the purpose at hand: most of the subsidies go to the middle class and only a small proportion of the money reaches those who most need assistance. When contrasting flat-rate and earnings-related benefits systems, the same argument is used: the former costs less and is more effective at alleviating poverty; the latter attracts greater political support from the middle class that wants to get even.

Both sides of the debate can point to particular policies as supporting evidence. Advocates of categorical programs cite the popularity of social security in a number of countries. Advocates of means-testing counter it with the example of welfare programs, such as the RMI or the RSA in France, which are effective at alleviating poverty with few resources. In any case, over the last decades, elections have been won or lost because of the threat of social protection reforms. Some of these reforms, which were rejected by the voters, seemed to be fair from the usual equity-efficiency trade-off. This points to the necessity for social scientists to move from the couple equity-efficiency to a *ménage à trois* with equity, efficiency and political sustainability.

In this debate one often finds the grass greener on the other side of the Channel. British economists tend to underline the pitfalls of a meagre social protection based on means-tested or flat-rate benefits, whereas the Continental economists find their Bismarckian earnings-related programs expensive and inefficient. In that respect the recent evolution is quite interesting. EU governments tend to be less ideological and more pragmatic. For example, in Bismarckian countries where earnings-related benefits and employer/employee contributions are the 'official' doctrine, one progressively slides towards a system of flat-rate benefits and general tax revenue financing.

In theory moderate levels of social spending could produce low poverty rates if resources were well targeted and yet it remains the case that almost no country achieves a low poverty rate with a low level of social spending. Large, universal welfare systems, while on paper being least distributive, distribute in fact the most. This has been dubbed the *paradox of redistribution* by Korpi and Palme (1998). One of the reasons for the paradox relies on the fact that sufficient political support requires a universal system close to the Bismarkian one. Moene and Wallerstein (2001) and Casamatta et al. (2000) show that a certain dose of Bismarck is needed to create a majority coalition comprising the least well off but also the middle-class. This means that some redistributive inefficiency, what has been labelled the *Matthew effect*, is needed to insure the political sustainability of the welfare state. We come back to this in Chapter 8, which deals with the efficiency of the welfare state.

In a survey (Eurobarometer 2011), Europeans were asked about their preferences for the welfare state and about their views on responsibility. The questions they were asked are the following:

Which of these two statements comes closest to your view?

1) *Higher level of health care, education, and social spending must be guaranteed, even if it means that taxes might increase*
2) *Taxes should be decreased even if it means a general lower level of health care, education and social spending*

Which of these two statements comes closest to your view?

1) *Your Government should take more responsibility to ensure that everyone is provided for*
2) *People should take more responsibility to provide for themselves*

Table 5.4 displays the results of this survey.

From this table, it appears clearly that Denmark, Luxembourg, the Netherlands, and the UK are in favour of a generous welfare state, as opposed to Germany, Greece, Portugal and Italy. The position of the UK and Germany is quite surprising. On average, Europeans seem to be in favour of more social spending (63 per cent). Regarding the issue of responsibility, the majority is in favour of a universal coverage regardless of responsibility. The countries that seem to be responsibility prone are Denmark, Luxembourg, the Netherlands, and the UK.

Table 5.4. Two views on the welfare state

	Preference for the welfare state		Responsibility	
	1	2	1	2
Belgium	56%	27%	47%	44%
Denmark	80%	14%	42%	50%
France	65%	16%	51%	36%
Germany	54%	28%	57%	34%
Greece	54%	21%	76%	15%
Ireland	59%	15%	59%	26%
Italy	53%	18%	64%	20%
Luxembourg	72%	11%	32%	49%
Netherlands	79%	10%	27%	65%
Portugal	53%	18%	50%	32%
Spain	62%	21%	70%	21%
UK	74%	16%	42%	48%
EU12	63%	18%	51%	37%

Source: Eurobarometer EB74.1 (2011)

Types of Social Protection

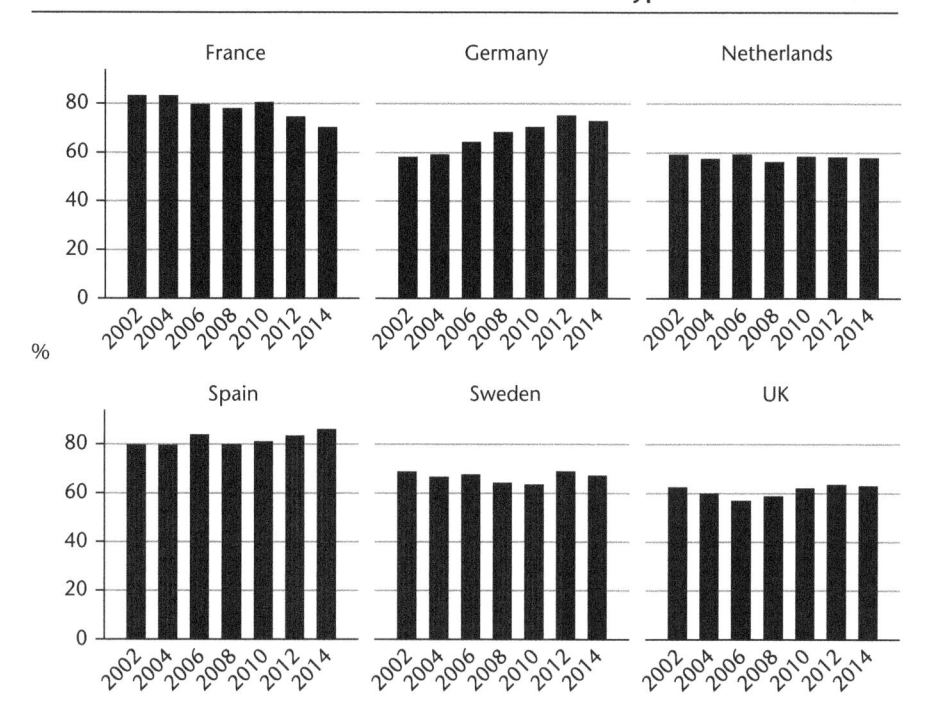

Figure 5.1. Percentage of people who agree or strongly agree that government should reduce differences in income levels
Source: ESS Round 1 to 7: European Social Survey Round 7 Data (2014). Data file edition 2.1. NSD: Norwegian Centre for Research Data, Norway—Data Archive

Along the same line, the European Social survey publishes on a regular basis data on preferences for redistribution. Figure 5.1 presents the percentage of people who are in favour of redistribution in six countries over the period 2002–2014. There are clear differences across countries, with France and Spain showing the strongest preference for redistribution. Over time, the percentage is quite stable except for France where it is decreasing and Germany where it is increasing.

In a recent paper, Olivera (2015) analyses the determinants of those preferences for redistribution in thirty-four European countries over the six available waves of the European Social Survey. He shows that, at least in Europe, growing income inequality leads to more individual support for redistribution.

5.4. Styles of Welfare State

Lately, a number of economists have considered a more pragmatic distinction, that between European and American-style welfare states. Their aim is to explain differences in redistributive policies between most European countries and the US. Instead of focusing on history and traditions, they base their explanation on the self-fulfilling role of agents' preferences, beliefs, and their induced norms of behaviour.

It seems widely accepted that redistribution is more easily supported if the focus is on bad luck rather than on individual responsibility or if it covers poverty driven by exogenous events rather than deprivation resulting mostly from laziness. It is sometimes asserted that Europeans put more weight (more probability) than Americans on random causes than on individual responsibility in order to explain poverty and deprivation.[7] Naturally, this conjecture cannot be tested empirically in an unambiguous way.

Benabou and Tirole (2002) use the concept of cognitive dissonance to explain individual belief in a just world. They show that, starting from the same initial conditions, society can evolve in two distinct directions and end up in two contrasting welfare states. The first is characterized by a high prevalence of the belief in a just world together with a relatively laissez-faire public policy. Both characteristics are mutually sustaining and generate an optimistic view of the world. The second welfare state is characterized by more realistic pessimism and tends to be more generous, which in turn reduces the need for individuals to invest in positive beliefs. In this welfare state there is less stigma on the poor: one does not blame poverty on a lack of effort or will-power.

Bisin and Verdier (2004) focus on the interaction between redistribution policies and ethical beliefs, particularly the so-called 'work ethic'. Ethical beliefs are not given, but evolve over time, partially driven by parental education. Parents try to shape their children's beliefs according to their own beliefs. Redistribution is chosen through majority voting in a setting where the individual's work ethic is private information. The final solution, that is the long run redistribution equilibrium, may depend or not on the initial distribution of preferences. There are cases where multiple equilibria result from the same initial conditions, some with generous redistribution and some without.

Along the same lines, Lindbeck (1995a,b) analyses the interaction between welfare state disincentives and the evolution of the work ethic.[8] There is also the work of Hassler et al. (2003) which leads to multiple equilibria of redistribution. They study a dynamic model with repeated voting: agents vote over distortionary income distribution, knowing that their votes will influence the next period vote. These models are theoretical. There are also papers that try to test differences in beliefs and norms between Europe and the US. Alesina et al. (2001), for example, present a study of the determinants of welfare state

---

[7] See Alesina and Angeletos (2002).   [8] See also Lindbeck et al. (1999).

policies. They conclude that none of the economic, political, and sociological factors they examine can explain the differences between the US and Europe. The explanation is to be found elsewhere. According to the *World Value Survey*, less than 40 per cent of Americans believe that luck determines income, while this percentage is close to 60 per cent for Italians, the Spanish, Germans and the French.

These are just a few representative samples of work aimed at explaining the emergence of two styles of welfare state, without resorting to what some economists consider as ad hoc assumptions: exogenous differences in values, traditions, or preferences. One cannot but be ill at ease with some of these contributions: behind a rigorous methodology they hide some value judgements. To start with, opposing the US (and generally the Anglo-Saxon world) to Europe (or Continental Europe), is a bit simplistic. Europe is very heterogeneous as it appears in Table 5.4. With characteristics such as social spending, unemployment rates, savings rates, age of retirement, or education, it is difficult to find the US as an outlier. More seriously, this type of work tends to consider the US style as being the only sustainable welfare state.

5.5. The Active Versus Passive Welfare State

Within Europe, one finds two contrasting views of the welfare state: a passive and an active view. The notion of the active welfare state includes two ideas. On the one hand, there is the goal of a high employment rate and full responsibilization. On the other hand, there is the pervasive concern for offering protection to those who are excluded from the labour market. By default, a passive welfare state is one in which unemployment is viewed as a fatality and individual responsibility for being poor or unemployed is discounted.[9]

Admittedly this distinction is impressionistic. It appears in the opposition between two forms of socialism: traditional socialism that supports a regime where free enterprise co-exists with central regulation of the economy, some socialized production, and welfare programs, and liberal socialism, or social democracy, that supports economic interventions to promote social justice within the framework of a capitalist economy.[10]

This distinction separates Europe with an East–West dividing line that goes through Belgium. Actually, the concept of activation divides Belgium between the Flemish North and the French-speaking South. In the North, policymakers speak of responsibilization in health care, compliance in unemployment

[9] See Vandenbroucke (2001), De Lathouwer (2004).
[10] One of its modern version is the third way advocated by Giddens (1998).

insurance, workfare for the unemployed young without incurring negative reactions from the unions or from the political left. In the South, these ideas are too often labelled as socially regressive. In that respect Belgium is an interesting real life laboratory. The two main regions have the same legal and fiscal institutions, and yet their views of the welfare state are quite opposite.[11] At the same time, Flanders has an unemployment rate of 5 per cent or half of what it is in the French-speaking region. Is this the cause or is it the consequence? Very likely both. In the activation approach, there is the idea that one has to fight both unemployment and poverty. As the US and the UK examples show, one can have quasi-full employment as well as striking poverty.

Activation advocates argue that most schemes in traditional social protection do not encourage people to be active. Thus they should be abolished, or adapted in order to prevent the social safety net from becoming an 'inactivity trap'.[12] Moreover, the active welfare states should be proactive in preventing people from running to social aids (unemployment, disability, exclusion). There is the presupposition that individual vulnerability is at least in part socially determined and that intervention strategies are needed, for example, in the field of training and education. The active welfare state intervenes on a tailor-made basis. Target groups and goals have to be identified carefully and programs must adjust to individual situations. Nothing should be taken for granted. There should be a constant questioning of whether the existing programs are appropriate to solving social problems, and not the other way around.

In almost all European countries, some types of activation have been installed in the welfare state with more or less success. Success depends in large part on the way reforms are presented. It is important to explain to the unions, the political left, and above all to the citizens, that an active welfare state is as protective as it is active. However, even with the best pedagogy, there will always be some resistance from some groups who stand to lose something in the process of reform.

A good example of activation is the Danish 'flexicurity' approach,[13] which combines flexibility (a high degree of job mobility), social security (a generous system of unemployment benefits) and active labour market programs. Flexibility seems to work, at least, in Denmark where both unemployment and

---

[11] As an example, some time ago, the then Belgian Minister of Employment, Frank Vandenbroucke, one of the outspoken advocates of activation, introduced a reform allowing the federal agency that pays unemployment compensations to control the search efforts for employment of the unemployed. This reform was easily accepted in the north of the country, but fiercely rejected in the south by people who refuse this transformation of the federal agency into what they dubbed the 'National Office of Massive Exclusion.' Interestingly, acknowledging the difference in unemployment rates between the two regions, the Minister suggested that the controls ought to be less frequent where the rate of unemployment is the higher. This was considered discriminatory by some French-speaking political analysts.
[12] See Cantillon and van den Bosch (2002), Nolan and Marx (2000).   [13] See OECD (2004).

poverty are low. We come back to this in the chapter on unemployment. Compared to Belgium and France, Danish unemployment compensations are high, but after a short period there is an obligation to participate in activation programmes.

Besides the extent of activation, one can also evaluate welfare states according to two characteristics: individualization and responsabilization. Responsibilization is a concept close to that of activation: it refers to the process whereby subjects are rendered individually responsible for situations, which previously would have been recognized as resulting from bad luck. Individualization of social rights means equal access to the labour market for women and men and, through work, access to social rights for all insured workers. As a consequence, derived rights, linked to family relationship, granted to the spouse/partner not involved in employment, might be abolished. It can be stated that in Europe the legislation on social protection is characterized by an increasing degree of individualization of social rights and of responsabilization of citizens.

The area where individualization may be costly is that of welfare policy, as the following example shows. Suppose we have to provide a welfare compensation to a single individual and a couple. They have no resources to start and we can only spend 1800€ a month. Individualization implies that everyone receives 600€ with the consequence that the couple consumes 1200€ and the single 600€. It would seem fairer to allocate this limited budget using the equivalence scale according to which a couple needs 1.5 times what a single needs. Hence, the couple receives 1080€ and the single individual 720€.

5.6. Alternative Approaches

The approach adopted in this book is pragmatic and purposely balanced. We consider that priority should be given to the objectives of social protection: insurance against life uncertainty and poverty alleviation regardless of the institutions called for: the state, the market and the family. These are only viewed as different means to achieve these two objectives. In that respect, we are at odds with social philosophers and political scientists who tend to privilege one of these three institutions over the two other ones.

In his taxonomy of welfare states, Esping-Andersen (1990) distinguishes three views. First, there is the Anglo-Saxon view favouring individualism and markets, with the state and the family as nominal residual players. This view is associated with John Locke's tradition. Secondly, there is the Scandinavian view favouring the state along with the values of social democracy, universalism, egalitarianism, and comprehensive social citizenship. This approach is in line with Jean-Jacques Rousseau's tradition. Here both the family and the market are extras.

Finally, there is the Continental version involving France and Germany, where the central locus is the firm viewed as a family, and the southern countries where the family is the main player. In this view which is consistent with the philosophy of Thomas Hobbes, both the state and the market are residual players. The key concepts are those of corporatism and of solidarity within the firm and within the family.

We thus have several triptychs. On the left, one finds the state, the virtue of equality, Rousseau, social democracy. In the centre, one can see the family and the firm, the virtue of fraternity and solidarity, Hobbes and a corporatist society. On the right, there is the market, the virtues of freedom and liberty, Locke and a market economy. The approach chosen in this book is not to focus on just one of the panels of these triptychs, but on them all.[14]

5.7. Conclusion

In this chapter we have surveyed a number of taxonomies of social protection programs existing in the European Union. The main interest of these classifications is that different programs have different implications in terms of equity, efficiency, and political sustainability.

We first focused on the characteristics of redistribution and generosity. We then introduced other features, such as the opposition between the active and the passive welfare state, or between two sources of social exclusion: bad luck or lack of responsibility. Finally we distinguished among three types of European welfare states based on their geography: Anglo-Saxon, Nordic, and Continental.

---

[14] For an excellent discussion of these alternative views, see Masson (2004, 2009), who applies them to intergenerational transfers.

6

Social Protection and Globalization

> **KEY CONCEPTS**
>
> HDI, human development index
> OMC (Open Method of Coordination)
> posted workers
> prisoner's dilemma
> profit shifting
> race to the bottom
> social dumping
> tax competition
> yardstick competition

6.1. Introduction

Europeans are divided over two opposite approaches regarding globalization. The first one, which is dominant and named *pensée unique* (one track viewpoint) in France, consists in viewing economic integration with mixed feelings of hope and resignation. That is, hope that globalization will ensure steady growth and full employment for years ahead, and resignation regarding the diminishing role of national governments in economic and social policy. The second approach, epitomized by the various populist movements, sees both globalization and competition as responsible for persistent unemployment, and implies the abdication of politics in favour of economics. This quite radical view presents the choice offered to European voters between the (German) social democratic model and the (American) capitalist model as equivalent to a choice between the plague and cholera.[1]

---

[1] See on this Ravallion (2003) and Agenor (2002).

In this chapter we discuss two basic ideas. The first one is that technological change as much as (if not more than) globalization leads to increasing income disparities; accordingly, European unemployment is caused by attempts at fighting these inequalities. The second one is that globalization, and specifically factor mobility, make it difficult for national governments to conduct any redistributive policy, thus leading to what is sometimes called 'the race to the bottom', or 'social dumping.'

6.2. Benefits of Globalization

Over recent decades, the economies of European countries have moved along two distinct tracks, neither of which has offered a compelling model for current public policy. The economies of Ireland and the United Kingdom, like those of North America and Australia, have been creating a lot of jobs, while suffering from wage stagnation and growing inequality. By contrast, economies in Continental Europe have featured growing wages and more modest income gaps, but have been far less successful at job generation. Must we simply decide between wage stagnation and double-digit unemployment? Or might there be a third way, one that combines jobs with decent compensation for workers, low poverty rates with employment? Arguably these are the fundamental questions facing all European governments. We shall deal with them in Chapter 12. For the time being, let us look at the causes of these evolutions.

There is a tendency to blame unemployment or poverty on globalization: since growing trade with countries abundant in unskilled labour increases the premium on skill, this would explain inequality in North America and unemployment in Europe. This idea is attractive as it offers a broad common explanation for what is happening in the two sets of countries. Furthermore, it ties the labour market trends in advanced nations to the growth of international trade and the rise of newly industrialized countries. Finally, the idea of factor price equalization is well grounded in economic theory. As Krugman (1996) puts it: 'All in all, the proposition that globalization explains the simultaneous growth in inequality and unemployment makes a nice, intellectually appealing package; it is not surprising that it should command wide acceptance' (p. 21). Then Krugman bluntly adds: 'Unfortunately, empirical research is nearly unanimous in rejecting the idea that imports from the Third World have been a major factor in reducing the demand for less-skilled workers.' Indeed, one observes a consistent increase in the ratio of skilled to unskilled workers employed within each industry, despite the rise in the relative wage of the skilled. Thus one has to look elsewhere for the source of growing inequality and of rising unemployment.

It now appears to be widely accepted that the increase in the skill premium is primarily the result of technological change, including the digital revolution. The fact that both the relative wage and the employment of skilled workers have increased simultaneously indicates a change in the production functions that raises the marginal product of the skilled, relative to the unskilled. In countries such as the United States, and to some extent the UK and Ireland, where relative wages are highly flexible, the result is the growth of earnings inequality along with full employment. In European countries, where relative wages are rather fixed, one can only avoid such growth at the cost of unemployment. Furthermore, the effects of low-wage exports on employment are also negative (Krugman 1995) not because of the trade itself, but as a consequence of minimum wages. Also, a number of people have remarked that there is nothing new in the phenomenon of globalization. World markets achieved an impressive degree of integration during the second half of the nineteenth century.

Long-term comparisons show a trend towards regionalization as well as globalization of trade. For example, in the early fifties the five most important European trading partners of Belgium and Luxembourg accounted for less than half of total imports and exports; today, this share is approximately 70 per cent. What can we conclude from these figures? First, that globalization is not a new phenomenon. Secondly, that it cannot be considered as the main cause, or at least not the direct one, of increased unemployment. Thirdly, that it is largely responsible for the economic expansion of the last decades. However, there is a problem with economic integration particularly restricted to a regional area such as the EU: it raises the economic cost of redistributive policy, and thereby threatens a basic function of the welfare state.

Although the net cost of globalization is still debated, its political cost is undisputed. In a recent paper, Dani Rodrik (2017) analyses the surge of populist movements across Europe and America. The main argument of his paper is that 'advanced stages of globalization are prone to populist backlash' and the specific form populism takes will depend on the different societal cleavages that politicians can exploit to promote anti-establishment movements. One observes left-wing populism when 'globalization shocks take the form of trade, finance, and foreign investment' and right-wing populism when 'the globalization shock becomes salient in the form of immigration and refugees'. By advanced stage of globalization, Rodrick means that the efficiency gains of globalization are dominated by the redistributive losses that comprise loss of jobs, low wages, and poverty. Rodrik argues that this advanced stage occurred in the past in the late nineteenth century. He dates the first self-consciously populist movement in the US to the 1880s in opposition to the Gold Standard. Today we are experiencing the same situation.

6.3. Tax Competition and Race to the Bottom

Even though economic integration is not responsible for increased income disparities, it is often argued that it imposes new constraints on the ability of governments to engage in redistributive policies.[2] The potential mobility of factors of production, in response to differentials in taxation or benefits, underlies traditional arguments for centralization of the redistributive functions of governments. Increased internationalization of factor markets implies that such a central government, that is, one whose geographical extent coincides with that of the relevant factor markets, does not have the power of a national government. There is thus a clear divorce between the political geographical coverage and the economic one. This is surely true of the EU, particularly regarding the mobility of capital. The mobility of labour is still low compared, for example, to that within the USA; yet it represents quite a threat.

Capital mobility explains why it is now impossible for European governments to effectively tax interest incomes. At best, these are subject to a withholding tax of 20 per cent that has to be contrasted with marginal rates above 50 per cent on labour income[3]. This makes financing of the welfare state regressive and difficult, particularly in countries with a high outstanding debt. With labour mobility, the prognosis is even more pessimistic. As Sinn (1990) puts it, discussing European integration with increasing mobility, and no cooperation among governments, labour mobility could lead to 'the death of the insurance state.' He goes on:

> Any country that tries to establish an insurance state would be driven to bankruptcy because it would face emigration of the lucky who are supposed to give, and immigration of the unlucky who are supposed to receive. Voting with one's feet would only work if it could be limited to the young, and if the middle-aged managers and successful entrepreneurs could be prevented from migrating—a rather awkward idea. A Europe with competing tax systems and unrestricted migration would be like an insurance market, where the customers can select their company and pay the premium after they know whether or not a loss has occurred (p. 502).

The perverse effect of governments competing for tax base was first underlined by George Stigler (1965) in an often quoted paper on the limits of local government. Indeed, one can view European governments as local governments lacking a central (supranational) authority. Stigler also noted that

---

[2] For a survey of the literature, see Cremer and Pestieau (2004), Cremer et al. (1997). See also Razin and Sadka (2005) who strongly believe that tax competition will eventually lead to the decline of the European welfare states. They argue that the US welfare state, which is mainly organized at the federal level, is more sustainable than the European ones.

[3] This is the dual income tax system, also known as the Nordic tax system or the Nordic Dual Income Tax.

Social Protection and Globalization

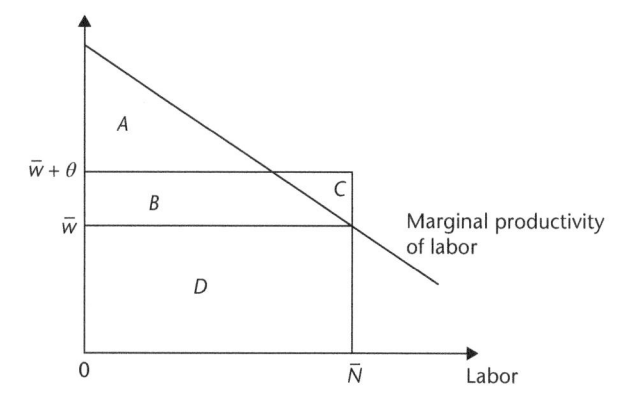

Figure 6.1. Race to the bottom

the current organization of local governments would make it impossible for any of them 'to obtain money from the rich to pay for the education of the children of the poor, except to the extent that the rich voluntarily assumed this burden' (p. 172).

To illustrate the issue at hand, we take the example of a small open economy whose national production results from the joint use of immobile capital and mobile unskilled labour. Figure 6.1 represents the marginal productivity of labour. In an autarchy the 'national' workers, $\bar{N}$, are paid their marginal productivity, $\bar{w}$. The wage bill is thus equal to area D, and aggregate capital income including profits is equal to area $A + B$.

There are few capital owners in this country, and they are willing (or forced) to devote part of their income to a redistributive transfer equal to θ. This implies that workers now receive a total amount of $B + C + D$ or $(B+C+D)/\bar{N}$ per unit. The capital owners now receive $A - C$. Suppose now that this economy is open to migration, and that the world wage rate is $\bar{w}$. This would have two consequences. First, as long as the offered wage is above $\bar{w}$, there would be some inflow of workers. Second, this inflow would only stop for $w = \bar{w}$ and thus $\theta = 0$. Without restriction to entry (which would be inefficient) or discriminatory treatment of newcomers (but this is ethically questionable), redistribution would be impossible.

Clearly, this is the extreme example of a small open economy that cannot retaliate. But even when a country can retaliate, redistribution will generally be lower than in an autarchy or in a cooperative setting. What is central to this phenomenon is the competition among national governments that leads them to reduce production costs, and hence social benefits. We here face quite a paradox: economic competition is generally deemed desirable, whereas political competition conveys inefficiency.

In order to illustrate this process of perverse competition and, more generally, the pitfalls of individualism, the economist uses a sort of fable known as 'the prisoner's dilemma.' This is the story of two people caught in possession of stolen goods. They are suspected of having stolen them, but there is no proof. Theft is punished by three years' imprisonment, while the simple possession of stolen property carries only a one-year sentence. The two people are questioned in separate rooms. Each can either deny having taken part in the crime, or admit to it, and in so doing implicate the other. If only one prisoner admits guilt, he is freed, and the authorities shift all the blame to the other prisoner, sentencing him to six years of imprisonment. If both prisoners deny all participation in the theft, they get only one year in prison. If they both admit, they are sentenced to three years prison. Table 6.1 shows the various possibilities of this 'game.'

The figures given represent the years in prison that prisoners A and B, respectively, would get for their choices. If each one could be sure that the other one would say nothing, both would obtain the best solution for themselves. But, they will end up admitting their crime because they do not trust each other. Prisoner A tells himself that if he chooses to say nothing, his partner will not hesitate to betray him in order to escape prison, thus condemning him to six years' of imprisonment.

'The prisoner's dilemma' applies to a great variety of economic and political situations. It illustrates the cost of individualism and non-cooperation. It is a perfect description of the fiscal game in which the European nations are engaged, a game which tends to exempt capital income from taxation in order to attract it. By refusing to cooperate, each one ends up with a solution which is disadvantageous for everyone: zero taxation on that income and high taxation on other types of income. Table 6.2 illustrates this fiscal game in two countries: Borduria and Syldavia. The figures show the hypothetical level of well-being attained by each of these two countries in the four possible cases. The idea is simple: if one country taxes capital income heavily and the other hardly does so, it is to the full advantage of the latter where the capital will flow in. This country gets some tax revenue and benefit from a larger stock of capital for national production.

Table 6.1. Prisoner's dilemma

	Prisoner B Confess	Prisoner B Deny
Prisoner A Confess	3/3	0/6
Prisoner A Deny	6/0	1/1

Table 6.2. Tax game: capital income taxation

		Borduria	
		Do not tax	Tax
Syldavia	Do not tax	80/80	110/60
	Tax	60/110	100/100

Note that if we consider two countries of different size, tax competition can improve the welfare of one of them. One thinks of Luxembourg, which clearly benefits from the inflow of capital from neighbouring countries. One can, however, show that the gains of the smaller country are offset by the losses of the larger one.

As it appears tax competition is inefficient, all those who view the government as a benevolent maximizer of citizens' welfare oppose it. It is however welcome by those who view the government as a Leviathan and see such competition as a useful device to lower taxes and public spending.[4]

6.4. Some Evidence

As just shown, the race-to-the-bottom hypothesis appears reasonable, at least in theory. Yet up to now there has been little supporting evidence.[5] Essayists usually cite anecdotes about firms moving from France to Scotland in order to benefit from better fiscal arrangements, or of executives leaving Paris for London, where taxes are lower.[6]

One of the problems with this issue of supporting or non-supporting evidence is that there is no clear-cut way to test the reality of a race-to-the-bottom. We will use two types of evidence: one looking at the change in the tax burden of capital (generally highly mobile) and labour (still not very mobile), and the other one showing the effect of economic openness on the redistributive effort of national governments. A race-to-the-bottom would imply that the net taxation of labour increases relative to that of capital and that international openness leads to less redistribution. As we shall see, the evidence for this is not conclusive.

It indeed appears that for most European countries, effective taxation of both labour and capital income has been rather stable over recent decades.

---

[4] See on this Edwards and Keen (1996).
[5] The recent history in the US is in that respect enlightening. At first sight the generosity of social policies of the states during the period 1994–2002, which is a period of devolution, has not changed. Yet looking at the content of their policies, one observes a retooling of programs with two consequences: increased interstate and intrastate inequality. See Meyers (2004).
[6] See Pestieau (2004).

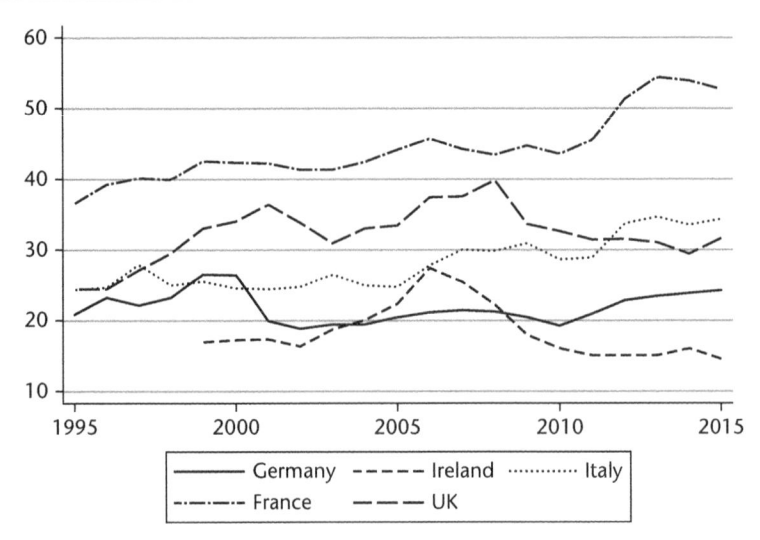

Figure 6.2. Implicit tax rate on capital
Source: European Commission (2017b)

The sharp drop in statutory tax rates on capital income could suggest that governments are not insensitive to the threat of tax competition. However changes in effective tax rates are negligible as appears in Figure 6.2.

The evolution of tax rates does not reveal the various implications of globalization. Behind those numbers, there are realities that illustrate the damage that globalization may have on government revenue and social protection. These realities have names: tax havens, profit shifting, digital firms and posted workers.

Tax havens are low-tax jurisdictions that provide individuals and multinational companies with opportunities to escape taxes. They cause the world's governments to lose hundreds of billions of dollars every year. Since the financial turmoil of 2008, this worrisome issue has dominated the political agenda around the world, and it has given rise to tensions over austerity and wealth inequality. Zucman (2015) found that 10 per cent of European wealth is held offshore implying a cost of $75bn in tax revenue. Despite recent policy initiatives (automatic exchange of bank information) much remains to be done. Well-defined sanctions are missing.

Base erosion and profit shifting are tax-planning strategies used by multinational companies, that move profits to low or no-tax locations where there is little or no economic activity. These techniques are particularly used by the famous GAFA, an acronym for Google, Apple, Facebook, and Amazon, and other technological firms, which do not pay taxes in countries where they operate. These techniques are also used by the collaborative economy, sometimes called the sharing economy, which covers a great variety of sectors and is rapidly emerging across Europe. They range from sharing houses and car journeys to domestic services. The best known are Uber and Airbnb. Not only do these multinational firms avoid paying taxes in countries where they operate but some of them are accused of not ensuring adequate consumer and social protection.

Turning to labour mobility, which remains lower than capital mobility, we have the issue of posted workers that leads to some sort of social dumping. Around 2 million postings are recorded in the EU in the sectors of construction, manufacturing industry, and personal services. Posting involves workers being temporarily employed in another EU country, but still being taxed in their home country and subject to its social protection. Whether they are paid the same rate as the workers in the host Member State where the work is performed is the nub of the debate on social dumping. Actually employers are not obliged to pay a posted worker more than the minimum rate of pay fixed by the host country and they have sometimes paid them even less.

In this way posted workers have a positive impact on the home country, decreasing unemployment, and increasing household incomes and labour tax revenues. They also have an overall positive effect on consumers of the host countries but not on the workers employed in the sectors in which posting prevails. This creates tensions between home countries mostly from East Europe and host countries such as Germany, France and Belgium that attract the highest numbers of posted workers and want—as do many other countries—stricter rules to mitigate social dumping. This now looks like implying a different political East-West perception.

6.5. Incidence of Redistribution

We now turn to the evolution of income redistribution and poverty alleviation. Recent publications indicate that in most countries redistribution has stayed strong and that there is no clear tendency towards a race to the bottom. But this is not the only question. Another, possibly more relevant question, is whether or not there is a relation between openness and the variation in either the redistributive effort or in the performance of poverty alleviation. To measure openness we can use two indicators: the standard one, which is the ratio of exports plus imports divided by GDP and a more complex indicator that takes into account obstacles to international exchanges. They happen to be closely related; hence we only use the second one.

To measure the change in the effort of redistribution, we use three indicators. The first one is the variation in social expenditure, which truly denotes the financial effort made by society. The second one is the variation in poverty alleviation measured by the reduction in poverty due to social transfers. The

The Welfare State in Europe

third one is the variation in the reduction of inequality measured by the difference between the Gini coefficient of income before and after transfers. We take the last two decades, which is a period of rapid economic integration and for which we have good poverty and inequality data for a number of OECD countries. This data is presented in the appendix (Table A.6.1). In the majority of countries, social spending has increased over the decade in question, which is already revealing. In other words, globalization has not led to a reduction in redistributive efforts for most countries. The only exception is Sweden, which experienced a reduction in its social expenditures. In the Netherlands, poverty alleviation has decreased. Finally, the reduction in inequality has decreased in nine out of nineteen countries, including France, Germany, and in the Netherlands. Note, however, that in these three cases the reduction is always very small.

To see if globalization plays some role, we now look at the effect of our indicators of openness on changes in social spending and in redistribution. We use simple cross-national regressions, represented in Figures 6.3–6.5. Clearly it appears that there is a negative relation between openness and the effort in redistribution (DPS). There is also a negative relation between openness and change in poverty alleviation (DAP). On the contrary, the relation between openness and variation in inequality alleviation (DRG) is positive. Note however that these relations, positive or negative, are hardly statistically significant. This seems to indicate that openness has little influence on both the outcomes and the means of redistribution.

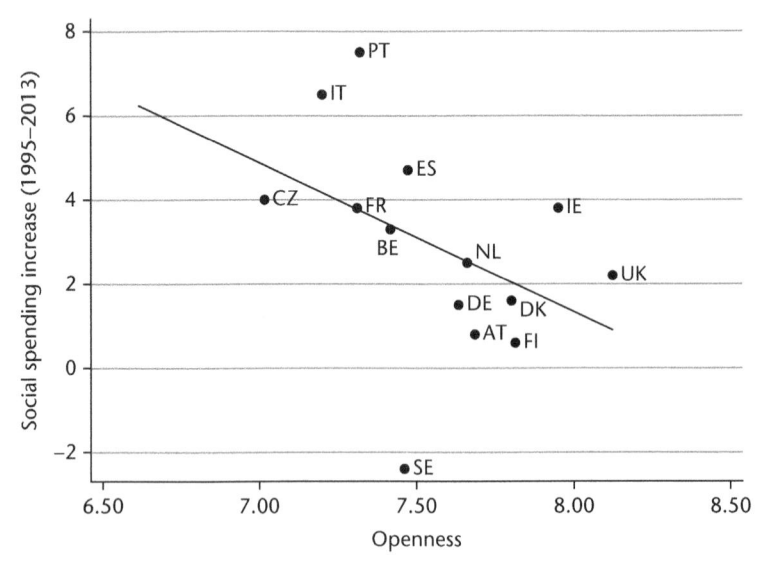

Figure 6.3. Social spending and openness
Source: See Appendix. Table A.6.1

Social Protection and Globalization

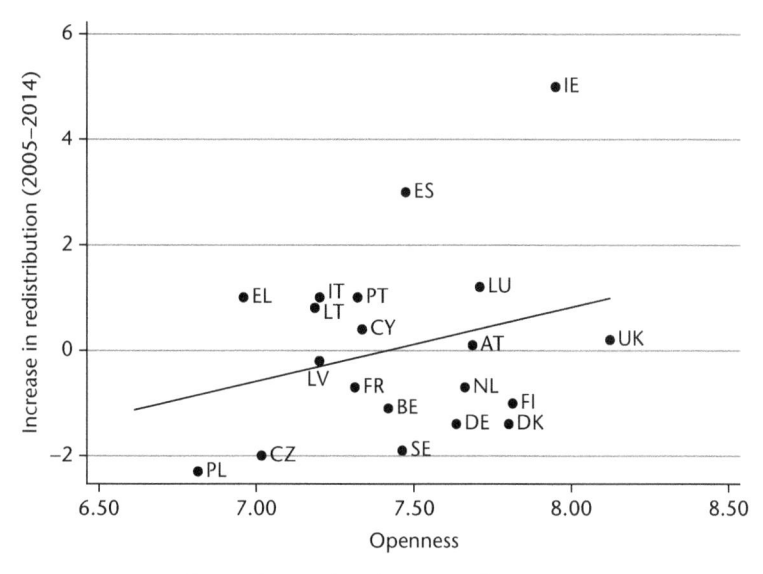

Figure 6.4. Redistribution and openness
Source: See Appendix. Table A.6.1

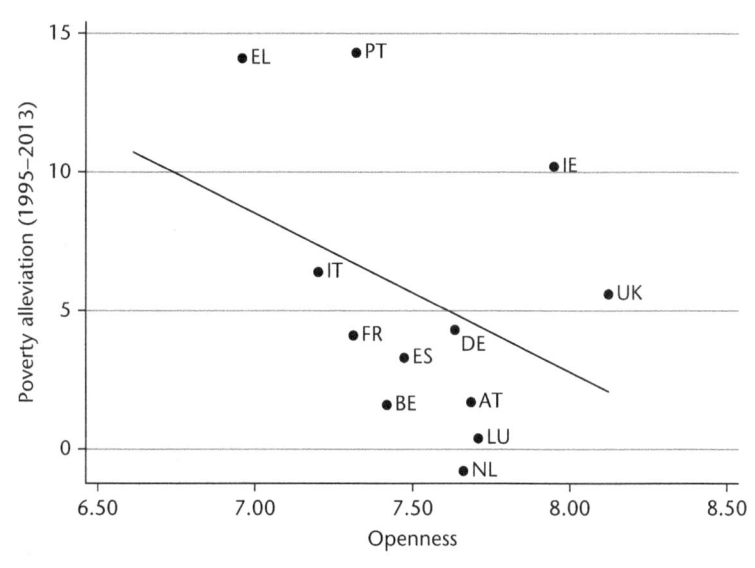

Figure 6.5. Poverty alleviation, and openness
Source: See Appendix. Table A.6.1

A number of arguments have been advanced to explain why there is no drastic decline in redistribution even though labour, and above all capital, are free to move within the EU and even outside. The cost of mobility, as well as the uncertainty concerning tax-transfer policies in host countries, can prevent the race to the bottom. Let us consider other reasons. First of all, it might be too early to draw a conclusion. There are clear resistances to reforms aimed at dismantling the welfare state. Vested interests can prevent governments from downsizing some redistributive programs. This is surely the case for public pension schemes. Not only are there lags in the behaviour of governments, but also in the availability of data. Data for the most recent years is not available and does not allow for a conclusion one way or the other.

In addition, national governments can be insensitive to factor movements, in particular those known as 'brain drain'. Also national institutions are far from being transparent, which means that an effective fiscal wedge may not be perceived as such. Moreover, to the extent that benefits are linked to past contributions, or at least that entitlement is not automatic, welfare-induced migration should be limited. This raises an ethical issue. There seems to be a trade-off between the generosity of the welfare state and the political treatment of immigrants. A country adopting a policy of 'guest workers' can afford a more generous social protection than a country that right away awards all the benefits of social protection to an immigrant and his/her family. Even without resorting to a supranational government, one can expect a European government to reach multilateral agreements to the benefit of all parties concerned. What really matters is to have a population that truly supports redistribution. Indeed one sometimes has the feeling that European integration is just an excuse for fading out preferences towards redistribution. Finally, it is often argued that economic integration may sometimes reduce some of the need for national redistribution. In a world of uncertainty, factor mobility can in itself provide a form of market insurance against income risk. Access to external markets may limit factor price variation through spatial arbitrage, as well as obviate the need for social insurance (Wildasin 1995).

To sum up, we have seen that in an increasingly integrated world, redistributive policies face the threat of a race to the bottom. But when looking at recent data, this threat does not seem to have been translated into reality: social redistributive policies are still alive and well. Yet, one is still left with the feeling that in the future the reasons just discussed will be less relevant, and that some race to the bottom will occur. The only way to reverse such an expected outcome is to rely on cooperation among national governments. In other words, the solution is to make supranational authorities responsible for redistributive policies. This is not out of reach, but it is up to the political will of each national government. Instead of waiting for the emergence of such a supranational government, a more pragmatic method has recently been proposed. It rests on the idea of governance by objectives and is called the Open Method of Coordination (OMC).

6.6. The Open Method of Coordination

Defining the OMC is not an easy task. It is a bit like the proverbial elephant: we may not be able to define an elephant, but we recognize one when we see one. If we don't have one to point to, we use words like 'trunks', 'tusks', 'ivory', 'mammoth'. The same holds with OMC. To define it we use words like 'benchmarks', 'yardsticks', and 'best practices'.

The OMC starts from the idea that each EU member state has its distinct history, and wants to run its welfare state its own way. Even though they face common challenges and risks, no country wants social uniformity, and all countries stand against additional transfer of national competencies to the EU, let alone harmonization for the sake of harmonization. The solution is in some kind of soft governance by objectives. It is here that the OMC, which was coined at the Lisbon meeting in March 2000, makes its appearance. The OMC is a multistage process. First, member states define clear and mutually agreed objectives. Then, on a regular basis, the best practices are identified for each one of these objectives. Hopefully, each member country will then try to fill the gap between its own practice and the best practice for each of the objectives.

OMC is close to what is called 'political yardstick competition'. This surfaces when the performance of governments in various jurisdictions becomes sufficiently comparable so that the voters, after making meaningful comparisons between jurisdictions, can reward or sanction their own government.

The OMC involves fixing guidelines, establishing indicators, and periodic monitoring. The commonly agreed upon indicators are of two kinds: the primary and the secondary. We focus on the primary, which encompass financial poverty, income inequality, and regional variation in employment rates, long term unemployed, joblessness, low educational qualification, low life expectancy and poor health. Table 6.3 gives the most recent available data for those indicators.

A number of questions come to mind. Why these particular indicators? Do some countries always come on top? Is it not naive to expect that comparing actual performance with best practice will be a sufficient discipline device, particularly when the gap between the two is wide? Finally, is it possible to reduce the number of indicators to one or two?

To make these indicators more comparable they can be normalized so that the minimum is 0 and the maximum is 1. In the Table A6.2 in the appendix we present those normalized indicators. It is thus tempting to add these eleven normalized indicators in order to get a synthetic indicator of exclusion. Adding them with equal weights of 1/11, we obtain the SPI, which stands for Sum of Partial Indicators. This average can be contrasted with the United Nations Human Development Indicator (HDI), which provides a qualitative measure

Table 6.3. Inclusion indicators (2014)

Countries	Ineq	Pov	Ppov	Rpov	Reg	Drop	LTU	CUN	Aun	Life	Health
Belgium	3.8	21.2	9.5	18.8	9.4	9.8	4.3	12.8	13	81.4	15.8
Bulgaria	6.8	40.1	16.5	33.2	6.4	12.9	6.9	16.1	12.9	74.5	21.9
Czechia	3.5	14.8	3.4	18.0	4.2	5.5	2.7	8.0	5.9	78.9	27.6
Denmark	4.1	17.9	–	18.5	1.8	7.8	1.7	8.0	9.8	80.7	20.2
Germany	5.1	20.6	9.5	23.2	4.0	9.5	2.2	8.9	8	81.2	26.8
Estonia	6.5	26.0	11.2	22.0	–	11.4	3.3	8.0	8.2	77.4	31.7
Ireland	4.8	27.6	–	17.2	–	6.9	6.6	16.0	13.5	81.4	13.5
Greece	6.5	36.0	14.5	31.3	4.8	9	19.5	11.3	18.8	81.5	15.7
Spain	6.8	29.2	14.3	31.6	10.9	21.9	12.9	13.0	15.3	83.3	18.9
France	4.3	18.5	7.9	16.6	6.3	9	4.2	11.9	11.3	82.8	23.5
Croatia	5.1	29.3	–	27.9	–	2.7	10.1	10.7	12.2	77.9	22.0
Italy	5.8	28.3	12.9	28.2	19.4	15	7.7	10.8	13.4	83.2	20.0
Cyprus	5.4	27.4	7.3	18.5	–	6.8	7.7	9.9	9.6	82.8	16.9
Latvia	6.5	32.7	10.8	23.6	–	8.5	4.6	8.3	9.4	74.5	37.1
Lithuania	6.1	27.3	16.0	22.7	–	5.9	4.8	10.9	11.2	74.7	37.2
Luxembourg	4.4	19.0	8.7	16.3	–	6.1	1.6	4.0	7.3	82.3	18.8
Hungary	4.3	31.8	8.6	22.3	6.6	11.4	3.7	10.9	9.7	76.0	26.7
Malta	4.0	23.8	10.6	17.8	–	20.3	2.7	8.7	7.4	82.1	21.9
Netherlands	3.8	16.5	7.7	16.9	2.6	8.7	2.9	7.0	9	81.8	17.3
Austria	4.1	19.2	8.5	20.1	5.2	7	1.5	6.2	8.6	81.7	21.6
Poland	4.9	24.7	10.7	23.2	5.5	5.4	3.8	9.4	9.9	77.8	28.1
Portugal	6.2	27.5	12.0	30.3	3.6	17.4	8.4	7.7	9.6	81.3	35.7
Romania	7.2	39.5	20.2	35.1	7.0	18.1	2.8	11.4	10.9	75.0	20.4
Slovenia	3.7	20.4	9.5	22.0	–	4.4	5.3	4.5	9.6	81.2	24.2
Slovakia	3.9	18.4	–	29.0	7.4	6.7	9.3	10.1	8.4	77.0	22.7
Finland	3.6	17.3	7.0	13.9	5.2	9.5	1.9	4.9	10.2	81.3	24.2
Sweden	3.9	16.9	6.6	20.4	2.8	6.7	1.4	6.5	10.3	82.3	16.0
UK	5.1	24.1	6.5	19.6	4.8	11.8	2.2	14.2	10.1	81.4	20.9

Notes:
Ineq: Inequality of income distribution (income quintile share ratio)
Pov: At-risk-of-poverty rate after social transfers
Ppov: At-persistent-risk-of-poverty rate
Rpov: Relative median poverty gap
Reg: Dispersion of regional employment rates
Drop: Early school-leavers
LTU: Total long-term unemployment rate
CUN: Children aged 0–17 living in jobless households
AUN: People aged 18–59 living in jobless households
Life: Life expectancy at birth for men
Health: Self-defined health status by income level

Source: Eurostat (2017a)

of national welfare, and in which the level of income plays an important role. The two rankings are correlated[7].

In Chapter 8, we use a subsample of these indicators to assess the performance of the welfare states. As we show for EU15, the performance of European welfare states has been increasing and converging over the last two decades. This seems to imply that the OMC is working.

6.7. Another View

Besides economists, social scientists are also concerned with the issue of globalization. They tend to focus on the emergence of a global capitalist empire in which national welfare states occupy a less central position than before. Sociologist Manuel Castells (2000), to take a well-known and typical example, argues that the modern state is facing a rapid decline. According to him, the planetary expansion of information networks is at odds with national state institutions and hierarchies: 'Networks dissolve centres, they disorganize hierarchy, and make materially impossible the exercise of hierarchical power without processing instructions in the network, according to the network's morphological rules. Thus, contemporary information networks of capital, production, trade, science, communication, human rights, and crime, bypass the national state, which, by and large, has stopped being a sovereign entity' (Castells 2000, p. 19). This view is questioned by Beland (2005), according to whom it seems to oversimplify the impact of economic and social globalization on state institutions and protection. 'Not passive victims of the globalization process, West European and North American policymakers have generally played the game of economic integration in order to gain electoral power and push for their own political agenda at home. Promising more prosperity as a consequence, these actors stress the fact that economic integration could benefit their country, and even stimulate welfare state development and coordination' (Beland 2005, p. 36). Now, we do not deny that European integration has a number of positive implications for the population. The question that we want to raise in this chapter is that of the perenniality of social protection and redistributive policies.

6.8. Conclusion

In this chapter we have distinguished two levels of analysis of the alleged effect of globalization on income distribution. The first level pertains to the

---

[7] The HDI is a composite index of life expectancy, education, and per capita income. Up to 2010, it used an uniformly weighted sum of these normalized indicators. Since 2010, it uses a geometric mean.

The Welfare State in Europe

distribution of earnings and income before taxation and transfers. The second one concerns the redistributive capacity of the welfare state. It would seem that technical progress is responsible for increasing wage disparities between skilled and unskilled workers, and that in that respect the role of globalization is overstated. However, globalization can explain why national governments find it more and more difficult to redistribute income. Indeed factor mobility leads to fiscal competition and social dumping in an economic union, without a central government to control for externalities induced by mobility.

Appendix

Table A.6.1. Openness and redistribution

Count	DAP	POV	DRG	GIN	DSE	OP
AUT	1.7	14.1	0.1	27.6	0.8	7.7
BEL	1.6	15.5	−1.1	25.9	3.3	7.4
CZE	–	9.7	0.4	25.1	4.0	7.0
DNK	–	12.1	−1.4	27.7	1.6	7.8
FIN	–	12.8	−1.0	25.6	0.6	7.8
FRA	4.1	13.3	−0.7	29.2	3.8	7.3
DEU	4.3	16.7	−1.4	30.7	1.5	7.6
GRC	14.1	22.1	1.0	34.5	–	7.0
IRL	10.2	15.6	5.0	30.8	3.8	7.9
ITA	6.4	19.4	1.0	32.4	6.5	7.2
LVA	–	21.2	−0.2	35.5	–	7.2
LTU	–	19.1	0.8	35.0	–	7.2
LUX	0.4	16.4	1.2	28.7	–	7.7
NLD	−0.8	11.6	−0.7	26.2	2.5	7.7
POL	–	17.0	−2.3	30.8	–	6.8
PRT	14.3	19.5	1..0	34.5	7.5	7.3
ROU	–	25.4	–	34.7	–	6.6
ESP	3.3	22.2	3.0	34.7	4.7	7.5
SWE	–	15.1	−1.9	25.4	−2.4	7.5
GBR	5.6	16.8	0.2	31.6	2.2	8.1
Period	1995–2014	2014	2005–2014	2014	1995–2013	1995–2013

Definition and source of variables

OP CATO trade openness, which measures the degree to which policies interfere with international exchange. It consists of four components: tariff rates, black market exchange premium, restriction on capital movement, actual size of the trade sector compared to the expected size.
Source: CATO (2015)

DSE Variation in the share of public social expenditure in GDP.
Source: Eurostat (2017c)

POV The poverty rate measured with a poverty line equal to half the median income.
Source: Eurostat (2017a)

DAP The increase in poverty alleviation, namely poverty with income before transfers minus poverty with income after transfers.

GIN The inequality index of GINI.
Source: Eurostat (2017a)

DRG The increase in inequality alleviation, namely GINI with income before transfers, minus GINI with income after transfers.

Table A.6.2. Normalized indicators: 2014

Countries	Ineq	Pov	Ppov	Rpov	Reg	Drop	LTU	CUN	Aun	Life	Health	Average
Austria	0.16	0.17	0.30	0.29	0.19	0.15	0.01	0.18	0.21	0.18	0.34	0.20
Belgium	0.08	0.25	0.36	0.23	0.43	0.31	0.16	0.73	0.55	0.22	0.10	0.31
Bulgaria	0.89	1.00	0.78	0.91	0.26	0.49	0.30	1.00	0.54	1.00	0.35	0.68
Cyprus	0.51	0.50	0.23	0.22	–	0.14	0.35	0.49	0.29	0.06	0.14	0.29
Czechia	0.00	0.00	0.00	0.19	0.14	0.06	0.07	0.33	0.00	0.50	0.59	0.17
Denmark	0.16	0.12	–	0.22	0.00	0.19	0.02	0.33	0.30	0.30	0.28	0.19
Estonia	0.81	0.44	0.46	0.38	–	0.40	0.10	0.33	0.18	0.67	0.77	0.46
Finland	0.03	0.10	0.21	0.00	0.19	0.29	0.03	0.07	0.33	0.23	0.45	0.18
France	0.22	0.15	0.27	0.13	0.26	0.26	0.15	0.65	0.42	0.06	0.42	0.27
Germany	0.43	0.23	0.36	0.44	0.13	0.29	0.04	0.40	0.16	0.24	0.56	0.30
Greece	0.81	0.84	0.66	0.82	0.17	0.26	1.00	0.60	1.00	0.20	0.09	0.59
Hungary	0.22	0.67	0.31	0.40	0.27	0.40	0.13	0.57	0.29	0.83	0.56	0.42
Ireland	0.35	0.51	–	0.16	–	0.14	0.29	0.99	0.59	0.22	0.00	0.36
Italy	0.62	0.53	0.57	0.67	1.00	0.61	0.35	0.56	0.58	0.01	0.27	0.53
Latvia	0.81	0.71	0.44	0.46	–	0.23	0.18	0.36	0.27	1.00	1.00	0.54
Lithuania	0.70	0.49	0.75	0.42	–	0.09	0.19	0.57	0.41	0.98	1.00	0.56
Luxembourg	0.24	0.17	0.32	0.11	–	0.10	0.01	0.00	0.11	0.11	0.22	0.14
Malta	0.14	0.36	0.43	0.18	0.05	0.91	0.07	0.39	0.12	0.14	0.35	0.31
Netherlands	0.08	0.07	0.26	0.14	0.21	0.25	0.08	0.25	0.24	0.17	0.16	0.16
Poland	0.38	0.39	0.43	0.44	0.10	0.06	0.13	0.45	0.31	0.63	0.62	0.37
Portugal	0.73	0.50	0.51	0.77	0.30	0.74	0.39	0.31	0.29	0.23	0.94	0.50
Romania	1.00	0.98	1.00	1.00	0.32	0.78	0.08	0.61	0.39	0.94	0.29	0.67
Slovakia	0.11	0.14	–	0.71	–	0.13	0.44	0.50	0.19	0.72	0.39	0.37
Slovenia	0.05	0.22	0.36	0.38	–	0.00	0.22	0.04	0.29	0.24	0.45	0.23
Spain	0.89	0.57	0.65	0.83	0.52	1.00	0.64	0.74	0.73	0.00	0.23	0.62
Sweden	0.11	0.08	0.19	0.31	0.06	0.13	0.00	0.21	0.34	0.11	0.11	0.15
UK	0.43	0.37	0.18	0.27	0.17	0.42	0.04	0.84	0.33	0.22	0.31	0.33

Source: Eurostat (2017a)

7

Welfare State and Economic Efficiency

> **KEY CONCEPTS**
> consumer's surplus
> corporatist economy
> deadweight-loss
> distortionary tax
> excess burden
> lump-sum tax

7.1. Introduction

European countries have experienced considerable improvements in wellbeing and standards of living over the past seventy years. This evolution includes widespread access to social protection benefits, a high degree of income redistribution, a reduction in absolute poverty and an increase in economic security for everyone. Such an achievement can be attributed to the development of modern welfare states and to several decades of unprecedented economic growth. Yet, over the last decade, a number of EU economies have experienced declining growth and increasing unemployment. Economists, like most people, have a short memory. They quickly forget the positive benefits brought about by the welfare state in terms of providing security and alleviating poverty and they blame it for slower growth. A number of economists now believe a retrenchment in social spending is necessary to revive economic efficiency and economic growth.

In this chapter, we shall discuss the arguments based on the disincentives embedded in the structure of the welfare state, and in its financing. In fact, most often the critique addressed to the welfare state can be extended to other forms of government spending. We shall also look at the aggregate evidence regarding the negative impact of the welfare state on the level or the growth rate of national income. The key issue is to figure out what we really want. Do we want the welfare state as it is, or a market economy with no social protection, or a market economy with protection provided by the private sector? In other words, the issue of the counterfactual is crucial when discussing the dismantlement of the welfare state.

7.2. Individual Behaviour

Studies of individual behaviour in the welfare state focus on the distortions that the welfare state carries with it. In these studies one looks at the effects of taxes and social insurance contributions, as well as at the effects arising from the expenditure side of the public budget: price subsidies, cash transfers and provisions of social goods like education or health care.

To illustrate these microeconomic effects, we first look at the effect of a wage tax on the welfare and the labour supply of workers. In Figure 7.1, Tintin's hours of work are plotted on the horizontal axis, and his hourly wage on the vertical. Tintin's compensated labour supply curve is labeled S_L: it shows the smallest wage that would be required to induce him to work each additional hour; or to put it otherwise, it gives the marginal disutility of providing one more hour of work. Initially, Tintin's wage is w and the associated hours of work L_1. For that amount of effort Tintin earns an income corresponding to the rectangle $0wdL_1$ for a disutility equal to the area $0adL_1$. His net gain (worker's surplus) is area *adf*.

Now assume that an income tax at a rate t is imposed. The after-tax wage is then $(1 - t)w$. What is Tintin's reaction going to be? It will depend on how he

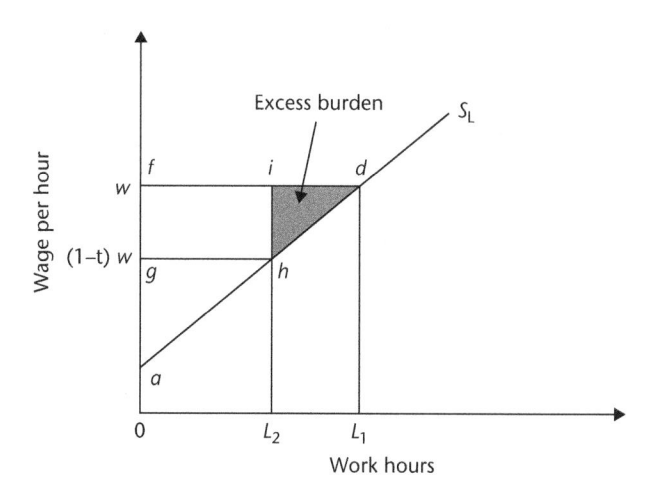

Figure 7.1. Excess burden of wage taxation

thinks that the tax proceeds are to be used. First, if he can expect that the tax proceeds will be integrally returned to him, then he will still choose L_1. Thus he behaves as though he were seeing through the fiscal veil and recognizes the one-to-one relation between the taxes he pays and the benefits he receives.

Secondly, if Tintin does not acknowledge such a relation, even though he eventually gets back his tax payment (area *fihg*), he supplies L_2 hours. His surplus after the tax is *agh*. The excess burden due to the tax-induced distortion is the amount by which Tintin's loss of welfare (*fdhg*) exceeds the tax collected. It is given by the triangular area *hid*. Quite often one approximates this excess burden, also called the deadweight loss triangle, by the formula:[1]

$$1/2wLt^2\varepsilon,$$

where ε is the compensated elasticity of work with respect to the wage.[2] Note that when only part of the tax proceeds is given back because the rest is used for redistributive purposes, the loss to the worker consists of the deadweight loss and the amount transferred to other individuals. Yet, from an efficiency viewpoint, only the deadweight loss can be viewed as a real efficiency loss.

The importance of the excess burden of labour-specific taxes depends on three factors: the compensated elasticity of work, the linkage between taxes and benefits, and the perception of such a linkage. It has been argued (Summers et al. 1993) that the last-named factor is related to labour market institutions. In 'corporatist' economies, wherein unions and management are in charge of wage and employment policy, taxes have a smaller distorting effect than they have in countries where individual workers make labour supply decisions. This argument is, in fact, used to explain why taxes tend to be high in these corporatist economies.

The effect of social protection on the incentive to work and on the efficiency of the economy can also be studied from the viewpoint of the beneficiaries. Unemployment or disability benefits and social security pensions would be truly non-distortionary if the probabilities of occurrence of the various states were exogenous. Yet, in reality, they can be influenced by the individuals' own actions. For example, the probability of unemployment is partly determined by the worker's choice of education and training, and by the intensity of his search for a new job, should he become unemployed. Social security can induce socially undesirable early retirement. Disability insurance can lead to more absenteeism on grounds of minor health complaints.

These work disincentives are increased when working implies high implicit or explicit marginal tax rates. This is the case of the poverty trap that results

---

[1] The surface of the shaded triangle on Figure 7.1 is equal to (ih*id)/2, with ih = tw and id = εtL = twdL/dw.

[2] Recent calculations suggest a reasonable value for ε around 0.2.

from the interaction between the tax and benefit systems. In some countries, individuals in low paid jobs have little incentive to increase earned income since this could result in the withdrawal of benefits. At best, they are no worse off following an increase in labour supply and at worst, they are less well off. In this latter case, marginal effective tax rate or the benefit withdrawal rate is greater than 100 per cent.

So far, we have discussed the effects of the welfare state on labour supply. But it also has effects on savings behaviour. Basically, social protection may depress individual savings by taking the decision of whether to insure or to save against risk out of the individual's hands. This critique is particularly addressed to pay-as-you-go social security which reduces private saving by guaranteeing retirees benefits financed by current workers. The effect of social protection on saving is a hot issue. However, the size of this effect is still debated.

From a review of the literature on the effects of the welfare state on labour supply and savings, we offer three remarks. First, most of this literature focuses on a fairly narrow range of questions that are studied because they lend themselves to feasible empirical work. It fails to address the more fundamental and lasting effects of the welfare state on work and saving behaviour. In that respect, Linbeck's (1995a, b) point is worth mentioning when he discusses the possible feedback from social policies to preferences and behaviour patterns. Accordingly, the challenge facing today's social protection is not only that the economic setting is totally different from that of the early fifties, but also that the individuals have tastes and political attitudes that may have fundamentally changed. This is very important. It means that rolling back social spending towards levels experienced in the fifties will not necessarily be accompanied by compensating responses from the private sector.

Second, by focusing on taxes and cash transfers one influences the conclusions drawn. Indeed, the provision of social goods, both private and public, could have a number of positive effects on the quality of the labour force. There exist several theoretical and empirical papers on endogenous growth that show that, through health care and education, the welfare state contribution to the stock of human capital can ensure higher growth rates.

Third, the micro-textbook approach to the disincentive effects of the welfare state neglects a fundamental issue: what would society be without a welfare state? In order to pass judgement on the strengths and weaknesses of the welfare state, its redistributive and insurance functions, we have to take a closer look at the performance of private insurance markets and at the working of an economy with huge and unregulated income disparities (Sandmo 1995). In the following section (that may be skipped) we come back to the concept of excess burden.

7.3. A Numerical Example

Suppose that the consumer worker's preference for consumption and leisure is represented by a simple logarithmic utility function:

$$u(c, 1 - L) = \log c + \log(1 - L)$$

where c is the level of consumption, or of disposable income, and L is the labour supply (total time available equal to 1). We see that both consumption and leisure $(1 - L)$ bring utility. Suppose also that consumption is equal to $(1 - t)wL + T$ where t is the (constant) payroll tax rate, w, the wage rate and T, some benefits transferred back to the consumer. If t, w and T are given, maximizing $u(c, 1 - L)$, subject to the budget constraint brings a labour supply function and an indirect utility function, v, that depends only on t, w, T:

$$L = \frac{w(1 - t) - T}{2w(1 - t)} \quad \text{and} \quad v = 2\log[(w(1 - t) + T)] - 2\log 2 - \log[w(1 - t)].$$

We then distinguish among several cases:

Case 1: no taxation.

$$L_1 = 1/2 \quad \text{and} \quad v_1 = \log w - 2\log 2$$

Case 2: taxation according to the benefit principle (in other words, the consumer-worker knows at the outset that he will get back what he has paid for $(T = twL)$).

$$L_2 = 1/2 \quad \text{and} \quad v_2 = \log w - 2\log 2$$

Case 3: pure confiscatory taxation (the individual expects $T = 0$).

$$L_3 = 1/2 \quad \text{and} \quad v_3 = \log w(1 - t) - 2\log 2.$$

Case 4: distortionary taxation (the individual will ultimately get back his contribution but without seeing the direct link):

$$L_4 = \frac{1 - t}{2\ t} \quad \text{and} \quad v_4 = \log w + \log(1 - t) - 2\log(2 - t)$$

One easily checks that for $t > 0$,

$$v_1 = v_2 > v_4 > v_3.$$
$$L_1 = L_2 = L_3 > L_4.$$

Furthermore, $v_4 - v_2$ is what economists call the deadweight loss, the efficiency cost, or the excess burden of taxation.

Finally, one could also consider the case of a confiscatory tax that would not be distortionary. This is also called a lump-sum tax. Instead of collecting twL through a tax on wage, the same amount would be collected without affecting the labour leisure choice.

Case 5: non distortionary confiscatory tax ($T = -tw/2$)

$$L_5 = 1/2 - t/4 \quad \text{and} \quad v_5 = \log w - 2\log 2 + 2\log(2-t)/2$$

One sees that:

$$L_5 > L_3 \quad \text{and} \quad v_5 > v_3.$$

With a lump-sum tax as compared to a distortionary one, the utility loss is smaller and the labour supply is higher. It is important to note the difference between the excess burden of taxation and the income effect implied by a confiscatory (redistributive) tax. The first effect is a pure loss for the economy; it corresponds to a drop in GDP, whereas the second effect is only a loss if the tax proceeds are wasted. In the standard case where the tax proceeds are redistributed to people who need them because of poverty or accidental loss, these proceeds bring more social utility as these people are likely to have a higher marginal utility of income than the taxpayers. Those five cases are illustrated in Figure 7.2 for an arbitrary utility function.

Now, when turning to those receiving social protection benefits, one observes the same two effects: an income effect and a distortionary effect. There is no distortion (substitution) effect when the benefits are unconditional, or when they are given to categories that are perfectly observable. When using the same utility function one can distinguish among four cases.

We assume that the individual is not subject to the wage tax, but he may be subject to a means test. We also consider the possibility of an individual voluntarily stopping working, and who then receives an unemployment compensation or disability benefit.

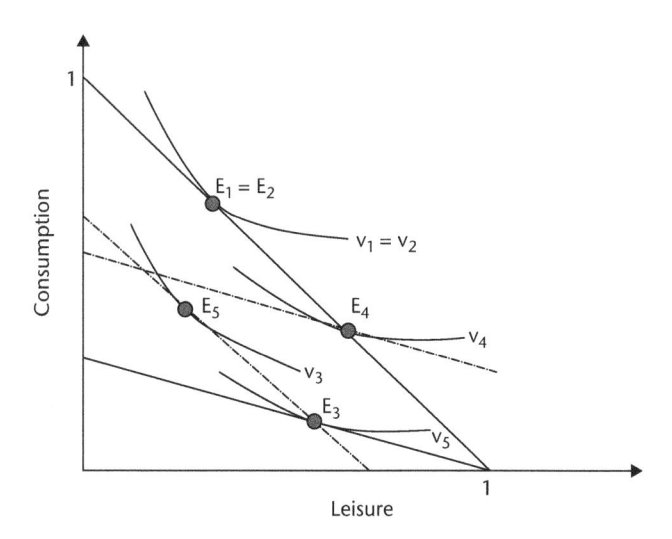

Figure 7.2. Disincentive for workers

Case 6: Zero transfer

$$L_6 = 1/2 \quad \text{and} \quad v_6 = \log w - 2\log 2$$

Case 7: Transfer T without means test

$$L_7 = \frac{w - T}{2w} \quad \text{and} \quad v_7 = 2\log[w + T] - 2\log 2 - \log w$$

Case 8: Transfer T with means test

$$L_8 = \frac{w(1-\tau) - T}{2w(1-\tau)} \quad \text{and} \quad v_8 = 2\log[w(1-\tau) + T] - 2\log 2 - \log[w(1-\tau)]$$

Note that in the case where $\tau = 100$ per cent corresponds to the so-called unemployment trap, one then has

$$L_8 = 0$$

Case 9: Discrete choice between working and receiving no benefit, or not working and receiving T

$$L_9 = 0 \quad \text{if} \quad \log T > \log w - 2\log 2$$

Those last four cases are represented in Figure 7.3. One readily sees that both the income effect and the distortion contribute to less work.

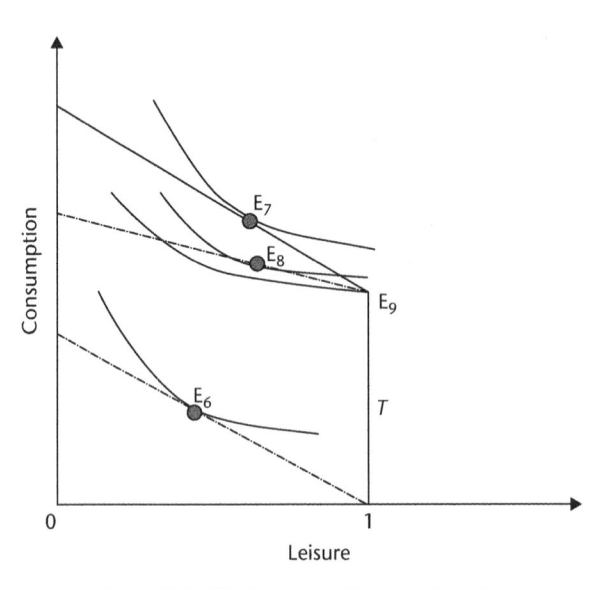

Figure 7.3. Disincentive for beneficiaries

7.4. Aggregate Evidence

An alternative approach to the study of the effect of social protection on economic performance is to test a macroeconomic relation. On the dependent variable side, one can look at the level of income or its growth rate. On the explanatory variable side, one can use either the level of social spending or the extent of income redistribution. At the outset, there are two problems with such an approach. First, any aggregate relation of that kind is a black box: we have no indication as to the mechanism that is at work. Second, there is the causality issue. Why couldn't we hypothesize that a growing economy implies a strong demand for social protection and redistribution policies? In that respect, let us observe that, following Kuznets (1955), there have been a number of studies that conjecture that in advanced economies, growth results in a decreasing disparity in income.

Using the level of GDP or its growth rate leads to different predictions. Consider first the effect of social spending on the level of GDP. A cut in social spending induces a temporary rise in the growth rate; GDP rises to its new equilibrium level, but there is no permanent increase in the rate of growth. Alternatively, there is the alleged effect of the level of transfers on the long-run rate of growth. Accordingly, a reduction in the welfare state is predicted to raise the growth rate permanently. Using the data of Chapter 3, Figure 7.4

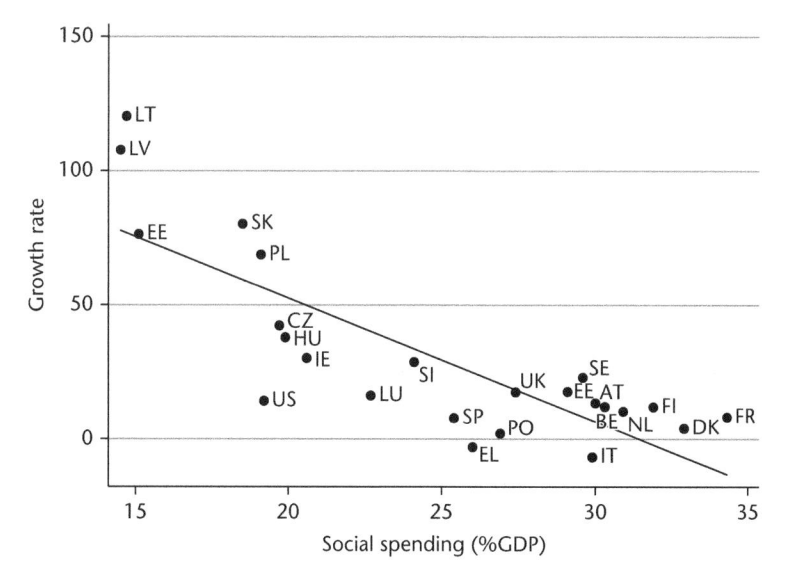

Figure 7.4. Social spending in 2015 and per capita GDP growth rate over 2000–2015
Sources: Eurostat (2017a), OECD (2017c)

shows the relation between average GDP growth over the period 2000–2015, and the social burden in 2015. The estimated regression line is given by

$$\text{GDP growth} = 144 - 4.59 \text{ social burden} \quad R^2 = 0.66$$

In contrast, we have the more ambitious study of Bellettini and Berti Ceroni (1999), who analyse the empirical relationship between social security expenditure and economic growth, using cross-country data for a sample of sixty-one countries and panel data for a sample of twenty industrialized countries. They find a statistically significant positive association between social security expenditure and growth. The estimated coefficient of social security expenditure seems robust to various forms of misspecification and appears to be larger in poor countries with relatively underdeveloped social security systems. As for the channels through which the positive effect of social security expenditure on growth should take place, their results seem to indicate that social security has a positive influence on human capital formation.

There are also theoretical predictions as to the effect of inequality on economic growth. Two mechanisms have been suggested by which redistributive policies could reduce aggregate growth. Post-Keynesian economists (Kaldor 1956) argue that since a high level of savings is a prerequisite of rapid growth and the marginal propensity to save increases with income, policies that redistribute income from the rich to the poor reduce saving and thereby growth. There is also the political economy argument (Persson and Tabellini 1994) that an initially unequal distribution of market income leads to political pressures for redistributive policies that distort economic incentives and thereby reduce growth. Thus, *ex ante* inequalities are ultimately bad for growth since they engender policies that are themselves bad for growth.

In these macroeconomic studies one finds the same problem as in the microeconomics ones. The welfare state and redistributive policies can also have a number of positive effects. Indeed it is clear that the welfare state can stimulate growth by a variety of ways: by improving the quality of human capital, increasing social cohesion, easing credit constraints, and fostering risk taking. One thus needs to look at the empirical evidence.

Atkinson (2000) presents a number of studies on the effect of social protection on growth. These studies use a variety of methods to overcome the usual econometric problems, including those of causality. Out of the ten studies listed, two find an insignificant effect of welfare state spending on annual growth rates; four find that social transfers are negatively associated with average growth; and another four find a positive relation between the welfare state and growth.

What can we conclude from the macroeconomic studies of the effect of welfare state spending on economic performance? There are three levels of answers. First, there is the answer of the laymen who are also voters. Basically, they would like to keep the benefits of the welfare state but pay a lesser price. Secondly, there is the empirical evidence which at this moment cannot provide a reliable guide to the likely implications of cutting welfare state spending. Thirdly, there is the theoretical understanding of the relation between the welfare state and economic performance, which is still in need of further investigation.

A recurrent issue in development economics is the relation between three concepts: poverty, inequality, and growth, which raises questions such as: is growth pro poor? Is inequality bad for growth? Can growth lead to less poverty but more inequality? There exist a huge number of articles and books, more empirical than theoretical, more positive than normative, on the effect of poverty or inequality on growth, and of growth on inequality or poverty.[3] Even though most of the discussion concerns less advanced countries, that is, countries without a sensible welfare state, it has some bearing on the theme of this chapter. In the ongoing debate, the poverty measure is absolute (e.g. equal to $1 a day), and the conventional wisdom is that growth reduces poverty, given that income inequality does not increase. Furthermore, high levels of inequality can depress the rate of growth because of its undesirable political and social impacts on crisis, political stability, and education. In other words, reducing inequality is good for growth and for poverty alleviation. Unfortunately, since the early mid-1980s, inequality has risen in many countries and often sharply.

7.5. An Historical View

While most of the debates over the efficiency of the welfare states deal with recent decades, it must be noted that Europe's welfare states are much older than that. In a provocative and challenging book, Peter Lindert (2004) offers a monumental history of two centuries of social spending, and he concludes that the big European welfare states—which are undoubtedly expensive—are surprisingly efficient. But, at the same time, they are less redistributive than one might expect. This conclusion surely goes against Ricardo's conjecture that Europe's redistribution would lead to the 'plague of universal poverty.'

Let us follow Lindert's main argument that deals with the efficiency of the welfare state, and particularly, of its financing. Compared with Americans, Europeans place far more of their tax burden on consumption than on income, thus doing less damage to the incentive to save and to work. Furthermore, also unlike the Americans, when they tax income they lean on labour rather than on capital. One knows that it is easier to discourage capitalists

---

[3] See, e.g. three books on that subject published by the United Nations Institute WIDER (World Institute for Development of Economic Research) in 2004.

from investing than workers from labouring. Even today, Europeans treat capital better than earnings. Note that as far as incentives are concerned, the marginal tax rates are those that matter, and the gap between marginal rates of capital income taxation in Europe and in the US is quite astonishing.

Let us now look at the other side of Lindert's conclusion: this structure of taxation is efficient but wholly inequitable. It is known that capital owners, who tend to be richer, get off lightly while labour carries a heavier burden because of lower disposable income and higher unemployment. Lindert's conclusion is interesting for two reasons: it covers two centuries and goes against the tide. It also needs to be qualified in a number of aspects. First the European and American tax systems have evolved and converge somehow. In addition, the efficiency of the tax system is just a part of the efficiency of an economic system. On the redistributive side, one realizes today that little redistribution is achieved through the tax system. Most of the redistribution is implemented by social insurance (health and pensions) and by public spending (education).

7.6. Conclusion

At the end of this chapter one is left with very mixed impressions. The question we started with was whether or not the welfare state was responsible for the decline in economic performance. At the micro level, social protection brings distortion in the choices of contributors and of beneficiaries. Yet, the empirical evidence indicates that the cost of these distortions is rather limited. At the macro level, one cannot infer much from a negative relation between the social burden and GDP growth. If there is any relation between these two variables, it is the result of a very intricate model that appears to be a black box.

Having said this, three conclusions emerge. First, the welfare state is likely to have modified the preferences of individuals. By overprotecting certain categories of people, and, not necessarily the neediest, it leads to a loss in the spirit of responsibility and initiative. The second conclusion is that the decline in economic growth and pressured public finance—regardless of whether or not its cause is the development of the welfare state—calls for its partial retrenchment. Finally, most of the work on the effect of the welfare state on growth and unemployment deals with a relatively short and recent period. A longer run view such as that of Lindert might be useful.

8

Performance and Efficiency of the Welfare State

> **KEY CONCEPTS**
> best practice frontier
> convergence
> Matthew effect
> productive efficiency

8.1. Introduction

In general, when one considers the concept of efficiency coupled with the welfare state, one immediately thinks of the effects on the efficiency of the economy of the welfare state, notably the taxes implied and the benefits generated. This question has been widely discussed in recent works.[1] One of the main charges addressed to modern welfare states is that they impair economic performance and international competitiveness. It was the topic of Chapter 7. Another charge, just as widespread, concerns their inefficiency in providing social services, and their responsibility for the proliferation of costly transfer programs that miss their target populations. This second charge is thus different from the first one, although not totally unrelated. It concerns the economic efficiency of the welfare state per se, and it is the topic of this chapter.

Each type of social expenditure has what could be called a target population, which it reaches via a more or less lengthy process. To take an example, the fact that 100 million Euros are devoted to social housing does not mean that the natural beneficiaries of this type of program, namely needy households, will receive a service equivalent to that amount. At each stage of the process

---

[1] For a survey, see Atkinson (1995). See also the work of Lindbeck (1995a,b).

that provides such a service dysfunctionings may appear, with the consequence that the amount initially intended for this service is greatly reduced.[2] At the production stage, corporatism, self-interest, and mere incompetence can lead to the first failures in functioning. Further down the line, at the allocation stage, the benefits, if any, may be attributed to population groups that do not really need them, while neglecting those for whom they could be vital. This is another type of failure.

We have just mentioned two forms of failure in functioning, 'productive inefficiency' and 'distributive inefficiency.' The first has been widely studied by production economists, and it applies to components of the welfare state that involve the production of services. This is the case of hospitals, schools, day-care centres where services (outputs) are produced out of some human and material resources (inputs). The second has been studied particularly by economists and sociologists, and concerns income transfer programs, particularly means-tested ones. Note, however, that agencies in charge of these transfer programs, for example, the social security administration, can also be inefficient if they require excessive administrative costs.

In this chapter we will discuss those types of inefficiency with a particular focus on productive inefficiency. We will present a methodology that is not often applied to the welfare state: the efficiency frontier approach.[3] Our main purpose is to show that one can measure inefficiency in the welfare state, not just talk about it in abstract terms, as is often the case. In so doing, we want to address a number of policy questions. When inefficiency is detected, can it be corrected? Can it be explained? Is it inherent to the public sector? In other words, would privatizing some of the activities of the welfare state wherever possible increase their efficiency? Our motivation comes from a conviction that removing these efficiency slacks could alleviate part of the financial strains that burden most welfare states. Too often we hear unqualified statements as to the inefficiency of government action. These, in turn, can be used to justify hasty dismantlement or privatization of a specific program or service. We believe that the welfare state, like any accused, is entitled to a due process and particularly to a fair trial. If then its inefficiency is proved without extenuating evidence, then measures of rolling back or of privatizing can be taken.

Even though we believe that efficiency studies of components of the welfare states are desirable and needed, we do not think that this methodology can apply to the welfare state as a whole. We will argue that for such a level of aggregation we should restrict the performance analysis to the outcomes and not relate it to the resources involved. As an illustration, we then turn to an

---

[2] This argument is different from that of the leaking bucket.
[3] Already mentioned in Chapter 6 about the OMC.

evaluation of the performance of all the European welfare states and its evolution over time, using frontier techniques. The results confirm that countries with the lowest performance grew faster and that we observe a path towards convergence.

The rest of the chapter is organized as follows. The next section is devoted to the distributive inefficiency that arises in the allocation of social transfers or services. Section 8.3 deals with the administrative cost of transfer and social insurance programs. Section 8.4 introduces the efficiency frontier approach. This approach can be applied to a number of specific social services. Section 8.5 is devoted to a performance analysis of the whole welfare state. The final section discusses the causes of inefficiency in social spending and presents a few recommendations.

8.2. The Matthew Effect

One can speak of the distributive inefficiency of social policy when programs that have been implemented do not help to remove the insecurity of existence from beneficiary households or individuals, despite sufficient resources to achieve this objective. How can this phenomenon be explained? Simply by the fact that needy households do not exercise their right to benefit from these social protection programs, while other households not suffering from precarious conditions do benefit from them. Furthermore, this inefficiency is not limited to social protection in the strict sense of the term, but also to a number of social facilities and services: study grants, social housing, social assistance, and so on. This phenomenon of unequal and inappropriate distribution of the state's social expenditure has been studied under the name of the 'Matthew effect.'[4] For cultural and institutional reasons, well-off social groups often benefit from social provisions intended for disadvantaged groups. These are stopped by administrative complexity and by fear of stigmatization. Admittedly, the Matthew effect does not explain everything; some new types of poverty and exclusion are not being provided for in the existing social assistance programs.

The Matthew effect has been widely studied in a number of European countries, including Belgium (Deleeck (1979)) and the UK (Le Grand (1982)) in the 1970s and 1980s. It has received less attention over the following

---

[4] The concept of 'Matthew effect' is widely used by sociologists in different areas. It was first introduced by Robert Merton (1968) and then by Herman Deleek (1979). It is named after the 'Parable of Talents' as told in the Gospel according to Matthew: 'For to everyone that has, more will be given, and he will have abundance; but from him who does not have, even what he has will be taken away' (Matthew 25–9). Recently Paul Krugman (*New York Times*, June 1 2004) has introduced the concept of Dooh Nibor Economics (Robin Hood in reverse) to characterize large scale transfer of income from the middle class to the very affluent.

91

decades.[5] This might reflect the fact that today very few people believe that expenditure in social services benefits primarily the less well off. It came as a surprise when Peter Townsend (1979) concluded his survey on poverty in the UK: 'Contrary to common belief, fewer individuals in households with low rather than with high incomes receive social services in kind of substantial value' (p. 222). Today, most social scientists admit that social spending in areas such as education, health, transport, housing, is distributed in favour of the higher social groups.

As Le Grand (1982) puts it, there are different kinds of equality pertaining to social services: equality of public expenditure, equality of final income, equality of use, equality of cost and equality of outcome. He then studies whether public spending on health care, education, housing and transport promotes equality in any of its interpretations. Focusing on equality of public expenditure in Britain, he shows that the top socio-economic group receives up to 40 per cent more National Health Service expenditure per sick person than the bottom group, accounting for difference in age and sex. The top fifth of the income distribution receives nearly three times as much public expenditure in education per household as the poorest fifth. Public expenditure on housing favours the better off, with the highest group receiving nearly twice as much as the lowest. Finally, the richest fifth of the income distribution receives about ten times as much subsidy per household on rail travel, and seventeen times as much on private transport as the poorest fifth.

As another example of the Matthew effect, one can mention the use of subsidized child care in Belgium. In 1992, 28.2 per cent of households with children under three used that facility, with a wide dispersion across classes of disposable of income. The rate of participation was of 15.5 per cent for the bottom decile, 21.8 per cent for the fifth decile and 47.8 per cent for the top decile. This rather regressive effect still holds even after controlling for working mothers.[6]

Let us mention a more recent study. In response to structurally poor job prospects for the least skilled, Belgium has recently introduced a voucher system to boost domestic services employment. This service voucher system pays for a range of services like cleaning, washing and ironing. It is heavily subsidized: about 70 per cent of the cost of services rendered to individual consumers is borne by the state. Marx and Vandelannoote (2014) show that the principal winners are the generally highly educated, relatively well-earning service voucher users who can now benefit from reliable and better quality services than would otherwise be obtainable.

---

[5] At least in developed countries. In the less advanced countries, this issue has been widely studied by the World Bank with the famous concept of *'programs for the poor are poor programs.'*
[6] See Storms (1995).

This evidence can readily be applied to other countries with strong social policy. However, it calls for two caveats. First, as has often been noted, the political survival of the welfare state might require that not only the poor benefit from social policy, but also the middle class. In other words, without the Matthew effect there could be no social program at all[7]. Second, one has to keep in mind that, fortunately, the Matthew effect does not apply to the entirety of the welfare state. There are many redistributive programs that work, which explains the relatively good performance of the welfare state at fighting poverty and social inequalities.

8.3. Administrative Costs

In welfare and social insurance programs, productive activity is limited to one of financial intermediation. The question raised is that of the relative administrative costs associated with public and private intermediation. This has been particularly studied in the field of retirement and health care insurance for which there exist a number of empirical studies (Mitchell 1997). The current evidence pertains to international cost comparison of social insurance and cost comparison between private and social insurance.

The administrative costs of social insurance vary greatly across countries and institutional settings. Table 8.1 reveals that European countries spend less than 3 per cent of their annual budgets on social security in administrative costs. This ranges from a low 0.97 per cent in the UK to 6.07 per cent in

Table 8.1. Administrative costs as a percentage of social security benefit expenditures in Europe

EU28	2.89	Ireland	6.06
Austria	1.93	Italy	2.08
Belgium	3.03	Latvia	1.39
Bulgaria	2.10	Lithuania	2.21
Croatia	1.74	Luxembourg	1.41
Netherlands	5.50	Poland	2.21
Czechia	2.91	Portugal	1.47
Denmark	3.76	Romania	2.06
Estonia	1.21	Slovakia	2.61
Finland	2.50	Slovenia	1.58
France	4.04	Spain	1.81
Germany	3.85	Sweden	1.93
Greece	1.58	United Kingdom	0.97
Hungary	1.29		

Source: Eurostat (2017c).

---

[7] Marx et al (2015). This point is related to the paradox of redistribution discussed in Chapter 5.

Ireland. Part of the explanation for these marked cost differences is that social security systems vary across countries in terms of the particular mix of social assistance and insurance, and in terms of the types of payments offered. Another part of the explanation lies in the economies of scale. It appears, from a multivariate comparison of social security costs in a sample of countries, that a one per cent increase in participation raises costs by only 0.6–0.9 per cent. The same study shows that a universal demogrant system is significantly less costly to administer than a means-tested or an earnings-related program (Mitchell 1997).

A comparison of publicly managed insurance systems with privately managed alternatives indicates that, in general, the latter is considerably more costly. In the US it is estimated that roughly 12 per cent of the revenue of the health insurance industry goes on administrative expenses. This percentage is well above the cost of state-managed health insurance in European countries, and even in the US. As noted by Diamond (1992), this high percentage is primarily a reflection of returns to scale in transactions including advertising and commissions. In part it is also due to adverse selection because of the need to underwrite in details. Finally, it can be attributed to the high turnover that characterizes private health insurance. The same cost difference is observed in retirement insurance. For example, it is now clear that the Chilean private pension system that many consider as a model is very expensive, a lot more expensive than well-run, unified, government-managed social security systems (Valdes-Prieto 1998 and Gill et al. 2004).

It is important to recognize those cost differences. Too many people think of privatization as a route to greater efficiency and lower costs. Yet as early as 1942, Beveridge (1942) referred to a 'markedly lower cost of administration in most forms of state insurance.' In defence of private insurance, a number of observers note that it is likely to offer better and more diverse services in exchange for these higher costs. There would be a trade-off between diversity and transaction costs that requires further study.

So far, the focus is on the efficiency of social insurance programs and their administrative costs. In this particular activity the index of performance is unidimensional; thus measuring the efficiency of insurance programs is quite easy. The difficulty arises when there are several kinds of services produced or provided, and resources used. We now turn to this problem.

8.4. Doing Better with Less. Productive Efficiency Studies

For an economist, an activity is called productively inefficient if the same production of goods and services can be carried out with fewer resources, or if more can be produced with the resources used. To illustrate this concept

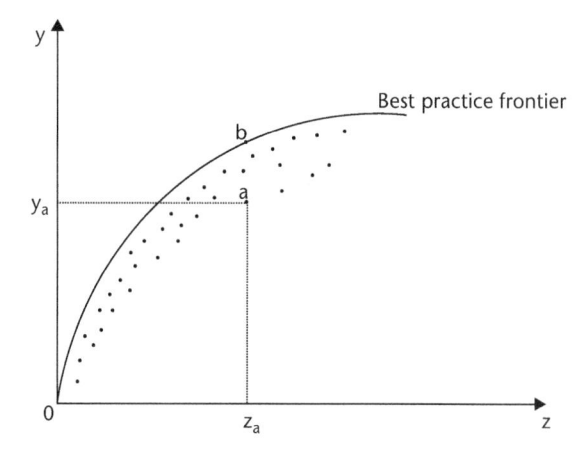

Figure 8.1. Productive inefficiency

a figure may be helpful. Being restricted to two dimensions, we consider an activity a that produces a service y_a out of an input z_a. Figure 8.1 represents such an outcome, as well as a curve that represents the productive efficiency frontier. This curve is the yardstick with respect to which the efficiency of a can be assessed. The relative vertical distance between a and this frontier measures what we call the productive inefficiency of a. Note that such a measure can readily apply to a setting with multiple outputs and inputs, possibly including quality indicators.

The measuring of productive efficiency would be a rather simple exercise if the efficiency frontier were known. Unfortunately, this is not the case as the true frontier cannot be found in the blueprints of a social engineer. It must thus be inferred from the reality; that is, constructed from a sample of possibly inefficient observations. The dots on Figure 8.1 represent such a sample.

There are different types of method for inferring an efficiency frontier from a sample of activities. They vary from the estimation of a pre-specified production function to the construction of a stair-shaped envelope of the input–output points (Free Disposable Hull, FDH). One of the most popular methods is the DEA, to which we come back in the next section. Whatever the method chosen, parametric or not, stochastic or deterministic, one should realize that the productive inefficiency so measured is, of course, a relative one. Hence, one often uses the term 'best practice' frontier. This frontier is made up of those observations that appear to be the best ones in the sense of some posited assumption of dominance.

For that reason the choice of the sample of observations is crucial. It is important that they originate from similar conditions as to the technology. To take the case of a cross-section sample of retirement homes, the question of spatial homogeneity is quite relevant. It is not impossible that geographical or institutional differences go a long way towards explaining variations in performance. Part of the efficiency assessment exercise consists in accounting for these differences.

One can see right away the limitations of the efficiency frontier approach for the purpose at hand. First, it only applies to components of the welfare state in which there is production of services: hospitals, social security administration, social work. Secondly, since the method is comparative, it concerns activities with a large number of comparable productive units. Note, however, that in certain instances intertemporal or international comparisons can enlarge the sample of activities whose performance is to be assessed. As appears clearly from Figure 8.1, productive inefficiency measures waste of resources. Why produce only a when b is attainable?

It is clear that productive efficiency should not be the sole objective of social policymakers. There are other objectives for sure: first of all, achieving some redistribution as we have seen, but also fostering employment and growth while keeping within the financial constraints. Some of these objectives are not always compatible. Productive efficiency is, indeed, the only objective whose achievement does not impede the achievement of the other objectives. Producing too few services or employing too many resources, as compared to what is technically feasible, cannot be justified in terms of any of the other objectives traditionally assigned to the welfare state.

For a long time, there was nothing but anecdotal evidence to document the efficiency of the welfare state. Fortunately, over the last decades, there have been a number of studies that have used the productive efficiency approach to measure the efficiency of various sectors of the welfare state. Going back to Figure 8.1, the procedure is quite standard. We collect data on a sample of activities that can be represented by dots. Then we construct a frontier that essentially envelops that data. For each observation, for example, a, one calculates its degree of productive efficiency or the ratio az_a/bz_a. This ratio would be equal to one, if the observation were lying on the frontier. The last stage attempts to explain, when possible, some of the observed efficiency slacks.

There exist a number of studies[8] that are surveyed in different papers. A sample of them is given in Table 8.2. They concern different areas of social spending, such as health, education, day care, and retirement homes. These studies lead to three conclusions: (i) there are serious productive inefficiencies; in other words, more and better could be done with less; (ii) these inefficiencies are not specific to a particular type of organization (non-profit, state-owned,

---

[8] Pestieau and Tulkens (1993), Lefebvre et al. (2017).

Table 8.2. Efficiency studies

Areas	Production unit	Studies	Country	Productive efficiency (in %)
Health	Hospitals	Biorn et al. (2003)	Norway	79 to 82
		Herr (2008)	Germany	86
		Gok/Sezen (2011)	Turkey	51 to 71
		Varabyova/Schreyogg (2013)	Cross-country	77 to 86
		Kittelsen et al. (2015)	Nordic countries	77 to 90
		Mukherjee et al. (2010)	US	72
		Van Ineveld et al. (2016)	Netherlands	85 to 90
Social	Retirement homes	Bjorkgren et al. (2001)	Finland	85 to 89
		Garavaglia et al. (2011)	Italy	80 to 86
		Ni Luasa et al. (2017)	Ireland	55 to 62
		Dulal (2017)	USA	92
Education	High schools	Waldo (2007)	Sweden	66 to 73
		Haelemans et al. (2012)	Netherlands	78
		Johnes et al. (2012)	UK	75 to 86
		Cherchye et al. (2010)	Belgium	74
	School districts	Banker et al. (2004)	USA	71
		Ferrera et al. (2011)	Spain	82
	Universities	Abott/Doucouliagos (2003)	Australia	94 to 96
		Anthon et al. (2012)	US	76
		Johnes (2006)	UK	95
		Barra et al. (2015)	Italy	64 to 72
Community	Municipalities	Erlandsen/Forsund (2002)	Norway	76 to 93
		Storto (2013)	Italy	85 to 88
		Struk/Matulova (2016)	Czechia	47 to 50

for-profit); (iii) competition, autonomy, and flexibility could help to reduce a substantial proportion of these inefficiencies.

For a long time, there was a strong belief among economists that public sector managers, unlike their private sector counterparts, do not have to worry about losses, or become the victims of takeovers. Hence, they have little incentive to carefully monitor the activities of their enterprises or services. But it is now widely accepted that the productive efficiency of a public or private activity depends on both the market environment and the institutional setting in which it operates. A privately owned monopoly or a regulated firm may produce very inefficient results, while a publicly owned operation that is subject to a lot of competition and few legal restrictions may produce quite efficiently. This is a theoretical statement backed up by a number of empirical studies. It implies that, to enhance efficiency in the welfare state, it is important that it opens its operations to competition, and if necessary, that it allows private companies to compete along with public ones for contracts to supply particular services.

This conclusion is at odds with the one reached on financial intermediation where being a single provider was cost efficient. The reason for this contradiction lies in the underlying technology. Activities such as day-care centres or retirement homes quickly reach their optimal scale; in other words, multiplying them is scale efficient and allows for some form of competition. On the other hand, in activities such as social security or unemployment insurance, fixed administrative costs can be spread over a large group of people, and their scale economies dominate the potential gains arising from competition.

8.5. The Performance of the Welfare State

In the previous section we have seen that many components of the welfare state can be submitted to the test of best practice and that such exercise is useful to improve its overall efficiency. These studies concern micro units such as postal services or hospitals. They would not be relevant for aggregates such as the health or the education systems, and even less so for the welfare state as a whole. For example, public spending in health is not closely related to the quality of health in a nation or a region, for at least two reasons: health depends more on factors such as the living habits or the climate than on spending; and spending can be higher where it is needed, namely in areas of poor health. For these reasons, when dealing with such aggregates we prefer to restrict our analysis to the quality of outcomes and not to the more or less efficient relation between resources used and outcomes. This does not imply that public spending is worth nothing; it just means that it is part of a complex process in which other factors play a crucial and complementary role. Another reason why using social spending is not appropriate comes from the fact that social spending as measured by international organizations is not a good measure of real spending. It does not include subsidies and tax breaks awarded to schemes such as mandatory private pensions or health care and it includes taxes paid on social transfers.[9]

To illustrate the difference between efficiency studies as advocated in the previous section and the performance approach used in this section, we could use the analogy of a classroom. It makes sense to rank students according to how they perform in a series of exams. Admittedly we can question the quality of tests or the weights used in adding marks from different fields. Yet in general there is little discussion as to the grading of students. At the same time we know that these students may face different 'environmental conditions' which can affect their ability to perform. For example, two students can obtain the same grades but the one coming from an underprivileged family

---

[9] See Adema et al. (2011) for the definition of gross and net social spending. See also chapter 3.

can be considered as more deserving or meritorious than the one whose material and family conditions are ideal. That being said there exists no ranking of students according to merit. The concept of 'merit' is indeed too controversial. By the same token, we should not attempt to assess the 'merit' of social protection systems or the public sector as a whole.

The problem becomes one of aggregation of outcome indicators. We use five normalized outcome indicators—which concern poverty, inequality, unemployment, education, and health—for the twenty-eight European Union member states, fifteen historical members (EU15) and 13 newcomers (EU13), over the period 2005–2014. By normalized we mean that each indicator will go from 0 to 1. The country with the highest value for life expectancy and the lowest for the four other indicators gets 1 and the country with the lowest indicator for life expectancy and the highest for the four other indicators obtains 0. These normalized indicators are given in Table A.8.1 in the Appendix. For poverty and inequality, Czechia has the highest score and Romania the lowest. For unemployment, Sweden and Greece rank first and last respectively. For health, we have Spain and Bulgaria, and for education Croatia and Spain. We clearly see that countries such as Sweden and Czechia perform well and countries such as Bulgaria and Romania poorly. The case of Spain is interesting; it has the highest score for health and does poorly otherwise. To be able to compare the overall performance of these welfare states we use two methods of aggregation. The first one simply adds the normalized indicators with identical weights; we label it *SPI* for sum of partial indicators. The second one is the *DEA* (data envelopment analysis) that is widely used to construct best practice frontiers. This technique gives different weights to each indicator and each decision unit, here each national welfare state. So doing, we expect that the weight given to a partial indicator and to a specific country reflects the importance that this country gives to this indicator. We thus meet the concern of political scientists that different welfare states can have different priorities.[10] We however depart from the standard use of DEA in two ways. First, we assume a unitary input, thus focusing on the performance and not the efficiency of welfare states. This approach, which has been labelled *benefit of the doubt*, is now widely used to measure the performance of welfare states.[11] The second departure from standard DEA is that we impose a 10 per cent floor on the weights to avoid a country that has a maximum score on one partial indicator and poor scores on the others (typically Spain) being awarded a maximum score on overall performance.

---

[10] See, e.g., Esping-Andersen (1990).
[11] See Coelli et al. (2010), Cherchye et al. (2004), Lefebvre et al. (2017), Lefebvre and Pestieau (2015).

Table 8.3. Performance indicators EU 28: 2014

Countries	SIP	Ranking	DEA	Ranking
Austria	0.826	5	0.992	8
Belgium	0.759	10	0.941	10
Bulgaria	0.297	27	0.372	27
Croatia	0.569	19	0.828	17
Cyprus	0.713	11	0.928	11
Czechia	0.856	1	1.000	1
Denmark	0.821	6	1.000	1
Estonia	0.435	23	0.611	22
Finland	0.833	4	1.000	1
France	0.802	9	1.000	1
Germany	0.695	13	0.890	13
Greece	0.370	25	0.404	26
Hungary	0.606	18	0.728	19
Ireland	0.701	12	0.895	12
Italy	0.550	20	0.800	18
Latvia	0.393	24	0.429	24
Lithuania	0.471	21	0.527	23
Luxembourg	0.804	8	0.983	9
Malta	0.667	16	0.706	20
Netherlands	0.846	2	1.000	1
Poland	0.650	17	0.859	15
Portugal	0.451	22	0.654	21
Romania	0.235	28	0.286	28
Slovakia	0.818	7	1.000	1
Slovenia	0.669	15	0.834	16
Spain	0.332	26	0.409	25
Sweden	0.844	3	1.000	1
UK	0.674	14	0.873	14
EU28	0.632		0.784	

Source: Authors own calculation based on Eurostat (2017a)

Table 8.3 reports the indicators as well as the rank of each country in 2014. As it appears, following the SIP approach, we have, at the top, the Nordic countries, plus Austria and the Netherlands. But we also have new entrant countries (EU13) doing quite well, like Slovenia or Czechia, which are at the top. At the bottom, we find Bulgaria, Greece, Latvia, Romania and Spain. Turning to the DEA approach, the ranking changes a bit. We have several countries with the maximum score: Czechia, the Netherlands, Slovakia, France, and the Nordic countries. In the bottom, we have the same countries as with SPI. A few comments are in order. First, note that a score of one indicates that the country is on the best practice frontier[12]. This is not unusual in a DEA analysis where the number of dimensions (variables) is large relative

---

[12] With the unconstrained DEA there would be twice as many countries with a unitary score.

Performance and Efficiency of the Welfare State

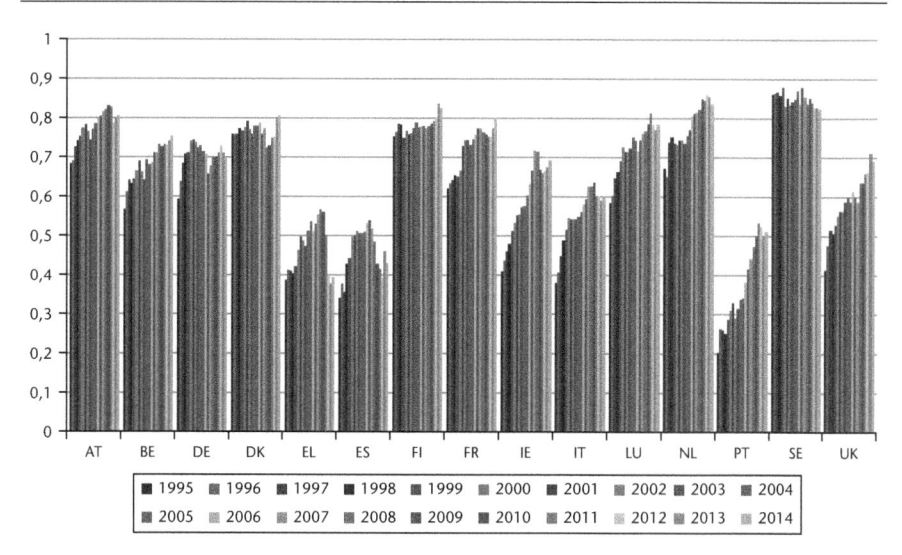

Figure 8.2. Evolution of SPI performance indicators, EU15 1995–2014
Source: Author's own calculations based on Eurostat (2017a)

to the number of observations. Second, the average DEA score is 0.784 versus the mean SPI score of 0.632. The DEA scores tend to be higher because of the unlimited freedom to choose outcomes' weight (even with the constraint of 10 per cent) compared with SPI uniform weights assumption. Third, the DEA rankings are 'broadly similar' to the SPI rankings. However a few countries do experience changes, such as France or Slovakia. The correlation between the two indicators is quite high (0.974 Spearman correlation).

For EU15, we have data over the period 1995–2014. Thus, it is interesting to see whether we observe specific trends and particularly convergence towards welfare state performance among the EU countries, the aim of the OMC strategy. For this purpose, we compute year by year performance indexes—SPI and constrained DEA—and their rate of change using the 2005–2014 normalized indicators.

The results by year and by country are reported on Figure 8.2 for the SPI performance. It is interesting to note that in most cases one observes an improvement over the twenty-year period, particularly in countries that were lagging at the beginning. It should be noted however that the countries that have been hit by the great recession have a declining performance at the end of the period. This is the case for Greece, Portugal, Italy, and Spain. Note also that the decline observed in Sweden is part of the convergence process. Figure 8.3 presents a test of convergence for the DEA performance. One sees a

The Welfare State in Europe

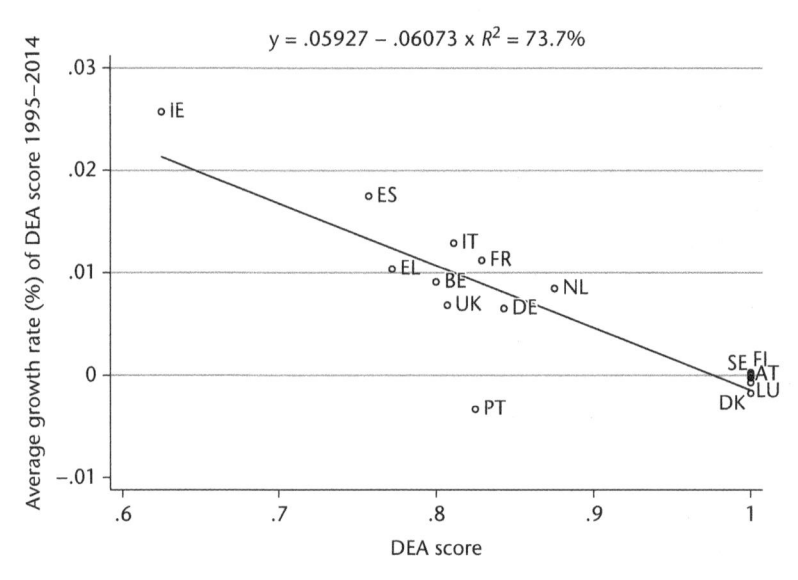

Figure 8.3. Convergence of DEA performance indicators, EU15 1995–2014
Source: Author's own calculations based on Eurostat (2017a)

clear negative relation between the initial performance score and its rate of change over the period. Summing up, the results reported here confirm some convergence in performance among these fifteen European countries as in Coelli et al. (2010).

8.6. Conclusion

Among the critiques levelled against the welfare state is inefficiency in distributing benefits and in producing services. This is often been followed by a call to roll back some programs and entrust others to the private sector, the implicit assumption being that one can do as well with a leaner welfare state, and that the private sector is naturally more efficient. In this chapter we have tried to tackle the question of definition and measurement of the efficiency and the performance of the welfare state.

The welfare state consists of two types of programs: transfer programs, such as welfare, social security, unemployment insurance, and the production of services such as hospitals, day care, and schools. The issue of efficiency in transfer programs has to do with whether the transfers are made to the right people and whether the financial intermediation is cost efficient. The issue of efficiency in the provision of services can be expressed in terms of resource utilization. In other words, can we produce the same quantity and quality of services with fewer resources, or conversely, can we produce more and better services with the same amount of resources?

We have seen that clear inefficiencies exist in the distribution of services. Because of administrative complexity or fear of stigmatization, the neediest people can fall outside of the protection of the welfare state. As far as the administrative cost of social insurance, particularly health and retirement insurance, a single public provider tends to be cheaper than a multiplicity of private firms. Finally, in the production of services, there are clear efficiency slacks, but they are not really dependent on ownership—public or private. What seems to matter is competition and autonomy.

Finally, we have argued that efficiency studies cannot be applied to the whole welfare state and that an evaluation of its performance, abstracting from social spending, is preferable. This performance study indicates a clear process of convergence among the countries of EU15.

The conclusion one can draw from this chapter is clear. First, one has to fight the Matthew effect, and if this is not possible, one needs to make transfers transparent and universalistic. Secondly, one has to keep administrative costs at their current level, while at the same time maintain the quality of services provided. Thirdly, one has to introduce competition and autonomy in the management of social services. With an energetic efficiency-enhancing approach, the welfare state can recoup its credibility and recover desperately needed resources.

Within the expression 'welfare state', one tends to focus on 'welfare' and forget 'state.' An efficient functioning of the welfare state requires that the state, represented by the central government, play an important rule. Decentralization of decisions can be desirable for productive efficiency reasons. However, the main objectives of reduction of poverty and inequality across the national territory are to be entrusted to a central authority.

The Welfare State in Europe

Appendix

Table A.8.1. Normalized Partial Indicators EU 28: 2014

Pays	Poverty	Inequality	LT unemployment	Life expectancy	Early school drop-out
Austria	0.714	0.838	0.994	0.807	0.776
Belgium	0.623	0.919	0.840	0.784	0.630
Bulgaria	0.214	0.108	0.696	0.000	0.469
Croatia	0.370	0.568	0.519	0.386	1.000
Cyprus	0.695	0.486	0.652	0.943	0.786
Czechia	1.000	1.000	0.928	0.500	0.854
Denmark	0.844	0.838	0.983	0.705	0.734
Estonia	0.214	0.189	0.895	0.330	0.547
Finland	0.799	0.973	0.972	0.773	0.646
France	0.766	0.784	0.845	0.943	0.672
Germany	0.545	0.568	0.956	0.761	0.646
Greece	0.195	0.189	0.000	0.795	0.672
Hungary	0.656	0.784	0.873	0.170	0.547
Ireland	0.578	0.649	0.713	0.784	0.781
Italy	0.370	0.378	0.652	0.989	0.359
Latvia	0.253	0.189	0.823	0.000	0.698
Lithuania	0.390	0.297	0.812	0.023	0.833
Luxembourg	0.565	0.757	0.989	0.886	0.823
Malta	0.597	0.865	0.928	0.864	0.083
Netherlands	0.877	0.919	0.917	0.830	0.688
Poland	0.526	0.622	0.867	0.375	0.859
Portugal	0.364	0.270	0.613	0.773	0.234
Romania	0.000	0.000	0.923	0.057	0.198
Slovakia	0.688	0.946	0.785	0.761	0.911
Slovenia	0.812	0.892	0.564	0.284	0.792
Spain	0.188	0.108	0.365	1.000	0.000
Sweden	0.649	0.892	1.000	0.886	0.792
UK	0.539	0.568	0.956	0.784	0.526

Note: Poverty is defined as the share of persons with an equivalized disposable income below the risk-of-poverty threshold, which is set at 60% of the national median equivalised disposable income (after social transfers). Inequality is defined as the ratio of total income received by the 20% of the population with the highest income (top quintile) to that received by the 20% of the population with the lowest income (lowest quintile). Income must be understood as equivalised disposable income. Long term unemployed (12 months or longer) as a share of the total active population harmonised with national monthly unemployment estimates. Life expectancy as the number of years a person may be expected to live, starting at age 0. Early school drop-out as the percentage of the population aged 18–24 with at most lower secondary education and not in further education or training

9

Social versus Private Insurance

> **KEY CONCEPTS**
>
> adverse selection
> commitment
> in kind transfers
> moral hazard
> new social question
> targeting
> self insurance
> workfare

9.1. Introduction

Up to now we have been mainly concerned with social insurance, neglecting the role of private insurance as an alternative means of protection. In this chapter, we look at the role of the public versus the private sector in the provision of insurance in light of recent economic and social developments. We believe that the comparison between those two types of insurance cannot be addressed in the same way as seventy years ago, when the welfare state started. Social insurance is now experiencing a number of difficulties. Some of these are linked to recent developments such as fiscal competition, the declining credibility of the state, evolving labour markets, public opinion resisting redistributive policy, and an increasing demand for protection. First, let us clarify some conceptual issues, and give some figures for the evolution and the relative strength of social versus private insurance.[1]

---

[1] See on this Poterba (1996) and Pestieau (1994).

9.2. Social Insurance

9.2.1. *The State, the Market, and the Family*

The title of this chapter implies that the state and the market are the two institutions concerned with reducing the risks individuals face. In other words, we are neglecting the oldest and still important protection that is provided by the family.[2] Historically, the responsibility for providing security has rested with the family, or rather with the extended family or the 'village.' Risks such as disability, unemployment, retirement, or disease that are today essentially borne by social insurance programs, and those such as fire, street accidents, and sudden death that are now borne by private insurance companies, used to be accommodated, at least partially, by the family or by the employer. Then came the private insurance industry to bring more adequate protection. Later, it was felt that the market was not providing appropriate coverage against some important risks; as a result governments became increasingly, indeed predominantly, involved in the provision of insurance.

Does that mean that the role of the family is now nil? Not really. Indeed, the family still plays an important insurance role that is widely documented in the study of altruism, exchange, and bargaining within the family. In some instances, either it replaces the state or the market, or it offsets their action; in other instances, it has a rather supplementary role (Becker 1991, Kotlikoff and Spivak 1981). During the great recession, the family played an important role in reducing income inequality through the pooling of resources. However this effect weakened as the crisis progressed.[3] It is important to note that in countries that witness a retrenchment in social protection programs, there is an acute need for families to protect their members against risks such as loss of earnings. Some governments even tend to use family altruism as an alibi for cutting social protection spending. As an illustration, Table 9.1 provides data on the relative importance of the state, the market, and the family for the resources of elderly people of a sample of European countries.

9.2.2. *The Specificity of Social Insurance*

What is specific in social insurance relative to private insurance? As observed by Tony Atkinson (1991), there is no easy answer to this question. Is it the publicness of the provision? Not really—since one can have social insurance benefits distributed to individuals by private organizations. This is the case in

---

[2] This can be viewed as an extended from of self-insurance.   [3] Eurofound (2017).

Social versus Private Insurance

Table 9.1. Resources of elderly people

Country	State	Market	Family
Austria	93.2	3.4	3.4
Germany	88.2	8.3	3.5
Sweden	82.1	15.5	2.4
Netherlands	94.5	3.9	1.6
Estonia	94.4	1.6	4.0
Italy	90.0	3.0	3.0
France	96.3	1.3	2.4
Denmark	76.3	21.5	2.2
Switzerland	67.7	30.7	1.6
Belgium	94.6	2.1	3.3
Czechia	84.7	1.4	13.9

Source: SHARE, 5th wave, 2013, authors' calculation

Belgium for health care. On the other hand, in many countries, such as France, there are a number of state-owned insurance companies involved in private insurance. Is the specificity of social insurance the mode of financing? Even though social insurance is often associated with the functioning of the labour market and financed by payroll taxes, there are countries such as Denmark where it is exclusively financed by general revenue. We should add, in this respect, that the decline in regular salaried employment contributes to loosening the link between social insurance and the labour market.

The most specific feature of social insurance is undoubtedly that it is mandatory and universal. But again, as stated by Stiglitz (1983), one often confuses 'the question of whether individuals are to be insured with the question of who is to provide the insurance. The view that society must take measures to ensure that everyone is insured against certain major risks does not, in itself, imply that the government should directly provide that insurance.' Yet, compulsion is not enough to characterize social insurance. In a number of countries, car insurance and fire insurance are compulsory, and yet one does not consider this to be social insurance. This leads us to an additional specificity: social insurance is not based exclusively on an actuarially sound basis, but involves some redistribution. In other words, social insurance can be explained not only by a 'merit good' kind of argument but also by equity considerations. This latter feature is a prerequisite for universal access.

Two remarks are in order. First, even private insurance schemes are quite often forced to effect some redistribution. For example, life insurance companies are not always allowed to distinguish insurees according to sex or occupation. Hence, they redistribute from men to women, and from low life-expectancy occupations to high life-expectancy occupations. Secondly, the most extreme social insurance program, as far as redistribution is concerned, would be the proposal for a basic income scheme: a basic allowance

The Welfare State in Europe

would replace most social insurance transfers. As pointed out by Atkinson (1991), one should not speak of social insurance in that case. One could, however, speak of social protection without any attempt to mimic private insurance. We come back to the basic income in Chapter 13.

9.2.3. Expenditure for Insurance, Private, and Public

In Figure 9.1 and Table 9.2, we contrast spending on social and on private insurance. This calls for a couple of remarks. First, social insurance, proxied by social protection spending, dominates private insurance over time and across countries; it is almost five times as important in most countries. There are two exceptions: Ireland and, above all, Luxembourg. It should be noted in that respect that the figure for private insurance includes activities outside the country. Secondly, looking at the cross-section presented in Figure 9.1, one notes a slight substitution effect with some countries relying more on private than on public insurance (the UK, the US and, clearly, Ireland) and others relying more on public than on private insurance (the Nordic countries Austria, France, Belgium and Italy).

Figure 9.2 gives the ratio of private insurance to social insurance spending for six countries and the period 1983–2014. This ratio increases everywhere but with some fluctuations. In particular, one observes some decline at the

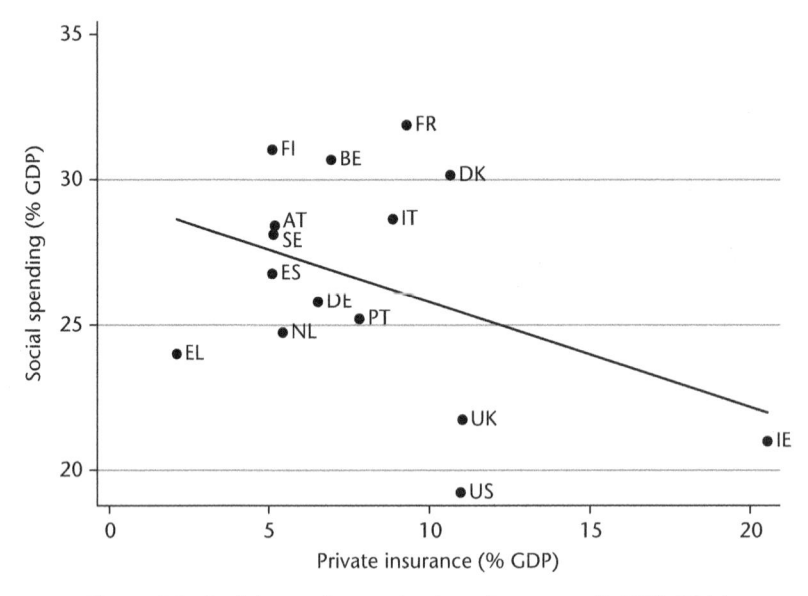

Figure 9.1. Social spending and private insurance % GDP, 2014
Source: OECD (2016c, 2016d)

Table 9.2. Social protection and private insurance in Europe, 2014 (% GDP)

Country	Private insurance	Social protection
Austria	5.2	28.4
Belgium	7.0	30.7
Czechia	3.6	20.6
Denmark	10.6	30.1
Estonia	3.2	16.3
Finland	5.1	31.0
France	9.3	31.9
Germany	6.5	25.8
Greece	2.1	24.0
Hungary	2.6	22.1
Ireland	20.5	21.0
Italy	8.9	28.6
Luxembourg	44.0	23.5
Netherlands	5.4	24.7
Poland	3.2	20.6
Portugal	7.8	25.2
Slovakia	2.9	18.4
Slovenia	5.0	23.7
Spain	5.1	26.8
Sweden	5.1	28.1
UK	11.0	21.7
USA	11.0	19.2

Source: OECD (2016c, 2016d)

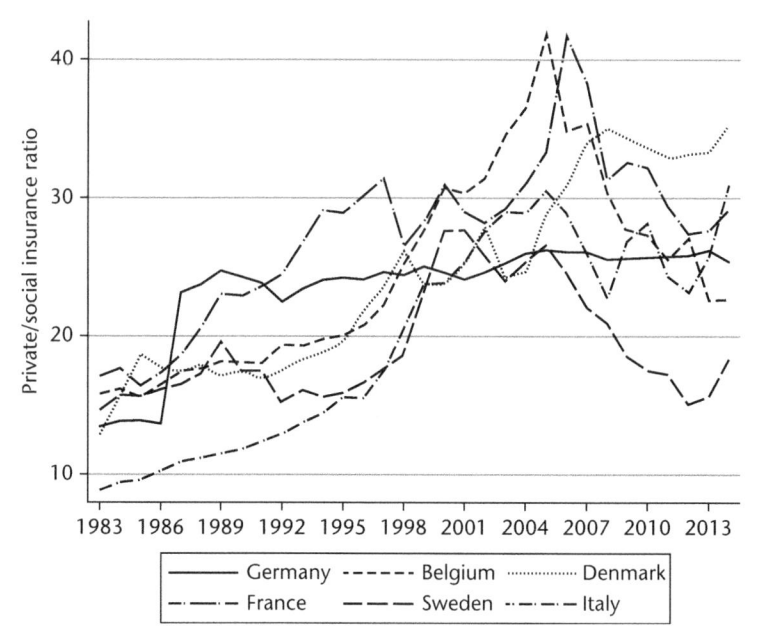

Figure 9.2. Private to social insurance ratio
Source: OECD (2016c, 2016d)

time of the great recession. The largest increase in the share of private insurance is in Denmark and the lowest is in Italy.[4]

9.2.4. Charity

Besides the market, the state and the family there is a fourth channel of social protection, namely, charity. Among many domains, charity contributes to that of poverty alleviation. And some people have argued that charity could efficiently substitute for the state in a number of areas. More so in Anglo-Saxon countries than on continental Europe. There indeed exists a political philosophy, dubbed compassionate conservatism, which stresses using traditionally conservative techniques in order to improve the general welfare of society. One of these techniques is charity. This viewed has been espoused by former U.S. President George W. Bush, and also in in the United Kingdom by former Prime Minister, David Cameron. The advocates of this view focus on alleged crowding-out effects that are created whenever government takes over any function previously left to voluntary actions. They believe that public welfare programs crowd out private charity but also family support systems and they are convinced that downsizing these programs would be socially desirable.

Without minimizing the role of charities and volunteering, one has to be cautious regarding the relative merits of charity and social protection. First, the theory of private contributions to public goods indicates that it necessarily leads to an underprovision of these goods because of free riding. In reality, charitable contributions represent a negligible amount relative to social spending. Second, unlike social protection, which is supposed to be universal, most charities are targeted on special beneficiaries. These remarks apply particularly to religious charitable organizations. The same remark about non-universality can be addressed to the family: it is clearly better to be needy in a well-to-do family than in a poor one. A third remark concerns the fact that charitable contributions benefit from tax deductions whose generosity varies across countries. These deductions can be costly and their desirability can be questioned. In other words, the forgone revenue could have been better used for financing social protection.

---

[4] We are not trying to explain why private and above all social insurance developed at the end of the nineteenth century and particularly after 1945. According to Ewald (1986), the emergence of the welfare state is linked to the construction of social risks and to the reconfiguration of personal responsibility.

9.3. Standard Cases for Social Insurance

9.3.1. *Market Failures*

In general, economists are interested by the failure of the market to provide adequate mechanisms allowing individuals to divest themselves of the risks they face, and by the role of the state in taking over some risk bearing. Quite interestingly, they are much more interested by this rather recent evolution than by the earlier one wherein the market progressively replaced the family in providing insurance protection. The standard examples of market failure are social risks, moral hazard and adverse selection.

Social risks are those risks faced by society as a whole and which are not diversifiable. Two types of social risks come to mind. First, there are all those low probability environmental or man-made hazards such as earthquakes, floods and large-scale fires. Secondly, there are events such as wars or heavy recessions. As regards to the first type of risks, individuals tend to have no interest in protecting themselves with insurance. They rely on society to help them in the unlikely case of a disaster, which in turn tends to affect their location decisions particularly in hazard-prone areas (Kunreuther 1978). We have here a typical case of moral hazard. Regarding the second type of risks, one often considers that society does better than an insurance company, particularly by engaging in risk sharing across generations. Long-term variations in public debt are often interpreted as a way of sharing the costs of wars or of heavy recessions between generations. It remains the case that most existing social insurance programs are not based on this argument of intergenerational risk taking. As to the first type of social risk, reinsurance could be the solution.

The *moral hazard* problem arises when the individual's incentives to avoid the insured-for event decrease as more insurance is provided. One consequence of this incentive problem is that insurance companies are reluctant to write unlimited insurance. It explains in part the limitations of insurance provided by the private market and the resulting reliance on social insurance. Note, however, that the government faces the same trade-offs between risk reduction and incentives as the market. On this ground, the traditional family has a clear edge (Arnott and Stiglitz 1991) to the extent that members feel concerned as much by the welfare of the family as a whole as by their own welfare. There are two types of moral hazard, ex-ante and ex-post, and both are different. Ex-ante moral hazard describes behaviour prior to an event occurring. For example, suppose a person, who has no health insurance, proceeds with her daily activities in a cautious manner because she knows she has to pay for hospital bills if she gets hurt. As soon as she decides to get health insurance she begins to engage in hazardous activities. To avoid such behaviour, it is common to introduce some co-payment. Ex-post moral hazard refers to the behaviour of an insured person after an event occurs. For example, a person who is fully insured would be tempted to overconsume medical services in case of health problems. Again to avoid ex post moral hazard one has to restrict the extent of insurance coverage.

The problem of *adverse selection*, which confronts private insurance markets and leads to reliance on social risk-taking, arises because the insuree knows more about the likelihood of occurrence of the insured-for event than the insurer. There is thus an incentive for the worst risks to sign up for insurance and for the best risks to self-insure. The state has an advantage over the market because it can make insurance compulsory. In so doing, the problem of adverse selection is avoided but the insurance scheme is no longer actuarially fair: good risks pay for bad risks. It remains the case that making participation mandatory would suffice to solve the problem of adverse selections in private insurance markets.

The administration of privately-managed health or retirement insurance is often considered costly as we have seen in the previous chapter. As discussed in Chapter 8, this argument pertains to increasing returns to scale in transactions, and it is often used in favour of social insurance. Nobody will deny that these problems, social risks, moral hazard, adverse selection, and to a lesser extent increasing returns are serious imperfections of private insurance markets. The debate is whether or not public provision is an improvement. Some economists would argue that there are cases where social insurance is inferior to even poorly functioning private insurance arrangements. These are cases where 'non-market failures' arising from public provision of insurance are more severe than the private market failures it is alleged to address. Leonard and Zeckhauser (1983) argue, for example, that 'moral hazard may be a more significant problem for publicly provided insurance because there is less financial incentive for the government to structure its insurance contracts efficiently' (p. 150).

To sum up, the problem of moral hazard, adverse selection, and social risks do not really make a convincing case for social insurance. As to the increasing returns argument, it mainly applies to health and old age insurance. Note finally that there are risks that seem to be insurable and that are hardly covered by the private market. Examples of that are the risk of dependence and the risk of mortality. We will come back to what has been called the long-term care insurance puzzle and the annuity market puzzle.

9.3.2. *Social Insurance as a Redistributive Device*

There is a second type of rationale for social insurance that is also often questioned, namely the objective of redistribution. In an ideal world, what economists call a first-best, redistribution ought to be achieved through non-distortionary income taxation that would include transfers to the needy.

Indeed, such redistributive taxation has been presented as a sort of insurance contracted by individuals behind the veil of ignorance, that is, before knowing anything about, for example, their own ability, health status and other characteristics (Varian 1980). Then why use social insurance programs to achieve such redistributive goals and not rely on income taxation? The answer is that we do not live in a first-best, but rather in a second-best world where the government pursues its redistributive tax policy with little information about the individuals' characteristics. In such a world, one can show that providing private goods including insurance benefits to everyone regardless of their contributions, can be desirable. This argument has been particularly developed for education, pensions, and health insurance (Rochet 1991, Cremer and Gahvari 1997, Boadway and Marchand 1995, Cremer and Pestieau 1996, Boadway et al. 2003). In the appendix to this chapter, we illustrate the implications of asymmetric information for redistributive policies.

When talking about redistribution and social assistance, it is worth noting that some programs have targeted neither the poor nor the vulnerable, but rather the so-called 'losers.' Powerful groups in some countries, developing and developed ones, have demanded and received unemployment benefits and severance compensations as the price for agreeing to economic reforms. Those people are not usually the neediest in society. Yet their political voice is louder than that of the truly poor, and governments have often not been able to resist using such programs in order to gain political support (Fields and Mitchell 1993).

The argument of redistribution through social insurance can be fostered by an argument of altruistic externality. This latter argument is particularly used to justify the norm of universal access to health care. It applies less to the other types of social protection programs. When social insurance is mainly conceived as an instrument of redistribution, insuring people against poverty rather than against specific events such as unemployment or disability, the typical insuree is no longer a 'worker' but a 'citizen.' This raises the issue of entitlement. In a world of increased integration and cheap mobility, there is a natural trend to develop rules of exclusion. Witness the creation of a 'fortress Europe' that imposes barriers on Asians and Africans seeking entry to EU member states and access to employment and social protection (Brown and Crompton 1994).

9.4. New Arguments Pro and Con

9.4.1. *Increasing Demand and Evolving Labour Market*

To begin with, let us mention two rather recent developments that affect the balance between private and public insurance; they pertain to an increasing demand for social protection and to the changing condition of the labour market. In spite of political and financial pressure to limit the social insurance budget, there are factors that tend to contribute to more and more public intervention in the field of social protection. Population ageing and structural unemployment are clearly two problems of today's economies that call for increasing rather than decreasing the scope of social insurance.

At the same time, changing conditions in the labour market may affect the functioning of social insurance. As forcefully shown by Atkinson (1991), social insurance, at least as far as unemployment and retirement are concerned, is historically linked to the labour market. Its development has to be found not so much in the failure of private insurance markets, as in the need to improve the working of the industrial labour market. Good theoretical arguments can be presented to show that such an approach is well-founded. One clear implication of such a view of social insurance is that it is financed by payroll taxes paid by either employees or employers, or both. This raises a serious problem. The share of individuals benefitting from regular steady employment is declining and getting quite small in a large number of countries. Put another way, there are more and more inactive people, unemployed and self-employed workers and those with temporary jobs, and fewer and fewer salaried workers with steady employment.

9.4.2. Payroll Taxation, Fiscal Competition, and Social Dumping

In the traditional view of social insurance, most revenue comes from payroll taxes, that is a wage-based levy that increases labour cost. In a closed economy setting this does not raise any difficulty. However in an open economy, particularly in a world of increased economic integration and competition, there is pressure on firms to lower their production costs and they will plead for limiting or even decreasing the social insurance budget. This phenomenon leads to what has been labelled 'social dumping', and results from fiscal competition. It occurs even when there is low labour mobility across countries. In a world without cooperation, each country competes for lower production costs and aims at ever decreasing payroll tax rates (See Chapter 6).

Two remarks on this: first, in countries where there is no direct link between the benefit and the revenue side, and where social insurance is financed by general (income and consumption) taxation, pressures for limiting social insurance are real, if not direct. Secondly, in countries where the link between the benefit side and the revenue side is tight, one could wonder why the agent cannot see through the social insurance mechanism that higher taxes imply higher benefits. After all, when an individual pays his car insurance premium he does not see it as a levy, but as a fair price for a particular service. This difference in perception between a payroll tax and an insurance premium is an important factor in the choice between one or another form of insurance.

There is another effect of globalization that affects the private insurance market. In an open economy, it is increasingly difficult for government to impose regulations on private insurers that can be redistributive. For example, the legal prohibition on discrimination against individuals according to their risk class in private health insurance is likely to be desirable from a social welfare viewpoint. Such a regulation will not be implementable when 'healthy' people realize that they can do better by buying a cheaper insurance policy in a neighbouring country. When this happens the government has to use other and less efficient redistributive tools.

9.4.3. *Credibility and Commitment*

Governments and parents both have the problem of commitment; they must bind themselves to courses of action they know to be desirable. For their own good, parents want to induce their children to be responsible, hence they restrict their protection to unavoidable risks. Yet, those children that Gary Becker (1991) calls 'rotten kids' have little incentive to abide by the rules as they know that their parents will be tempted to forgive them. Governments, particularly when they are responsive to citizens' concerns, are under constant pressure to move away from policies that are optimal in the long run. Two illustrations of this difficulty of commitment are public pension schemes in some European countries, and the federal insurance of savings and loan institutions in the US.

The crisis in the US savings and loan industry is symptomatic of problems with many government insurance and guarantee programs. These problems involve moral hazard, if not fraud, and arise in both government and private sectors. However, they tend to be less severe in the latter because private corporations cannot sustain huge losses without going bankrupt, nor can they rely on the taxpayers to pay for their financial ineptitude. The money-making objective of private companies is quite different from the objectives of a government agency. A private company would have no trouble deciding to terminate a program that involves substantial losses even if the program's purpose is to protect the life savings of small depositors. Long-term contracts among private agents are an important source of efficiency for markets. State sovereignty makes such contracts unenforceable among successive governments.

In a related area, private life insurance companies will always handle retirement on a purely actuarial basis even if this implies providing meagre benefits. A social security agency will have a terrible time resisting popular pressure if at some point the optimal pension scheme it adopted generates benefits that are deemed too low. Note that health insurance raises similar problems.

With ageing and technology, the demand for health care is really skyrocketing. Even though some sort of rationing à l' Oregon[5] cannot be avoided, it is difficult for public programs to do it the only decent way, out in the open. As seen below, in that respect health care is a particular case in social insurance.

9.5. The Limits of Redistributive Policy

Social policy can be hampered by the fact that the social planner is not much prone to redistribution. Another factor that can have the same effect is the lack of information that the central planner possesses. Quite often it does not really observe the characteristics of either the individuals or their behaviour. This is what is called private information. In that case, the contributors to social policy, generally well to do and healthy individuals, may be tempted to behave, as they were the potential benefiters, poor and disabled individuals. To avoid such an outcome, which would lead to the collapse of the policy, the social planner is forced to give the contributors an informational premium that ensures that they will reveal their true types, with the implication that the redistribution gets more restricted.

These are second best policies. They often comprise features that would never be observed in a first-best setting. We now consider three such second-best policies. They imply in kind transfers, targeting, and workfare. We choose a society comprising two types of individuals, on the one hand, skilled and healthy individuals and on the other hand, unskilled and disabled individuals. The government would like to redistribute resources from the first to the second.

Assume that the disabled individuals need a special medical treatment such as a dialysis but that disability cannot be observed. An egalitarian government could divide the available resources such that every individual receive the same amount, but clearly the disabled will be worse off than the able individual. By providing a transfer in kind, namely, free dialysis, a more egalitarian outcome can be achieved as the healthy individual has not incentive to use this transfer.

We now take a society again comprising two types of individuals but with the disabled being divided in two subgroups, those whose disability is visible and those whose disability is not common knowledge. In a first best setting, the government would redistribute from the healthy to the disabled so as to achieve a social optimum. In the second best setting, this redistribution would be restricted by the threat of the healthy mimicking the disabled. In that case,

---

[5] In 2008, Oregon began an expansion of its Medicaid program for low-income adults. Because officials could not afford coverage for all those who wanted to enroll, they decided on the novel approach of allocating the limited number of available slots by lottery.

it can be shown that it is desirable to treat differently the two types of disabled people. Those who can be tagged as disabled would be better treated than the others because the healthy cannot mimic them.

Finally, there is workfare, which is an alternative, and controversial, way of giving money to otherwise unemployed or underemployed people, who are applying for social benefits. Again in a society where the government cannot sort out skilled from unskilled individuals, conditioning social benefits upon a particular type of work or of training makes it unpalatable for the skilled to mimic the unskilled. In the appendix, we develop those three points analytically.

9.6. Implications and Conclusion

Let us summarize the main points made in this chapter. Table 9.3 sketches the case for government versus market intervention in the field of insurance. First, one must realize that the public sector is subject to many of the same incentive problems that lead to private insurance market failures. Secondly, on the revenue side, fiscal competition and economic integration make it increasingly more difficult to maintain 'generous' social protection programs regardless of their objective: insurance or assistance. Thirdly, the recent evolution of employment conditions leads to a widening gap between social protection programs and labour markets. Fourthly, recent economic and demographic developments call for increased public intervention in the area of redistributive income maintenance.

The lesson one can draw from these facts is clear. It is not certain that social insurance, or rather social protection, can pursue its two traditional objectives: insurance and assistance. Such a duality of objectives has not raised any difficulty in the past. Today, in a number of countries, it is unaffordable to provide insurance and at the same time take care of the needy. Furthermore, these objectives may interact inefficiently. On the one hand, redistribution is

Table 9.3. Comparative advantage of social over private insurance

Argument	Advantage
Large risk	nil when reinsurance is possible
Intergenerational smoothing	high
Moral hazard	negative
Adverse selection	nil if insurance is made mandatory
Administrative cost	noticeable particularly in the field of health care
Redistribution	high
Financing Annuities, long-term care	negative because of tax competition and social dumping high
Commitment	negative
Single provision	high in the field of health care

often used as a veil behind which allocative and even distributional dysfunctionings occur. On the other hand, sticking too closely to the insurance principle or, to put it differently, to the Bismarckian idea of social insurance, makes true redistribution impossible.

It has been shown that keeping the Bismarckian principle unchanged for the basic pension systems in France, Germany or Belgium, in a setting of demographic ageing and of pay-as-you-go financing, could rapidly lead to pockets of poverty among the elderly. For this reason, one should think of reshaping social protection in the direction of uniform transfers to all current beneficiaries of its various components. If these transfers were fixed at a decent level, the cost for public finance would be high, possibly higher than the current one. Individuals with middle or high income could supplement these transfers by private insurance programs (presumably without tax advantages).

Health insurance would also have this feature of universal access to a basic policy collectively decided. Diamond (1992) and others suggest combining universal access and competition among insurers and providers. The entire population would be divided into many large groups. Within each group, optimal social insurance principles could be applied with private insurance companies competing for these groups. Financing would be done by a combination of taxes and out-of-pocket payments for premiums and there would be some redistribution across groups. Within a group, selected insurance companies would offer supplementary policies to provide additional coverage for those who could afford it. In such a setting there would be no connection between health insurance and employment.

We believe that social protection should progressively abandon some of its insurance missions and focus on uniformity of benefits.[6] Financing should come from general revenue and be increasingly disconnected from the labour market. This way, private insurance would be allowed to provide additional coverage for those who found the basic policy insufficient and could afford to supplement it. Such a proposal is quite consistent with the three-pillars approach that is here extended to all traditional areas of social protection.

Appendix

Redistributive Policy under Asymmetric Information

In this appendix, we want to show how the government, a benevolent welfare maximizer, can be led to adopt policies that would be ill-advised in a setting of

---

[6] This view is at odds with Barr (1992, 1998), who focuses on the insurance dimension of the welfare state.

full information. We choose three cases, each involving a society made of two types of individuals.

The first type, denoted A for able, comprises individuals who are skilled and healthy. The second type, denoted D for disabled, consists of individuals who are either disabled or unskilled.

In each case, we will contrast the solutions that emerge under full information and that one has to adopt when the individual characteristics are not observable by the government. Asymmetric information leads the government to adopt policies of in-kind transfers, tagging, and workfare that are all questionable for ethical reasons but turn to be unavoidable in a second-best setting. In each case, we adopt different objective functions for the sake of simplicity:

- Equal utilities for in-kind transfers
- Maximum sum of utilities for tagging
- Minimum poverty for workfare.

1. Transfer in Kind

We consider two individuals with utility:

$$U_A = y_A \quad \text{and} \quad U_D = y_D - e^{1-z}$$

where U_i and y_i $(i=A,D)$ denote the level of utility and of consumption. Individual D needs some medical treatment costing z. With $z=1$, the disutility of being disabled is limited to 1 whereas without treatment ($z=0$), it is equal to 2.7.

If we want to equalize the utility of the two individuals for a total endowment of R, we would need $y_A = (R-2)/2$, $y_D = R/2$ and $z=1$. This allocation implies $U_A = U_D = (R-2)/2$.

If the government cannot distinguish between the two types, it would have no choice but to attribute to each $R/2$ and the result would be $U_A = R/2$ and $U_D = R/2 - 2$. In the latter we suppose that D chooses to invest in the medical treatment. Otherwise his utility would be lower: $U_D = R/2 - 2.7$.

A superior policy in this setting of imperfect information would be to supply for free the medical treatment and to allocate each type $y_A = y_D = (R-1)/2$. That way, individual A has no incentive to use the treatment, namely to mimic individual D, which would be the case if the government offered the disabled individual an income $R/2+1$. With this solution we have $U_A = (R-1)/2$ and $U_D = R/2 - 1.5$.

Comparing the three solutions, we conclude that the first best dominates the second best with in-kind transfer, which dominates the second best without in-kind transfer. This latter solution would correspond to the laissez faire with equal endowment $R/2$.

2. Tagging

We now assume that our society comprises n_A types A and n_D types D, but that a fraction γ of the latter can be identified, tagged, as D. We normalize the population such that $n_A = n_D = 1$. Type A has a productivity w and working involves some disutility ε; the productivity of D is nil. We use logarithmic utility functions:

$$U_A = \log y_A - \varepsilon \quad \text{and} \quad U_D = \log y_D$$

We here assume that the government maximizes the sum of utilities. This is a utilitarian objective. In other words it aims at maximizing:

$$\log y_A - \varepsilon + \gamma \log y_T + (1-\gamma)\log y_D$$

subject to the resource constraint:

$$y_A + (1-\gamma)y_D + \gamma y_T = w$$

where y_T denotes the consumption of the tagged individuals and it is assumed that the able individual works one unit of time. One easily checks that under perfect information the utilitarian solution yields:

$$y_A = y_D = y_T = w/2$$

and

$$U_A = \log \frac{w}{2} - \varepsilon < U_D = U_T = \log \frac{w}{2}$$

In contrast we note that in a pure market economy we have

$$y_A = w \quad \text{and} \quad y_D = y_T = 0.$$

Consider now the case where the government cannot distinguish between the types. The above first-best solution is not anymore sustainable, as the able individual will pretend that he is disabled and his utility would then be $U_A = \log \frac{w}{2}$, which is higher than in the first best because he is avoiding the disutility of effort. To avoid such a situation, the government has to make sure that type A gets as much utility as if he mimics the disabled type. Formally:

$$\log y_A - \varepsilon = \log y_D$$

The second-best problem we deal with can be expressed by the following expression to be maximized:

$$\log y_A - \varepsilon + \gamma \log y_T + (1-\gamma)\log y_D - \mu\left(y_A + (1-\gamma)y_D + \gamma y_T - w\right)$$
$$+ \lambda(\log y_A - \varepsilon - \log y_D)$$

where μ and λ are the Lagrange multipliers respectively associated with the resource constraint and the self-selection constraint. Besides these constraints, the first-order conditions for this problem are:

$$y_A = \frac{1+\lambda}{\mu}; \quad y_T = \frac{1}{\mu}; \quad \text{and} \quad y_D = \frac{1-\gamma-\lambda}{\mu(1-\gamma)}$$

Combining these three conditions, we get $\mu = 0.2$; $y_T = 5$; and $\lambda = 0.5(1-\gamma)/(2.5-\gamma)$, where we posit that the antilog of $\varepsilon = 1.5$.

The values of y_A, y_D, and y_T for different settings are given in the following table

Settings/Outcomes	y_A	y_T	y_D	Sum of utilities
Laissez faire	10	0	0	Minus infinity
First-best	5	5	5	$1.3978 - \varepsilon$
Second-best without tagging ($\gamma = 0$)	6	4	4	$1.3801 - \varepsilon$
Second best with tagging ($\gamma = 0.5$)	5.625	5	3.75	$1.3865 - \varepsilon$

Tagging brings more total utility than no tagging, but implies a horizontal inequity between the two types of disabled individuals.

3. Workfare

The concept of workfare can be interpreted in different ways. It can be viewed as a scheme that encourages direct employment to get individuals off the welfare roll or as a requirement imposed on unemployed to continue receiving their welfare benefits. In the latter interpretation, workfare is also viewed as a way to discourage able workers from drawing unemployment benefits. This is the view we adopt here.

We consider a society comprising two types of individuals with wages w_A and w_D such that $w_A > w_D$. They have a utility function:

$$U_i = y_i - \frac{h_i^2}{2} = w_i h_i - \frac{h_i^2}{2}$$

where h_i is labour supply and the disutility of labour is quadratic. In a laissez-faire setting, individuals would choose $h_i = w_i$ and end up with a utility $U_i = \frac{w_i^2}{2}$.

The objective of the government here is to make sure that type D individuals earn at least $z > w_D^2$, where z can be seen as a poverty line. In the first-best, this objective could be implemented by providing to each individual D a benefit b_D such that:

$$b_D = z - w_D^2$$

The first-best scheme would cost: $n_D b_D$ where n_D is the number of unskilled individuals.

Such a scheme is not sustainable as the type A individuals can claim being type D, when the government does not observe who is who. In that case, the second best solution amounts to providing every individual with a benefit:

$b = z - w_D^2$, which implies a total cost of $(n_A + n_D)b$.

We can show that under certain conditions one can achieve the same objective at a lower cost, by making the welfare benefit conditional upon supplying some work of length c. This work could consist of digging holes in the ground and filling them up as in Keynes. Its only role is to deter skilled individuals from drawing welfare benefits.

Now the benefit b^* is equal to:

$$b^* = z - w_D(h_D - c) = z - w_D^2 + w_D c$$

The problem is now to find the value of c and b^* that induce A to work normally and not to mimic D. This implies the following self-selection constraint:

$$\frac{w_A^2}{2} = w_A(h_A - c) - \frac{h_A^2}{2} + b^*,$$

where the right-hand side denotes the utility of A mimicking D. This can be written as:

$$\frac{w_A^2}{2} = \frac{w_A^2}{2} - cw_A + b^* = \frac{w_A^2}{2} - cw_A + z + cw_D - w_D^2$$

This yields the following value for the workfare variable c^*:

$$c^* = \frac{z - w_D^2}{w_A - w_D}$$

We now compare the cost of the universal transfer scheme and that of the transfer with workfare.

- Cost with workfare: $n_D(z - w_D^2 + w_D c) = n_D w_A c^*$
- Cost without workfare: $(n_A + n_D)(z - w_D^2) = (n_A + n_D)(w_A - w_D)c^*$

Workfare costs less than the universal transfer scheme and thus should be adopted if:

$$(w_A - w_D) > \frac{n_D w_A}{n_A + n_D}$$

Or

$$\frac{n_A w_A}{n_A + n_D} > w_D$$

In words, workfare should be chosen if the wage gap is important and if the relative number of disabled is low.

To sum up, we have presented three redistributive policies that would never be adopted in a full information setting and that furthermore can be objected to on ethical grounds. However in an asymmetric information setting, they bring the highest level of welfare.

10

Old Age Pensions

> **KEY CONCEPTS**
>
> annuity
> defined contribution
> notional defined contribution
> defined benefit
> dependency ratio
> effective retirement age
> fully-funded scheme
> lump of labour fallacy
> points pensions
> pay-as-you-go
> replacement ratio

10.1. Introduction

Pensions are the main source of income of older people in Europe. It is estimated that one European citizen in four depends directly on pension income. Thanks to pension systems, the majority of European retired workers enjoy today as good living standard as the average population.

Due to demographic ageing, the older people are a growing part of the population, which puts the pension systems under increasing pressure. Whereas they represent one of the biggest public expenditures in the European Union, the pension systems are facing the dual challenge of providing adequate income in retirement while remaining financially sustainable. If the main purpose of a pension system is to allow older people to enjoy decent living standards, its financial sustainability is an indispensable means to achieve it.

It appears that the cost of pension programs depends not only on increasing demographic aging, but also on labour force participation and on the effective age of retirement. Pension sustainability is thus related to the dynamics of the labour market, which affects employment at old age. Hence, most European countries have carried out gradual and substantial reforms over recent decades in order to enhance the financial sustainability of their public pension system. One of the main concerns in conducting these reforms is to make sure poverty among retirees is avoided.

10.2. The Pension Systems

Public pension systems are diverse and often involve a number of different programs that makes classification difficult. All the European countries have set up programs whereby workers are assured of a certain level of income upon their retirement. In each country, we find schemes that are part of a public retirement system and are mainly financed through taxes or social contributions. This constitutes what the World Bank and the OECD call the first pillar and is the main topic of this chapter.

In addition to that public retirement scheme, we find mandatory or voluntary contribution schemes financed by the employer/employee or the individual; namely the second and the third pillars. The presence and the importance of the three pillars vary widely across countries and the line between public, employer-related systems, and voluntary contribution can be thin. The first pillar is often seen as a means to prevent poverty and ensure redistribution, even though one also talks of a pillar zero that is means tested and provides benefits to those who are not covered by the first pillar. The second pillar, which is occupational and earnings-related focuses on an adequate pension in terms of replacement ratio. The third pillar is meant to provide an opportunity for individuals to save towards increasing their retirement income.

Table 10.1 shows that expenditures on old-age public pensions represent on average about 10 per cent of the GDP of the EU. In 2014, Austria, France, Greece, Italy, and Portugal had relatively high shares of pension expenditures as a proportion of GDP, while the Eastern and Baltic countries have relatively low shares compared to the EU15, excepted Slovenia. Between 2000 and 2014, the pension share has increased in most European countries with the largest increase being observed in Ireland, Finland, and Portugal. The last column of Table 10.1 gives the private pension funds assets as a percentage of GDP. This figure reflects the extent of collective precaution against the future. Here again we observe huge variety among European countries. It is a stock figure and cannot be readily compared to the flow of public pensions.

We have seen in Chapter 5 that one could broadly distinguish between two types of welfare state: the Beveridgean and the Bismarckian systems. This difference applies also to the way old-age retirement systems are organized.

Table 10.1. Expenditure on old-age pension: 2000–2014

	Old-age public pension (% of GDP)		Pension funds assets (% of GDP)
	2000	2014	2014
Austria	10.1	12.2	5.8
Belgium	6.7	8.6	5.9
Bulgaria	–	–	10.9
Czechia	6.5	8.2	8.3
Denmark	8.0	10.1	44.8
Estonia	5.9	6.5	12.8
Finland	7.3	11.4	50.8
France	10.2	12.6	0.6
Germany	8.4	8.2	6.6
Greece	9.7	11.3	0.6
Hungary	6.9	9.6	4.1
Ireland	2.4	4.9	49.1
Italy	11.1	13.7	7.0
Latvia	8.3	7.5	–
Lithuania	–	–	5.9
Luxembourg	6.6	6.7	2.8
Netherlands	4.9	6.2	178.4
Poland	8.5	9.1	8.0
Portugal	6.6	12.1	10.1
Romania	–	–	3.7
Slovakia	5.6	6.6	10.3
Slovenia	10.0	10.3	4.3
Spain	6.6	9.5	9.6
Sweden	8.6	9.6	9.1
UK	5.2	6.5	97.5

Notes: Pension funds assets correspond to all pension fund investments
Source: Eurostat (2017c) and OECD (2017d)

In the Beveridgian systems, all individuals are entitled to a basic level of income upon retirement at a flat rate and independently of occupation. People are free to supplement this income with occupational provisions as part of a contract with an employer or through collective bargaining. The Beveridgian system was put in place in the UK, Ireland, Denmark, and the Netherlands. It largely corresponds today to a system of a flat rate benefits complemented by an important, often mandatory or semi-mandatory, occupational scheme and a voluntary savings part (the second and the third pillars).

In the Bismarckian systems, people have a right to social security benefits only insofar as they acquire that right by work. Contributions through employment generate entitlement to benefits. Benefits are closely linked to occupation and income and thus they are earnings-related and profession-related, generally subject to maximum limits. This system has been followed in Germany, Belgium, Sweden, France, and the southern European countries, but also originally in most of the eastern European Member States. Here the role of occupational schemes is lower.

Although this division of systems has become less clear-cut over the years, the two models continue to typify the European pension systems. However, the distinction becomes to some extent arbitrary as both systems have evolved differently through reforms and economic situations.

Another important distinction concerns the way pensions are financed. The two major regimes are 'pay-as-you-go' (PAYG) and full funding. PAYG financing means that the current generation pays tax contributions to finance current payments to retired individuals. These contributions eventually add up to entitlement to pension benefits on retirement, but the link between contributions and benefits is rather loose. Fully funded pension schemes are characterized by employee contributions invested in a pension fund, which accordingly generates entitlement to a related benefit on retirement. First pillar pensions are generally financed on a PAYG basis, both in Beveridgian and Bismarckian systems, while second and third pillars are funded (except in France for occupational pensions).

The funded schemes come in the form of defined contribution (DC) or defined benefit (DB) principle. In a DB scheme, the pension benefit is defined as a percentage of earnings and employment career. The worker thus receives a pre-defined pension and does not bear either the risk of investment or the risk of longevity. This is also the principle behind most of the public PAYG retirement schemes. In a DC scheme, the benefit depends on the level of defined contributions and the returns on investments. In this case, the pensioner bears the risk of both longevity and investment.

As we will discuss in Section 10.4, recently several countries have reformed their system towards a notional defined contribution (NDC) principle. A NDC scheme is designed to mimic most of the features of a DC/PAYG scheme. The contributions are recorded in an individual account and a rate of return is applied on balances. The rate of return is set by the government and linked to wage or GDP growth. The individual accounts are notional in that the contributions create rights for the contributor but the balances exist only on the books of the managing institution. At retirement, the accumulated notional capital is converted into a stream of pension payments using a formula based on life expectancy. A variant is the point system (PS), as in Germany, which presents features close to an NDC system. In a point system, workers earn pension points based on their individual earnings for each year of contributions. At retirement, the sum of pension points is multiplied by a pension-point value to convert them into a regular pension payment.

10.3. Old-Age Poverty

An important goal of public pension schemes is to ensure that older people are protected against the risk of poverty and deprivation. While living standard in old age depends on private assets, notably home ownership, and occupational pension, public pensions are still the main source of income during retirement. The adequacy of benefits is an important feature of social policy towards the elderly.

Overall, older people in the European Union enjoy living standards close to those of the working age population. Table 10.2 shows the relative median income of the elderly. On average in the EU28, the median disposable income of people aged 65 or above stands at 93 per cent of the income of those aged 0–64. There is cross-country variability but, in most of the countries, the relative median income is above 85 per cent. It is even above 100 per cent in six countries: France, Greece, Hungary, Luxembourg, Romania, and Spain.

As to income inequality at old age, the disposable incomes of those in the top quintile are on average four times higher than those in the bottom

Table 10.2. Poverty and inequality at old-age (65+): 2015

	Relative median income	Poverty rate	Interquintile ratio (S80/S20)
Austria	0.98	13.2	3.7
Belgium	0.79	15.2	3.2
Bulgaria	0.71	31.7	4.5
Croatia	0.85	26.3	4.6
Cyprus	0.80	17.3	4.7
Czech R.	0.81	7.4	2.4
Denmark	0.77	9.1	3.2
Estonia	0.62	35.8	3.4
Finland	0.81	13.8	3.1
France	1.04	8.0	4.5
Germany	0.87	16.5	4.0
Greece	1.04	13.7	4.1
Hungary	1.01	4.6	3.0
Ireland	0.87	14.2	4.2
Italy	0.99	14.7	4.5
Latvia	0.65	34.6	4.2
Lithuania	0.73	25.0	4.2
Luxembourg	1.08	7.9	3.5
Malta	0.75	21.0	3.4
Netherlands	0.89	5.6	3.0
Poland	0.99	12.1	3.5
Portugal	0.92	17.0	5.0
Romania	1.00	19.4	6.2
Slovakia	0.91	5.6	2.3
Slovenia	0.90	17.2	3.6
Spain	1.01	12.3	4.3
Sweden	0.79	18.2	3.4
UK	0.88	16.4	4.2
EU28	0.93	14.1	4.1

Notes: The relative median income is median income of people aged 65 as % of the median income of people aged 0–64. The poverty rate is obtained with a poverty threshold calculated as 60% of the median income of the total population. The interquintile ratio is calculated as the ratio of total income received by the 20% of the population with the highest income to that received by the 20% of the population with the lowest income

Source: Eurostat (2017a)

quintile. Differences between countries are substantial, with ratios of more than four in fourteen countries.

The relative poverty of the elderly amounts to 14 per cent of the population in the EU28 but ranges from a low 4–5 per cent in Hungary, the Netherlands, and Slovakia to a high 35 per cent in Estonia and Latvia. Interestingly, in a majority of countries the poverty rate at old age is lower than for the total population. The pension systems seem thus effective in protecting living standard from work to inactivity. On average in the EU, the gross replacement rate, that is the ratio between gross pension benefit over the gross earnings, is about 60 per cent.

These figures demonstrate the importance of public pensions in allowing retired people to enjoy living standards which are, on average, close to those of the rest of the population. Moreover, in recent years (especially after the crisis), while the poverty rates increased for those below sixty-five; the rate went down for those aged over sixty-five. It is, however, important to note that these indicators do not take into account wealth such as home ownership and private savings. Older people tend to have accumulated more wealth than younger generations and it can be important in determining their well-being.

10.4. The Challenges of Pension Systems

The funding nature of the systems is at the heart of the problems they face. Because of demographic changes as well as a declining labour force participation at old age, the financial sustainability of the PAYG systems, mainly the first pillar, is not guaranteed and reforms are needed. In some countries there is a debate about a shift away from PAYG-financed pension schemes towards fully funded schemes, in both the first and second pillars, as a response to pressures of an ageing population, and the growing liabilities of basic retirement schemes.

10.4.1. *Population Ageing*

Due to a decline in fertility and an increase in life-expectancy, the population in Europe is ageing. This phenomenon has been in play since the Second World War and the projections of population for the forthcoming years confirm that trend. As Figure 10.1 shows for the EU28, but also for a selection of countries, the old-age dependency ratio, calculated as the share of individuals aged sixty-five and above compared to the population aged fifteen to sixty-four, will increase from less than 30 per cent in 2015 to almost 50 per cent by 2050. As a result, Europe is projected to move from four working-age people for every person aged over 65 to just two by 2050. This average trend

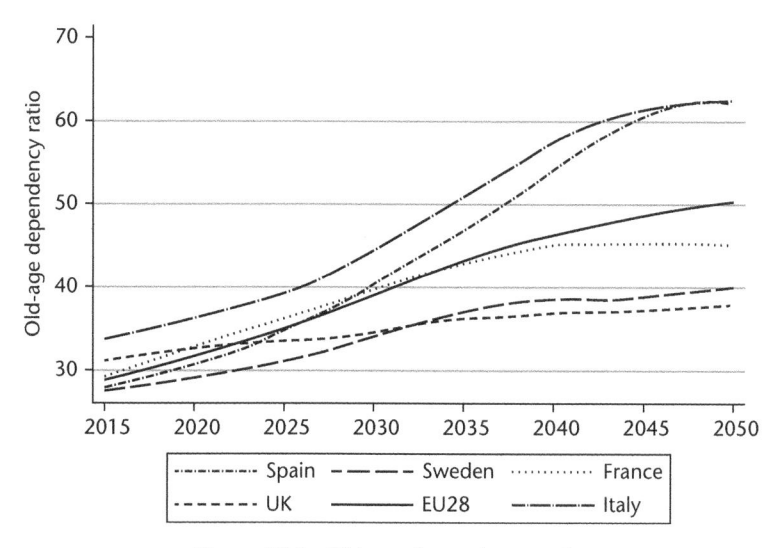

Figure 10.1. Old-age dependency ratio
Source: Eurostat (2017e)

hides heterogeneity among countries. In the southern countries like Italy and Spain but also in Greece and Portugal, the old-age dependency ratio is expected to rise a lot while in continental countries, such as France or Germany, the trend is close to the EU28. In the UK but also in the Nordic countries, the rise is smaller and the dependency ratio should be around 40 per cent in 2050. Note that to a large extent the standard old-age dependency ratio understates the real ageing process as it relies on the pivotal age of 65, which is well above the effective age of retirement.

The intensification of population ageing in the forthcoming decades will increase the difficulty for schemes to meet financial sustainability. This is particularly true in countries relying exclusively on PAYG where the ratio of workers (contributors) to pensioners (beneficiaries) is directly related to sustainability. In the long run the pension costs will increase and thereby constitute a strain on government budgets. An increasing dependency ratio will put a strain on the government budget in the sense that it will require relatively more to make ends meet in the future than today.

10.4.2. Employment of the Elderly

Population ageing is often cited as the reason for the financial burdens faced by the retirement programs but just as important is the labour force participation of older workers. The equilibrium of a PAYG system is based on the ratio of workers to retired people. However the labour force participation and

Table 10.3. Employment and activity rate of the elderly: 2016

	Population age 25–54		Population aged 55–64	
	Labour force participation rate	Employment rate	Labour force participation rate	Employment rate
Austria	85.1	83.6	51.7	49.2
Belgium	82.0	79.1	48.1	45.4
Bulgaria	88.9	76.2	58.8	54.5
Croatia	87.4	72.4	42.2	38.1
Cyprus	87.3	76.6	59.0	52.2
Czech R.	87.8	85.7	60.8	58.5
Denmark	81.2	82.5	70.6	67.8
Estonia	85.5	82.6	71.0	65.2
Finland	87.4	79.9	66.4	61.4
France	87.5	79.7	53.7	49.8
Germany	82.0	83.9	71.3	68.6
Greece	77.5	66.0	44.9	36.3
Hungary	86.8	82.2	52.1	49.8
Ireland	87.8	75.3	61.0	57.2
Italy	89.3	68.8	53.4	50.3
Latvia	87.2	79.7	67.6	61.4
Lithuania	86.1	82.7	70.0	64.6
Luxembourg	82.0	82.5	41.6	39.6
Malta	86.9	78.8	45.5	44.1
Netherlands	88.4	82.9	68.4	63.5
Poland	84.9	80.3	48.3	46.2
Portugal	89.1	80.2	58.5	52.1
Romania	81.9	77.6	44.2	42.8
Slovakia	90.5	80.0	53.9	49.0
Slovenia	87.6	83.5	41.2	38.5
Spain	86.3	71.5	59.2	49.1
Sweden	90.9	85.9	79.7	75.5
UK	86.1	82.9	65.8	63.4
EU28	85.5	78.7	59.1	55.3

Source: Eurostat (2017d)

the employment rates of those between fifty-five and sixty-five is very small in in a number of countries. Table 10.3 displays the employment and the labour force participation rates for the prime-aged workers (25 to 54) and the old-aged workers (55 to 64). The last category concerns those who are close to retirement. In the European Union, the employment and the participation rates of the elderly are, on average, 25 percentage points lower than for the prime-aged population. The employment rate ranged from 41.6 per cent in Luxembourg to 79.7 per cent in Sweden but in eight countries, less than 50 per cent of older workers are in employment. Since the mid-nineties, the employment rate of older workers is on the rise in most European countries. Some reforms have been implemented and the eligibility conditions for various programs have been restricted.

These numbers can be explained by a number of factors from both the demand and the supply side of the market but it must be emphasized that the provisions of a series of programs may also be responsible for the low employment of older workers. In most countries, public pension systems allow people to exit the labour force well before the statutory age of retirement, with or without adjustment in the value of retirement income. Furthermore, though not explicitly designed for this purpose, benefit programs such as unemployment or disability are used as exit routes from the labour force. Lastly, in many cases, mandatory early retirement schemes have been introduced in cases of excess labour due to sectorial slumps, sometimes with the requirement that the vacancy be filled with a younger (and cheaper) unemployed person.

Although early retirement and pension schemes in Europe are heterogeneous by nature, in most countries we find a series of possible pathways to retirement well before the statutory age of retirement. In some countries, such as the Netherlands, the exit route has been for long the disability program. In Belgium and in France, early retirement programs are widely used. As pointed out by Gruber and Wise (1999), this low participation in the labour market corresponds to an unused productive capacity that could contribute to the system. The reason is the availability and the generosity of the numerous social programs, in addition to public retirement, that provide a kind of implicit tax on continued activity. For a typical worker facing a possible exit route from the labour market, the decision is to work or not for another year. Another year of work means a delay in enjoying more leisure but it also means a delay in receiving benefits, which will be received for one less year then. In the absence of an actuarial adjustment that offsets the fewer years that benefits will be received, there is an incentive for workers to leave the labour force. This incentive effect has been confirmed empirically by dozens of studies and helps us understand why there are so few older workers in work; see Lefebvre (2013) for a survey of the evidence.

The low employment rate of older workers exerts pressure on the financial equilibrium of PAYG systems. Although most people who are knowledgeable about retirement systems recognize that these systems should be reformed to increase labour force participation and to restrain the growth of future costs, the reforms that are needed seem to be delayed. Two main arguments are usually put forward.

In many countries, the reluctance to implement reform is often related to a mistaken view of labour market functioning. Many of the early retirement opportunities were set up at the end of the seventies with the objective of tackling high and persistent unemployment. By encouraging older workers to leave the labour force, the goal was to free up jobs for young unemployed workers. The argument behind this reasoning was the idea of worksharing, or what is called the assumption of a lump of labour. This is based on the simple notion that, in a given period, a fixed amount of labour input required to produce a fixed volume of goods and services can be shared between persons who are already employed and those who are unemployed. It is usually argued that a trade-off can be made between the positively valued leisure of the older employed and the unwanted leisure of the younger unemployed.

There is no clear economic argument supporting the idea that early retirement schemes could have alleviated unemployment. Such an unemployment-reduction mechanism suggests a perfect homogeneity of workers, younger and older, while we know that differences exist between workers by age. Also the argument forgets that labour demand is not independent of economic conditions. Layard et al. (2005) provide a simple reasoning as to what we might expect from early retirement. If output is unaffected, those who most want to work will produce it. But output is not given and it will probably respond to increased early retirement. If the number of jobs remains unchanged, when workers retire, unemployment falls. Therefore, the low level of unemployment will cause inflationary pressure and the government, which has chosen a mix of inflation and unemployment, will let unemployment rise to its former level. The consequence is that there are now fewer jobs and the output is reduced. This is what Layard et al. (2005) call the lump-of-output fallacy. In a comparative study of twelve countries, Gruber and Wise (2010) provide no evidence that inducing older persons to leave the labour force frees up jobs for the young. If anything, the opposite is true; paying for older persons to leave the labour force reduces the employment rate and increases the unemployment rate of the young and of persons in their prime age working years.

Another argument that is also often presented to explain low labour force participation of older workers is their diminishing work capacity. In the public debate, one often-voiced concern about delaying the retirement age is that numerous workers do not have the capacity to work longer because of physical or mental health and exhaustion problems. This is true for a number of occupations that can be categorized as difficult or 'arduous'. One cannot then expect that a employee work should beyond the age of sixty, i.e., in the construction sector or in the heavy industry. However, the general health level of the population has increased a lot since the development of retirement programs. On average, life expectancy is now well above the statutory age of retirement in all countries. People in their 60s are in much better shape than their parents were at the same age suggesting that their health capacity to work is well beyond what it was. In a recent cross-country study, Wise (2017) shows that workers have substantial additional capacity to work beyond their current employment levels. As people live longer and healthier lives, it may be appropriate for policymakers to consider how these gains in life expectancy should be divided between years of work and retirement. The results show that the argument suggesting that increases in retirement age are constrained by the health of older workers does not hold for most workers.

10.5. The Future of Pensions

Given the challenges facing the pension systems there is an increasing need for reforms. The situation is by no means sustainable, particularly in countries relying exclusively on PAYG. In a PAYG system, one can express average pension benefit, p, as:

$$p = \frac{\tau w}{d},$$

where τ is the payroll tax, w, the wage level, and d, the effective dependency rate (number of retirees divided by the number of workers). The effective dependency rate differs from the old-age dependency rate (number of persons aged over 65 to the working age population), as it takes into account both the unemployment rate and the effective retirement age.

To meet the above constraint when the dependency ratio increases, one must adjust other variables. Either the contribution rate, τ, must increase or the level of pension, p, be reduced. One can also increase the labour participation of the young and of the old, or we rely on an increase in the wage rate, that is, productivity. One could naturally count on other sources of income: capital income arising from pension funds or regular saving. One can consider the possibility of borrowing further at the expense of future generations.

The problem of the sustainability of pension schemes in most European countries is that there is little room to adjust the main parameters. It is politically difficult to promote a reduction of replacement rates as much as it is economically risky to increase the payroll tax, especially given the tax competition running among countries in Europe. Since the crisis of 2008, productivity and GDP growth has been slow and the possibilities borrowing are limited. Moreover, the 2005 revised Stability and Growth Pact takes into account this discrepancy and requires implicit pension debt to be accounted for in the computation of the medium-term objective.

However, in order to enhance financial sustainability, while maintaining adequate pension income, most European countries have carried out gradual and substantial pension reforms over recent decades. The speed of reforms has intensified since 2000 and comprises a wide range of measures that try to modify the system rules and parameters. Those reforms are often implemented gradually over a long period in order to facilitate their acceptance by the population. Several countries, however, adopted radical reforms by changing deeply the nature of their public pension schemes or by fostering the introduction of new pillars.

The most common measure adopted has consisted of raising pension ages. Almost every European country has increased the level of early and statutory retirement ages. As the effective exit age from the labour market is often lower than the legal age of eligibility, most countries also change retirement incentives by closing or limiting access to pathways to early retirement. These measures comprise closing access to new entrants or increasing the number of years of contributions required to receive benefits. The introduction of bonuses for retiring after the normal pension age is an option as well as easing or even abandoning inefficient earning tests. The idea is to differentiate the age of eligibility to benefits and the age of retirement. Altogether, few countries attempt to reduce the relative pension generosity, which is politically hazardous.

The future of pension systems might imply more systematic reforms. At the end of the nineties, Italy and Sweden shifted their PAYG system to a NDC pension system with a gradual move from a dominant one-pillar system to a multi-pillar system. Germany also reformed its pension point system to present features close to an NDC system and encouraged private pensions. A common characteristic of the ground-breaking reforms introduced by these countries is that, besides the goal of enhancing sustainability, they have tended to substitute fragmented and complex schemes with a more unified public scheme.

The link between demographic challenges and social security benefits appears clearly in Figure 10.2, which presents the change in the relative share of old age benefits as a proportion of GDP between 2013 and 2060 according to forecasts by the European Commission (2015). The projections

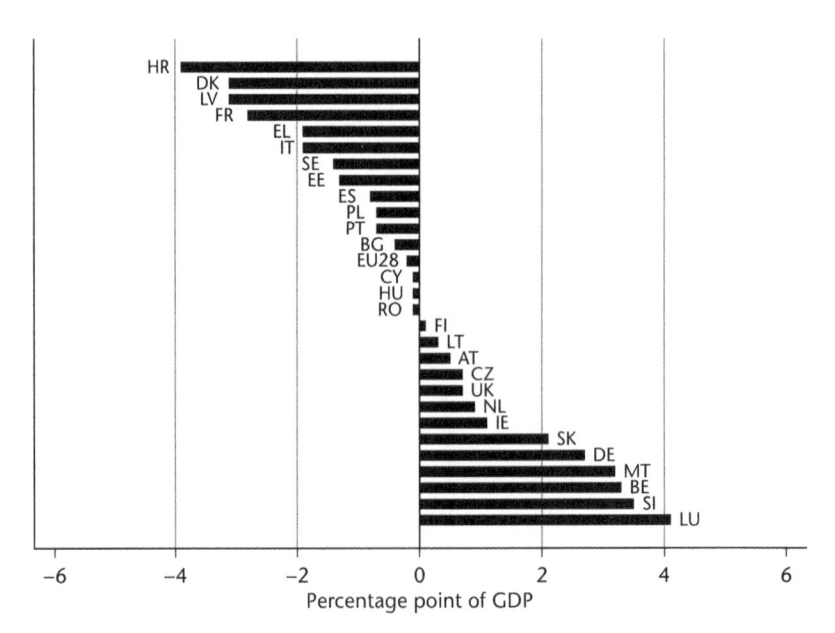

Figure 10.2. Change in gross public pension expenditure between 2013 and 2060 (in percentage points of GDP)
Source: European Commission (2015)

are based on assumptions with regards to demography, labour force, labour productivity and economic growth. They reflect, on the one hand, country-specific demographic dynamics. But they also rely on current retirement schemes as well as their ongoing reforms. The main drivers of the share of spending are the dependency ratio, the employment of 20–64 year-olds, replacement ratios, and the coverage rate.

In the EU28, the share of retirement pensions is expected to decrease by 0.2 percentage points (11.3 to 11.1 per cent) over the period 2013–2060. This EU average masks extremely varied situations. Croatia should record the highest decrease (−3.9 percentage points) along with Denmark, France and Latvia. Some countries are expected to also reduce the share of public pension but to a lower degree, like Greece, Italy, Sweden, Poland, Portugal and Spain. On the other hand almost half of the Member States will experience increases, with the largest in Luxembourg. The increase is projected to be high (around 2–3 percentage points) in Belgium, Germany, and Slovenia, and rather low in Czechia, Finland, and Austria.

These projections tend to provide good news at the global level and show that some countries that have introduced reforms to contain the cost of the retirement systems will be successful. They also show that for other countries, the rise in the share of pensions could be explosive. However, we need to be prudent with these figures. They are extremely sensitive to the macroeconomic and demographic assumptions. The future employment of the elderly and pension coverage depend not only on the rules governing the system but also on economic conditions as well as labour market functioning. Future crisis could affect the growth rate of the economy and its productivity, with outcomes much lower than expected.

One crucial issue will be to ensure that the ongoing changes in the pension schemes preserve as much as possible of the adequacy of pensions. It is important to ensure that public pensions contain appropriate mechanisms to address the needs of those who are less able to use the opportunities offered by pension systems. One can think of mechanisms such as minimum pensions or credits for inactive years during a career. It is also essential to pay attention to the workers who are unable to remain in the labour market up to the statutory age of retirement. When exit from the labour market cannot be prevented, for personal or work-related reasons, workers should benefit from an adequate pension.

10.6. Conclusion

The majority of European retired people enjoy as good standards of living as the average population. This is due mainly to quite generous retirement benefits coming from the public retirement systems. Except for some countries such as Denmark, the UK, or the Netherlands, the contribution of supplementary private pensions is negligible.

However, the pension schemes are facing important challenges related to their current and future financial sustainability. The low effective retirement age and consequently the low labour force participation of the elderly, combined with increased longevity and low productivity increases, make the future of social security rather gloomy. Obvious reforms are needed and have started to be implemented in a number of countries. These reforms most often consist of postponing retirement from the labour market by restricting access to early retirement and by raising the statutory retirement age. In some countries this age has even been linked to increases in life expectancy.

11

Health Care

> **KEY CONCEPTS**
> copayment
> cost-based reimbursement
> Health Maintenance Organization (HMO)
> managed competition
> QUALYS (quality adjusted life expectancy)
> single provider
> third-party payment

11.1. Introduction

Public health care systems are a crucial part of Europe's high levels of social protection and cohesion. They are varied as they reflect different societal choices. Despite organizational and financial differences, they are facing the same challenges. Population ageing and innovative technology lead to growing healthcare expenditure; health inequalities and inequities in access to healthcare do not seem to decrease. Dealing with health is quite different from dealing with unemployment, disability, or retirement. Health care is a unique commodity for a number of reasons. First of all, receiving it can be a matter of life or death and is thus subject to less economic rationality than other consumptions: health has no price. Also, health care spending has increased in recent decades more rapidly than most other social spending. Yet, what makes health care so different is undoubtedly the issue of incomplete information that generates moral hazard and adverse selection problems (see Chapter 9). There is also the paternalistic argument according to which people should be forced to have medical insurance for their own good, even against their own will. These specificities make it difficult to tackle the issue of cost containment and to face the urgent need for reform that most European

The Welfare State in Europe

countries now face. In the following pages, we first describe the recent evolution of health care spending. We then address the question of cost containment and of reform. Finally, we turn to the issue of inequities in health and in health care.

11.2. Expenditure on Health Care

Health expenditure results from a wide range of factors but the most important of them is undoubtedly the overall income level of a country. It is thus not surprising that high-income countries such as Germany (4003€), the Netherlands (3998€), and Sweden (3987€) are the European countries that spent the most in 2015. At the other end of the scale, Romania (816€) and Latvia (1030€) are the lowest spending countries. In the whole European Union, per capita health spending, adjusted for differences in purchasing powers, was 2781€ in 2015.[1]

If we look at health care spending as a percentage of GDP, the EU Members devoted a total of 9.9 per cent of their GDP to health care. Germany, France and Sweden each spent around 11 per cent of their GDP, closely followed by the Netherlands and Denmark. These shares remain well below that of the US where health expenditure accounted for 16.9 per cent of GDP. Romania, Latvia, Estonia, and Poland were the countries with the lowest share of health spending.

As Table 11.1 shows, the change in health care spending over the period 2000–2015 is as varied as its level. All countries experienced an increase, implying that health care spending increased faster than GDP. The change was very high in the UK (64.3) and in the Netherlands (51); it was very low in Lithuania (5.2), Latvia (5.7), and Luxembourg (2.5).

Figure 11.1 looks at the evolution of the share of health care spending in GDP over the longer period 1990–2015. In high spending and low spending countries, one sees that the great recession led to a temporary stop in the growth of health care. One also detects a clear convergence across countries.

The public sector plays a major role in the financing of health services: in two thirds of the EU more than 70 per cent of health expenditure is funded by the public sector. Table 11.1 shows the share of public finance in total financing of healthcare systems across European countries as well as the variation of that share over the period 2000–2015. Member States with a relatively low

---

[1] See OECD (2015).

Health Care

Table 11.1. Total spending on health and the relative part of public spending, 2000–2015

Country	Total spending on health (% GDP) 2000	2015	change 00–15 (in %)	Public health spending (% total) 2000	2015	change 00–15 (in %)
Austria	9.2	10.3	11.9	75.5	75.6	0.1
Belgium	7.9	10.5	31.9	74.6	77.5	3.8
Czechia	5.7	7.2	25.8	89.8	83.5	−7.1
Denmark	8.1	10.3	27.4	83.1	84.1	1.2
Estonia	5.2	6.5	26.1	77.0	75.7	−1.7
Finland	6.8	9.4	38.2	71.2	74.4	4.6
France	9.5	11.1	16.0	78.9	78.9	0.1
Germany	9.8	11.2	13.3	79.4	84.5	6.4
Greece	7.2	8.4	15.8	61.6	59.1	−4.1
Hungary	6.8	7.2	6.7	69.6	66.7	−4.2
Ireland	5.9	7.8	31.4	77.5	70.0	−9.7
Italy	7.6	9.0	18.7	72.6	74.9	3.1
Latvia	5.4	5.8	5.7	50.8	57.5	13.3
Lithuania	6.2	6.5	5.2	68.5	66.9	−2.3
Luxembourg	5.9	6.0	2.5	82.0	82.0	0.0
Netherlands	7.1	10.7	51.5	66.4	80.7	21.6
Poland	5.3	6.3	19.7	68.9	70.0	1.6
Portugal	8.4	9.0	7.1	70.5	66.2	−6.0
Slovak Republic	5.3	6.9	29.6	89.2	79.7	−10.6
Slovenia	7.8	8.5	9.8	72.9	71.7	−1.7
Spain	6.8	9.2	34.5	71.4	71.0	−0.5
Sweden	7.4	11.0	48.6	85.5	83.7	−2.2
United Kingdom	6.0	9.9	64.3	79.3	79.7	0.4
United States	12.5	16.9	35.2	44.2	49.4	11.7

Source: OECD (2017a)

share of public health expenditure are Greece (59 per cent of total health expenditure), Portugal (66.2 per cent), and Lithuania (66.9 per cent). Note that this is well above the 49.4 per cent of the US. Member States with the highest share of health expenditure funded by the government are the Netherlands (80.7 per cent), Denmark (84.1 per cent), Sweden (83.7 per cent), Czechia (83.5 per cent), and Luxembourg (82 per cent). Health spending is among the largest and fastest growing spending items for governments. Table 11.1 gives us the changes in the share of public health expenditure. We have about the same number of countries with a positive and a negative change. The largest increase is observed in the Netherlands and in Latvia. The largest decrease occurred in Slovakia. We note that countries that suffered from the financial crisis experienced a decrease in their share of public health spending (Portugal, Greece, Spain, Ireland).

Growing incomes, population ageing, rising expectations for high-quality health services and above all technological advances are expected to increase pressure for higher health spending. According to the 2015 Ageing Report (European Commission 2015), a further increase in the share of public health expenditure as a percentage of GDP is expected from now until 2060.

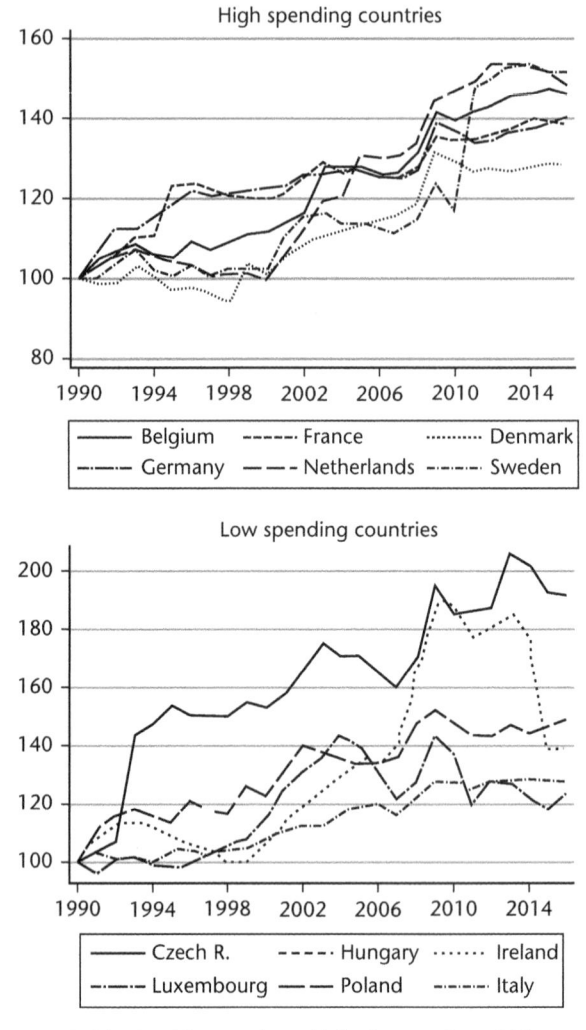

Figure 11.1. Public health spending (a) high spending (b) low spending
Source: OECD (2017a)

Depending of the chosen scenario, the increase in public expenditure on health will range from 2 to 4 per cent.[2]

To explain the rapid expansion of medical spending, a number of factors are often cited: ageing of population, income growth, third party payment, administrative costs, rapid advances in medical technologies and rising public expectations.

---

[2] European Commission (2015).

As already seen, the share of the population aged 65 and older is increasing everywhere in the EU. As the population ages, one expects health care expenditure to increase as well. At the same time, the population is aging in better health and what really costs are the last year(s) of life. To the extent that the demand for medical care increases with income and faster than income increases, the increase in health expenditure is in part a manifestation of a richer society wanting more health care. One also expects that the third party payment, which implies that only a negligible fraction of medical costs is paid by patients out of their pocket, will explain a fraction of the growth in medical expenditure. Administrative costs have also increased relatively faster than GDP.

There is now a wide consensus that these factors—ageing, income growth, third-party payment and administrative costs—can, at best, explain 40 per cent of the increase in medical expenditure. Accordingly, most of this increase is due to technological improvements: physician training, medical techniques, and equipment all of which have improved over time and will continue to do so in the future. This technology-based theory helps explain the increase observed in countries with different health care systems. All these countries have one thing in common—they all have been exposed to the same expensive innovation in technology. Clearly, it is important to understand the main sources of growth in expenditure in the debate on cost containment and on health care reforms.

Health care systems in Europe share common features:

- Third-party payment
- A single provider approach that implies offering all citizens, regardless of contribution and health status, a determined set of health services at low cost, if any
- Cost-based reimbursement: in most cases, health care providers are paid on the basis of the actual costs of treatment as opposed to capitation reimbursement. This latter technique used in the UK and in Health Maintenance Organizations (HMO) gives each health care provider an annual payment for each patient in his or her care.

Health care systems differ, however, in their source of financing, coverage, and means of delivering benefits. The Nordic countries, the UK, and Ireland finance their health care systems largely from general taxation. Other countries have predominantly insurance-based systems or a mixture of the two. Countries with insurance-based systems—Belgium, France, the Netherlands, Germany and Luxembourg—tend to have higher shares of expenditure on health care systems. This may be a result of higher quality care, or, more likely, a lower degree of control over expenditure and cost containment that is characteristic of an insurance-based system.

Access to some level of health care services in European countries is universal for all individuals. Individuals may opt out of obligations to state health care systems in Portugal or Italy by taking out supplementary coverage. In other European countries, supplementary insurance is available, but contributions to the state health care system remain obligatory. Countries with a large degree of insurance financing of their health care systems tend to have a larger market of private health care providers. In tax-financed schemes, the private market tends to be relatively less well developed.

One of the difficulties in assessing the performance of health care systems is how to measure their output. Just using indicators such as life-expectancy or mortality is clearly insufficient; it misses the qualitative dimension that is so important. One has to consider not only the number of years added to one's life but also their quality. Health economists are thus using the concept of quality-adjusted life years (QUALYS). It is interesting to check whether there is any link between health and health care spending. There is no clear relation between output indicators such as life expectancy at birth, healthy life expectancy, potential life years lost due to premature mortality, or infant mortality, and total costs of health care and input indicators such as total expenditure on health or total health employment. As seen above, one reason might be inefficiency.[3] Another reason may be that quality aspects are neglected for lack of data. In any case, it is well known that the nature of the environment and diet are likely to affect those health indicators as much as health care spending, as was forcefully argued by Illich (1976), who mentioned the case of Greece spending hardly 5 per cent of GDP for health care for a life expectancy that was well above that of the USA, which at that time spent almost three times more.

11.3. Cost Containment

Even though European countries spend much less than the US, both in relative and in absolute terms, cost containment is a priority. Since the early 1980s, governments have tried a number of strategies to reduce health care costs. Among the measures taken or discussed, are the move from cost-based reimbursement to capitation, the introduction of managed competition, the explicit introduction of quotas and the increased participation of well-to-do patients.

---

[3] See Osterkamp (2004).

Health Care

The movement towards capitation formulas and more generally to health maintenance organizations is under way in a number of countries. It is clear that cost-based reimbursement does not induce economizing on methods for delivering health care. But, at the same time, capitation-based reimbursement creates incentives to provide lower quality services. Managed competition is a combination of government regulation and market economy. The essential idea is to band people into large organizations that require health care providers, and even insurance companies to compete on price and quality to obtain their business. Co-insurance is increasingly imposed for two reasons. One is to curb moral hazard problems that lead to incremental costs. The other is to bring additional resources into the system. In a number of countries, coinsurance is quasi nil for low-income households and some categories such as the retired or the disabled. It can even increase with the income or wealth of households as it does in Belgium. In Belgium, the health care system includes the so-called *maximum billing*, according to which each household has an annual out-of-pocket maximum for all 'necessary health care expenses' that depends on its income.

When constraints are imposed on the supply side of the system, which is unavoidable in a single-provider country, rationing, whether implicit or explicit, is necessary. For equity and efficiency reasons it should be made explicit. In that respect, the Oregon experience is of great interest. Among the cost containment policies, the hardest to implement is, undoubtedly, the one pertaining to quotas. Every day tough choices are made, but generally they are implicitly based on ad hoc rules such as first come first served, or geographical distance. In 1990, the state of Oregon in the USA decided to tackle head-on the problem of expensive care for the many, and of little health care for some. The state decided to rank about 1600 medical procedures with a computer program that would balance the costs and benefits of these procedures. The objective was to eliminate coverage for those treatments that were disproportionately expensive. So doing, the state could double the number of poor people who were eligible for Medicaid, the government program of basic health insurance for the poor.

Of course, the list of treatments covered was controversial. Implementing it inevitably meant that the state would have to refuse to help some people who had so far benefitted from certain medical treatments, and that some of those people would die sooner than they otherwise would. Oregon taxpayers were not ready to provide everyone with all the medical care they could ever want. Scarcity cannot be avoided. In not implementing the Oregon list (which was the case), other choices were made that were socially less desirable but politically more acceptable, since they were made in the secrecy of the medical office. The Oregon plan proposed to shift medical care spending to treatments that provided greater public health benefits.

11.4. Inequality in Health and Health Care

As Table 11.2 shows, public health care covers the entirety of the population in most European countries. There are a few exceptions, including the Netherlands and Germany, where well-to-do households, whose income is higher than a specified amount, are covered by well-regulated private health insurance. In other words, everyone is covered for a wide range of health care. This does not mean that health consumption is totally free. As Table 11.2 also shows, out of pocket payment can be very important for a number of reasons. Among these reasons one counts high co-payments and the number of treatments that are not covered. Over the period 2000–2015, out of pocket payment increased quite a lot in several countries (Slovakia, Czechia, Ireland, and the Netherlands) and decreased in others (Poland, Luxembourg, Belgium). The country with the lowest out-of-pocket payment relative to total spending is France (6.8 per cent) and the highest is Greece (35.5 per cent).

Table 11.2. Public health care coverage and out-of-pocket payment

Country	% of covered population				Out-of-pocket(% of total spending)	
	1962	1980	2000	2015	2000	2015
Austria	78.0	99.0	99.0	99.9	17.8	17.9
Belgium	62.1	99.0	99.0	99.0	20.7	17.6
Czechiac	100.0	100.0	100.0	100.0	10.2	13.7
Denmark	95.0	100.0	100.0	100.0	15.4	13.7
Finland	55.0	100.0	100.0	100.0	23.2	19.9
France	–	99.1	99.9	99.9	7.3	6.8
Germany	85.9	92.3	99.8	100.0	12.0	12.5
Greece	44.0	88.0	100.0	86.0	–	35.5
Hungary	–	100.0	100.0	95.0	27.3	29.0
Ireland	85.0	100.0	100.0	100.0	12.1	15.2
Italy	88.0	100.0	100.0	100.0	26.5	22.8
Luxembourg	99.0	99.8	98.2	95.2	14.3	10.6
Netherlands	71.0	68.3	97.6	99.9	9.4	12.3
Portugal	20.0	100.0	100.0	100.0	25.0	27.7
Slovak Republic	–	–	98.8	94.2	10.8	18.4
Slovenia	–	–	98.0	100.0	–	12.5
Sweden	100.0	100.0	100.0	100.0	14.5	15.2
United Kingdom	100.0	100.0	100.0	100.0	11.5	14.8
United States	–	–	85.0	90.9	15.5	11.1

Source: OECD (2017a)

Assessing inequalities in health and health care is a very complex matter for two main reasons. First, these inequalities can been explained by different factors, which implies distinguishing between causal variables leading to ethically legitimate inequalities and causal variables leading to ethically illegitimate inequalities. An example of the former could be life-style choices; an example of the latter is social background. Whereas this distinction is theoretically clear, its implementation is not easy.[4] The second difficulty pertains to the interaction between health, consumption, and labour in individual wellbeing, which implies that a study of health inequality ought to be integrated in an overall evaluation of social inequality.

Given these difficulties, one has to resort to simpler and more widely available measures of inequality in both health and health care. Health disparities are apparent along many dimensions, including age, gender, race or ethnic group, geographic area, and socioeconomic status. One of the factors explaining those disparities is inequity in health care utilization. A number of studies have shown that for the same level of needs, the better-off are more likely to visit doctors—especially specialists and dentists—than those with lower incomes.

An indicator, which is frequently used to show barriers in access to health care, is patient self-reported unmet needs, due to excessive treatment costs, long waiting times, or having to travel to receive care. The EU-SILC collects data on unmet medical and dental care needs in a majority of European countries. Results are presented in Tables 11.3 and in Figures 11.2 and 11.3. For 2015, higher rates of unmet needs for medical examinations among the total adult population were found in Greece (12.3 per cent), Estonia (12.7 per cent) and Romania (9.4 per cent) and lower rates in the Netherlands, Austria and Slovenia. A large majority of countries were below the European average value of 3.2 per cent. Large disparities existed between quintile 1 (lowest income) and quintile 5 (highest income) in Belgium, France, Austria, and the Netherlands, but these countries happened to have a low rate of unmet needs.

Turning to the unmet needs for dental care among the adult population, the higher rates were reported in Greece, Portugal, Estonia and Latvia. Lower rates were found in the Netherlands, Austria and Slovenia. But inequalities within countries measured by the inter-quintile ratio were greater in countries such as Belgium, Portugal, Germany, and Sweden and lower in the UK and Romania.

The financial side is slightly easier to handle.[5] The question raised here is that of the distributive incidence of health financing in Europe. If it can be

---

[4] Fleurbaey and Schokkaert (2009).   [5] See De Graeve and Van Ourti (2003).

Table 11.3. Persons reporting an unmet need for medical acts because of problems of access: 2015 (%)

	Medical examination		Dental examination	
	Total	Interquintile ratio	Total	Interquintile ratio
EU 28	3.2	0.255	4.5	0.193
Belgium	2.4	0.042	3.7	0.039
Bulgaria	4.7	0.165	5.2	0.222
Czechia	0.8	0.333	1.1	0.185
Denmark	1.3	0.316	4.0	0.064
Germany	0.5	0.100	0.6	0.071
Estonia	12.7	0.708	11.1	0.173
Ireland	2.8	0.355	5.1	0.492
Greece	12.3	0.209	12.5	0.291
Spain	0.6	0.667	4.9	0.085
France	1.2	0.069	3.4	0.118
Croatia	1.9	0.154	1.0	0.190
Italy	7.2	0.092	9.9	0.164
Cyprus	1.5	0.063	4.1	0.090
Latvia	8.4	0.135	13.9	0.132
Lithuania	2.9	0.381	4.2	0.128
Luxembourg	0.9	0.143	1.1	0.027
Hungary	2.6	0.118	4.0	0.110
Malta	0.8	0.045	1.0	0.083
Netherlands	0.1	0.000	0.4	0.000
Austria	0.1	0.000	0.4	0.333
Poland	7.3	0.410	4.2	0.324
Portugal	3.0	0.094	14.6	0.092
Romania	9.4	0.410	8.6	0.500
Slovenia	0.2	0.667	0.5	0.077
Slovakia	2.1	0.414	2.7	0.226
Finland	4.3	0.446	5.2	0.569
Sweden	1.0	0.167	3.1	0.082
United Kingdom	2.8	1.036	3.0	0.444

Source: Eurostat (2017f)

shown that health financing is not regressive, namely that health spending, public and private, as a percentage of household income does not decrease with income, we can conclude that the welfare state fulfils its redistributive objective in this particular area. In such a study we have to consider the various sources of public finance but also expenditure from private insurance contributions and out-of-pocket payments. Not surprisingly countries that rely upon private sources tend to be regressive. Out-of-pocket payments are expectedly regressive everywhere and private insurance payments tend to be progressive only when they are supplementary to public financing. As to public financing itself, progressivity is expected particularly when it relies on income or payroll taxes and not on indirect taxes.

Table 11.4 gives the (Kakwani) redistributive indices for a number of European countries plus the US. Negativity (positivity) implies regressivity (progressivity).

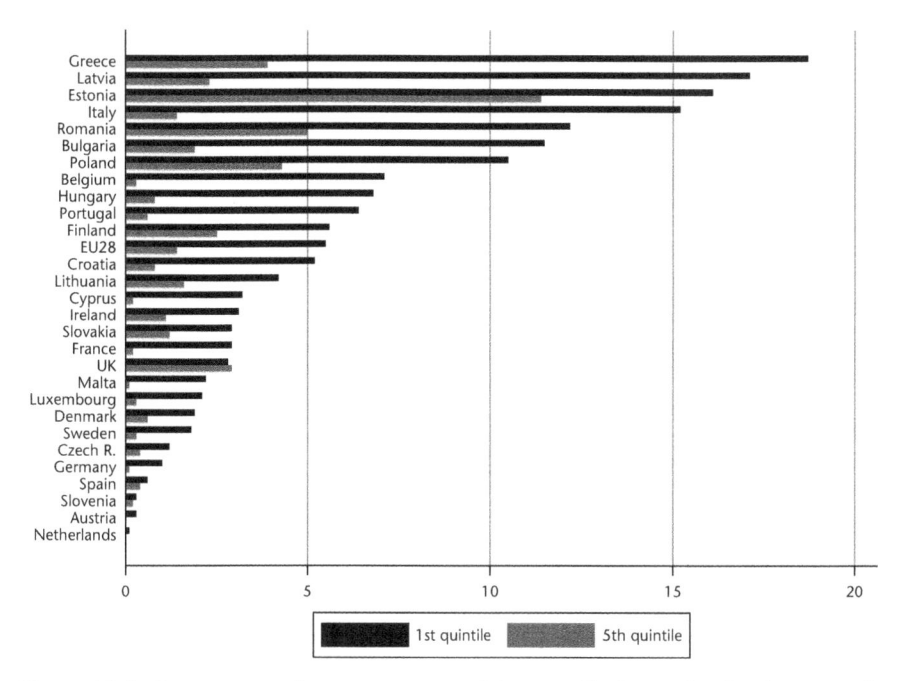

Figure 11.2. Persons reporting an unmet need for a medical examination because of problems of access (%)
Source: Eurostat (2017f)

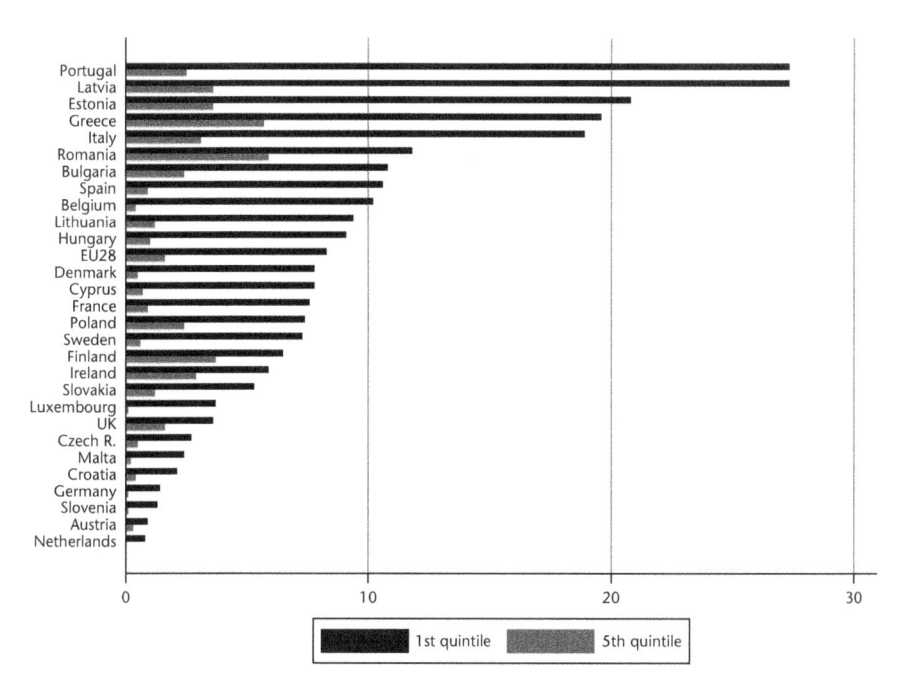

Figure 11.3. Persons reporting an unmet need for a dental examination because of problems of access (%)
Source: Eurostat (2017f)

Table 11.4. Redistributive indices for the financing source of health care

	Public finance	Private finance	Total
Finland (1994)	0.066	−0.198	0.060
France (1989)	0.111	−0.305	0.001
Greece (1989)	−0.053	−0.007	−0.045
Italy (1991)	0.071	−0.061	0.041
Netherlands (1989)	0.060	0.015	−0.035
Portugal (1990)	0.072	−0.228	−0.045
Spain (1990)	0.051	−0.163	0.000
Sweden (1990)	0.010	−0.240	−0.016
UK (1993)	0.079	−0.095	0.051
US (1987)	0.106	−0.317	−0.130

Source: De Graeve and Van Ourti (2003)

A lot of countries have near proportional financing systems. Countries relying on public financing and specifically on direct levies have a progressive system. This is the case of the UK and Italy.

A general observation that emerges from all this work is that larger inequalities in health and in health care are associated with the following features of the health care system:[6]

- Universal health coverage not achieved
- Large share of private financing and out-of- pocket payments
- Care not free at the point of delivery
- No gatekeeping system
- Mostly private provision of health care
- Non-existence of public screening programmes

11.5. Conclusion

It is clear that health care is in need of serious reform. The nature of this reform will depend on what the objectives are: purely budgetary, or with a strong concern for equity? There is increasing pressure to move towards at least partial privatization. It is important to keep in mind the pros and the cons of such a move. Table 11.5 summarizes the comparative advantages of private over public intervention. The case for a predominant public pillar supplemented by private insurance remains very strong.

Finally, it is worth noticing the impact that cheaper and more informative genetic tests can have on the future of health care systems and particularly

---

[6] Devaux and de Looper (2012).

Health Care

Table 11.5. Comparative advantages of private versus public health care insurance

Characteristics	Public insurance	Private insurance
Open to self-selection	No	Yes (in general)
Redistribution across risk classes	Yes	No (in general)
Redistribution across income classes	Yes	No
Equitable access	Yes	No
Open to moral hazard	Yes	Yes
Nature of contract	Collective and political	Individual and short-term
Preference matching	Weak	Yes
Administrative cost	Low	High
Competitive challenge	No	Yes

on their redistributive capacity. These tests allow individuals to obtain very detailed information on their genetic predisposition to several diseases, as well as prevention strategies and treatment. They can create a strong incentive for those with good genes to opt out of the system or at least to push for a lower involvement of the state in providing health care. The key issue is going to be to what extent individuals are forced to pass on test results to public and above all private insurers. This is clearly a political question with an international dimension.

12

Long-Term Care

> **KEY CONCEPTS**
> altruism
> exchange motive
> family norm
> informal care
> long term care insurance puzzle

12.1. Introduction

Due to the ageing process, the rise in long-term care needs constitutes a major challenge for the twenty-first century. Long-term care (LTC) concerns individuals who are no longer able to carry out basic daily activities such as eating, washing, dressing, etc. Nowadays, the number of persons in need of LTC is substantial. In Europe (EU27), the number of persons in need of LTC is expected to grow from 2.7 million in 2012 to 5.8 million by year 2060 (Lipszyc et al. 2012).

The expected rise in the number of persons in need of LTC raises the question of the provision of care. About two-thirds of LTC is provided by informal caregivers (mainly the family, i.e., spouses, daughters, and stepdaughters). The remainder of LTC is provided formally, that is, through services that are supplied by the state or paid for on the market. Formal care can be provided either at the dependent's home, or in an institution (care centres or nursing homes).

LTC services do not require high skills but they are, nonetheless, extremely expensive. The average private pay rate for a single room in a nursing home may exceed 40,000€ per year, which represents about three times the average pension.[1] Home-based LTC costs are also high. Those large costs raise the question of the funding of formal LTC. That question will become increasingly important in the future, where it is expected that the role of informal LTC provision will decrease. The implication of this is that financial risks associated with meeting LTC needs will grow and therefore the development of mechanisms for absorbing these risks will gain in importance.

Given that each person has a large probability of entering a nursing home when becoming old, and given the large costs related to LTC, one would expect that private LTC insurance markets would expand in order to insure individuals against the quite likely substantial costs of LTC. However, although markets for private LTC insurance exist, these remain thin in most countries. According to Brown and Finkelstein (2007), only about 9 to 10 per cent of the population at risk of facing future LTC costs have purchased a private LTC insurance in the U.S. This is the so-called 'long-term care insurance puzzle'. Because of various factors lying both on the demand side (myopia, denial of LTC, crowding out by the family, etc.) and on the supply side of that market (high-loading factors, unattractive reimbursement rules, etc.), only a small fraction of the population buys LTC private insurance. One can thus hardly rely only on the development of private LTC insurance markets to fund the cost of LTC.

In the light of the expected decline in informal care, and of the difficulties faced by the market for private LTC insurance, one would hope that the public sector would play a more important role in the provision and funding of LTC. Nowadays, in most advanced economies, the state is involved either in the provision or in the funding of LTC services, but to an extent that varies strongly across countries. Note, however, that the involvement of the public sector in LTC is, in most European countries, not as comprehensive and generous as it is for the funding of general health services. The LTC 'pillar' of the welfare state remains quite thin in comparison with other pillars of the social insurance system.

In this chapter,[2] we want first explain why informal care is expected to decline and why the private market has failed to play a role in covering LTC needs, and then advocate the development of social insurance for LTC that would meet two objectives: assist those who have no financial means nor family connections, and protect the middle class against the risk of financial bankruptcy.

---

[1] In France, nursing home prices range from 900€ to 4500€ per month, depending on location and ownership. The most expensive are private and in Paris and the least expensive are public and rural.

[2] For more details, see Pestieau and Ponthière (2017). For a survey of the economics of LTC, see Cremer et al. (2012).

12.2. Informal Care and LTC Private Insurance

Before considering the design of a LTC social insurance, let us examine the main reasons why the two other channels that could provide LTC, namely the family and the market, are defaulting.

We first consider the role of the family. It is expected that the family, which provides today the bulk of LTC, will be less active in the coming decades. A number of factors explain such a gloomy prospect. The drastic change in family values, the growing number of childless households, the increasing rate of participation of women in the labour market, and the mobility of children imply that the number of dependent elderly who cannot count on the assistance of either spouses or children is increasing.

At the same time, it is important to realize that, at least for heavy cases of dependence, informal care can be quite costly for caregivers. There exists a growing literature trying to assess the collateral costs that informal caring can represent for the caregivers. Several studies highlight that caregivers bear large opportunity costs because of care responsibilities (e.g., Van Houtven et al. 2013). Informal care may have adverse effects on multiple dimensions of the health of caregivers. The detrimental effects related to the physical aspect are generally less intensive than the psychological effects. Schultz and Sherwood (2008), Hirst (2005) and Burton et al. (2003) showed that moving into a demanding caregiving role (more than twenty hours per week of help for dealing with the basic activities of daily living) led to an increase in depression and psychological distress, impaired self-care and poorer self-reported health. A conjecture that would need testing is that those costs depend closely on the motives underlying caring: altruism, exchange, or norm. In other words, one would expect that informal care that rests on norm as opposed to altruism would involve more collateral costs. But in any case, we can expect, given the increasingly large literature on the costs of informal care provision, that the size of informal care will go down in the future and that such an evolution might be desirable given the collateral costs of care giving.

If the importance of informal care is likely to decrease in the next decades, can we count on LTC private insurance market to substitute for it? The literature on the LTC private insurance puzzle questions the capacity of the market to cover a large part of the population at risk of LTC costs. Actually, although LTC costs are high, and despite the large probabilities of becoming dependent in old age, the LTC private insurance market remains underdeveloped, in contradiction with the basic principles of insurance economics. One observes that individuals tend, because of either myopia or ignorance, to underestimate the risk of dependence, and thus do not feel the need to be insured against LTC.

Another possible explanation is that LTC insurance exhibits high prices that can be the consequence of adverse selection or administrative costs. Third, a number of families prefer to rely on informal caring, which is generally warmer and cheaper. Parents can avoid insuring to force their children to assist them in case of dependence and children can incite their parents not to insure to increase their expected bequests (see Pauly 1990). Fourth, there is the Good Samaritan argument: some families know that they can rely on means-tested social assistance such as Medicaid in the U.S or APA[3] in France. Even well to do families can resort to these programs through what has been called strategic impoverishment, meaning that parents transfer their wealth to their children so as to be under the threshold of means testing. Fifth, many insurance contracts have unattractive rules of reimbursement such as a monthly lump sum compensation that is insufficient and unrelated to the real needs of the dependent. Finally, there is often a denial of severe dependence; it is so awful that one prefers not to think of it, and thus does not consider purchasing a private LTC insurance.

Whereas those different factors may explain why the coverage of the LTC private insurance is so low, a key question is whether or not these plausible causes of the LTC insurance puzzle will persist in the future. If the answer is positive, this means that the market will not cover the mounting needs of LTC coverage and that the construction of a social LTC insurance is definitively a must.

12.3. Public Spending Projections

Before proceeding with the design of a LTC insurance scheme, let us look at the current and at the forecasted level of spending. To assess the expected increase in the need for LTC, one has to look at the forecasted increase in the share of the very old in the total population. Most dependent people come from that age group. The proportion of the EU28 population aged 80 years or over stood at 5.1 per cent in 2014 and is projected to rise by 7.2 percentage points to reach 12.3 per cent by 2080. Projections for 2080 indicate that among EU Member States, the share of the population aged 80 years or over will range from 7.4 per cent in Ireland to 16.3 per cent in Slovakia. These evolutions result from the combined effect of a slightly declining proportion of children and a continuously rising proportion of older persons.[4]

Future needs will depend on these demographic changes but also on the way the prevalence of disability per age will evolve in future years. Using

---

[3] Allocation personnalisée d'autonomie. [4] European Commission (2014).

The Welfare State in Europe

Table 12.1. Total Public Spending on LTC as % of GDP

	Level in 2013	Constant Disability	Demographic	Base case	High life expectancy
Belgium	2.1	3.5	3.6	3.9	4.1
Denmark	2.4	4.3	4.7	4.7	5.2
France	2.0	2.7	2.9	2.9	3.1
Germany	1.4	2.7	2.8	3.0	3.2
Italy	1.8	2.5	2.8	2.8	3.0
Netherlands	4.1	6.7	7.5	7.7	8.5
Spain	1.0	2.3	2.6	2.6	3.3
Sweden	3.6	4.9	5.2	5.5	5.7
U.K.	1.2	1.4	1.6	1.6	1.6

Notes: The constant disability scenario addresses the dependency factor in particular: it aims to capture the potential impact of assumed improvements in the health (or non-disability) status. The demographic scenario aims to isolate the size effect of an ageing population on public expenditure on LTC; for all types of LTC, expenditure per user grows in line with GDP per capita. The base case reflects in addition the highly labour-intensive characteristic of LTC services by letting in-kind LTC benefits profile grow in line with GDP per hours worked. The high life expectancy scenario assumes that life expectancy in 2060 is higher by two years than the demographic scenario

Source: European Commission (2015)

alternative scenarios one can forecast future needs and future costs. Table 12.1 provides the forecasts of public spending on LTC for the period 2010–2060 under various scenarios. This does not mean that the government will be alone in financing these additional expenses, nor that it reflects the real costs of public LTC as a percentage of GDP.

The scenarios differ in the way they anticipate the evolution of disability per age, the labour cost of long-term care, the level of demand for long-term care and the future growth rate. Table 12.1 indicates that in 2013 the share of public spending for LTC ranged from 4.1 in the Netherlands to 1.0 in Spain. These important differences are partially offset by a family solidarity that seems to be more important in the Mediterranean countries that in the Nordic ones. This has been called the North-South gradient. Recent evidence seems to indicate that this gradient is not as clear as initially expected. Solidarity would be strongest in the Mediterranean countries, followed by the Northern countries (and the Netherlands) and finally the remaining Continental countries. Constant disability captures the potential impact of health improvement and implies the lowest increase in public spending. The largest increase is obtained with high life expectancy, which is not surprising.

12.4. The Design of LTC Social Insurance

The state already plays some role in most countries but, as already mentioned, this role is still modest and inconsistent. The overall level of spending is low and the programs are scattered among the different levels of government. Typically, in Belgium for example, some programs are managed by the federal health care system and others, by the municipal authorities, without much coordination between the two. In a remarkable report for the UK, Andrew Dilnot (2011) sketches the features of what can be considered as an ideal social program for LTC. This would be a two-tier program. The first tier would concern those who cannot afford paying for their LTC and do not benefit from family support. It would be a means-test program. The second tier would address the fears of most dependents in the middle class that they might incur costs that would force them to sell all their assets and prevent them from bequeathing any of them. These two concerns and particularly the second are not met by current LTC practices. The proposal that individuals' contribution to their LTC costs should be capped at a certain amount, after which they will be eligible for full state support, is indeed attractive. It is in the spirit of Kenneth Arrow's (1963) theorem on insurance deductible. Arrow shows that it is optimal to concentrate insurance on the events with high levels of losses and to let individuals cover low losses themselves.[5]

The design of a public LTC scheme is not an easy task. It depends on the extent of political support for it; it also depends on the type of private insurance market that prevails and the structure of families involved. In particular, a key issue concerns assumptions about the motivations behind the behaviour of family members. For instance, children may serve as informal caregivers because of altruism, or because of a strategic motive, or because of a social norm[6]. Similarly, the dependent parent may either be altruistic towards his children, and purchase a LTC private insurance so as to minimize the cost imposed on his children, or, alternatively, behave in a more egoistic way and not purchase insurance, so as to force his children to provide informal LTC to him. Obviously, those different motivations lead to distinct behaviours, and, hence, will impact the design of public insurance.

Let us mention a couple of issues that have to be taken into account in such an endeavour. The first deals with the possibility of sorting out dependent people who cannot count on any assistance from their family and those who can count on such aid. Given its budget constraints, the government would like to distinguish between those two types of dependent and focus its attention on the first. It is not easy to implement such a selection. One way is to offer some free slots in nursing homes, the quality of services of which would be such that it would keep away altruistic families who otherwise would have liked to benefit from a 'free lunch'. This is a typical unpleasant solution that result from asymmetric information.

---

[5] Klimaviciute and Pestieau (2017) present a social insurance for LTC that pursues such an objective.
[6] See Klimaviciute et al. (2017).

Then there is the question of avoiding middle-class families taking advantage of welfare programs targeted on the poor. In many countries, individuals who could afford to pay for their LTC end up receiving benefits from the program. In other words, means testing is not always strictly enforced. Some individuals game the system by arranging complex asset transfers or insurance transactions that sidestep efforts to curb fraud. There is a range of strategies that lead beneficiaries to impoverish themselves so as to be eligible. This is called in the US the Medicaid impoverishment technique. A universal feature of this problem is the (im)possibility of recouping part of what has been paid by the government at the time of death. A related issue is that children be asked to finance their parents LTC expenses before the government intervenes. The law varies on that and so does the degree to which it is enforced. To take the example of France, where there are two means-tested programs for LTC, the PSD (Prestation Spécifique Dépendance) and the APA (Allocation Personalisée d'Autonomie). The first one can recuperate its participation on the estate of the beneficiary, whereas the second cannot. In Germany and in Belgium, the concept of means is extended to the children, as they are partially responsible for the caring of their parents. The crucial point is that for some reason, there very often appears to be a significant political resistance against the effective enforcement of some aspects of the means test, when the underlying program concerns dependent people. Attempts by the French PSD to recuperate expenses from the estate of a person who has benefited for years from means-tested services are perceived as unpopular by the majority of public opinion. In reality the rate of recovery is extremely low but ironically, the very hypothetical threat of recovery has led to a quite low take-up rate in France. This has induced the government to introduce the APA where such a requirement is not imposed.

12.5. Conclusion

This chapter started with an observation: LTC needs are increasing rapidly and neither the market nor the family seem to be able to meet such a mounting demand. Furthermore, the existing public programs are both insufficient and uncoordinated. For these reasons we advocate developing a full-fledge LTC public insurance scheme that would fulfil two objectives: assisting those who cannot count on any family assistance and do not have the financial means to purchase LTC services and providing the middle class with a program that would protect families against too costly spending.

13

Unemployment and Poverty

> **KEY CONCEPTS**
> flexicurity
> experience rating
> basic income
> minimum wage
> in-work poverty

13.1. Introduction

Labour market participation has always been at the heart of our welfare states. Employment is often the main source of income for the majority of households and most social insurance schemes were initially designed within labour market arrangements. This is the case not only for unemployment insurance, but also for retirement and disability insurance. In many countries, both benefits and contributions are settled through sectoral negotiations involving both unions and management with the state playing an increasingly active role as third party. Furthermore, as we have seen in previous chapters, there is an interaction between the state of the labour market, the level of wages and employment, and the nature of social protection.

The European labour market has experienced dramatic changes in the last two decades. The nature of employment is changing. There are more and more part-time and temporary jobs as well as more and more self-employed jobs. In a series of countries, recent employment growth has been driven mainly by part-time jobs, which has consequences for the financing and the survival of the welfare state. The increase of temporary and part-time jobs is often justified by the need for flexibility and one of the key issues in today's economies is how to keep a balance between the need for firms to adapt to ever-changing market conditions and workers' employment security.

The Welfare State in Europe

Labour market policies are evolving towards greater flexibility to boost the economy and improve the country's competitiveness. Reviewing European labour market performance, one realizes that income security and employment do not seem necessarily to be in conflict as there are countries which have succeeded in achieving both.

Another big challenge concerning the labour market is related to technological change and the rise of a new form of employment based on the utilization of computing platforms in order to facilitate peer to peer transactions between clients and providers of a service. This new sharing economy is dramatically changing the employment relationship and raises concerns over worker protection and government regulations and taxation.

13.2. Unemployment and Employment

First of all, it is important to define what we mean when we talk about the rates of employment and of unemployment because both do not reflect the same reality. The rate of unemployment is the ratio of employed workers to the labour force, which is the sum of employed and unemployed workers. The employment rate is the number of employed workers over the working age population (e.g., persons aged 15–64). In the denominator one thus finds the labour force but also all the people who are for whatever reason not involved in paid work: students, housewives, (early) retirees, disabled people, and so on. For that reason, one minus the rate of employment is much higher than the rate of unemployment and better reflects the idea of unused capacity. The participation rate (also called the labour force participation rate) is the ratio of the number employed and unemployed people to the working age population. It is a measure of the active part of the labour force. To summarize:

$$Unemployment\ rate = \frac{unemployed\ workers}{employed + unemployed\ workers}$$

$$Employment\ rate = \frac{employed\ workers}{working\ age\ population}$$

$$Activity\ rate = \frac{employed + unemployed\ workers}{working\ age\ population}$$

Recent data for the EU28 and the US are given in Table 13.1. The unemployment rate is the better-known concept. It has the advantage of being precise, and quite well agreed upon. As already seen, it is an indicator of social exclusion and it reports the burden for public finance of a bad labour market situation as most often implying the payment of unemployment compensations. As Table 13.1 shows, unemployment is on average higher in the EU

Table 13.1. Employment, activity and unemployment rates. Persons aged 15–64 (%): EU28 2016

	Employment rate	Activity rate	Unemployment rate	Long-term unemployment rate
Austria	71.5	76.2	6.0	1.9
Belgium	62.3	67.6	7.8	4.0
Bulgaria	63.4	68.7	7.6	4.5
Croatia	56.9	65.6	13.3	6.6.
Cyprus	63.4	73.1	13.0	5.8
Czech R.	72.0	75.0	4.0	1.7
Denmark	74.9	80.0	6.2	1.4
Estonia	72.1	77.5	6.8	2.1
Finland	69.1	75.9	8.8	2.3
France	64.2	71.4	10.1	4.3
Germany	74.7	77.9	4.1	1.7
Greece	52.0	68.2	23.6	17.0
Hungary	66.5	70.1	5.1	2.4
Ireland	64.8	70.5	7.9	4.2
Italy	57.2	64.9	11.7	6.7
Latvia	68.7	76.3	9.6	4.0
Lithuania	69.4	75.5	7.9	3.0
Luxembourg	65.6	70.0	6.3	2.2
Malta	65.7	69.0	4.7	1.9
Netherlands	74.8	79.7	6.0	2.5
Poland	64.5	68.8	6.2	2.2
Portugal	65.2	73.7	11.2	6.2
Romania	61.6	65.6	5.9	3.0
Slovakia	64.9	71.9	9.6	5.8
Slovenia	65.8	71.6	8.0	4.3
Spain	59.5	74.2	19.6	9.5
Sweden	76.2	82.1	6.9	1.3
UK	73.5	77.3	4.8	1.3
USA	69.4	72.6	4.9	1.0
EU28	66.6	72.9	8.6	4.0

Note: Long-term unemployment refers to people who have been unemployed for 12 months or more
Source: Eurostat (2017d) and OECD (2017b)

than in the US. There is a wide dispersion across countries with a low 4.0 and 4.1 per cent for the Czech Republic and Germany respectively and a high 23.6 per cent for Greece. Denmark, the United Kingdom, The Netherlands, Hungary and Romania do quite well whereas the other three large continental countries, Spain, France and Italy have disappointing records. As is shown later the advantage of the US over the EU is new. High unemployment is not a European trait; until the end of the 1960s unemployment was very low in Europe and the talk then was of the European unemployment miracle. The miracle came to an end in the 1970s when unemployment steadily increased. It kept increasing in the 1980s and, in spite of a slight decline in the mid-1990s, it has on average been very high with large cross-country differences since the early 2000s. The 2007 great recession has increased tremendously the unemployment rate in most European countries but since 2013, it has been gradually declining, showing its natural response to economic shocks.

The unemployment spell is also an important feature of the problem. In a dynamic labour market where job destruction is rapidly followed by the creation of a new jobs, the unemployment situation is transitory and is needed to adjust the labour force. In such a case, the unemployment duration is short and the workers go from one job to another. When the probability of being hired is small, the unemployment duration can be long. This represents an additional burden for the unemployment insurance system and it plausibly affects also individual well-being. The size of long-term unemployment indicates to what extent the labour market operates inefficiently and how precarious is the situation of job-seekers. On Table 13.1, large differences between countries are reported and the long-term unemployment rate follows the unemployment rate in relative terms; except for some countries like Sweden where the long-term unemployment rate is rather low compared to a high unemployment rate.

It is often believed that unemployment rates do not reflect the true state of non-employment as they does not comprise people who are more or less discreetly pushed out of the labour force: students beyond a certain age, soldiers, housewives or early retirees. Moreover, it does not take into account that the same rate of unemployment can hide different situations regarding temporary and part-time work. To address the first question, one increasingly uses the employment ratio.

Here again, it is lower in the EU (66.6 per cent) than in the US (69.4 per cent) with large cross-country differences. Greece, Italy, and Spain have a ratio below 60 per cent while France, Belgium, and Romania are well below the average. At the other extreme, Denmark, Germany, the Netherlands, Sweden, and the UK perform well and are above the US. We have already discussed one of the main factors of low employment ratios: the low rate of activity of aged workers. We can also add the differences observed in the female employment rate. The high level of employment observed in Sweden is also the result of the high employment rate of older workers (75.5 per cent) and a female employment rate above the EU average (74.8 per cent against 61.4 per cent). Overall in 2016, the employment ratio for male workers aged 55 to 64 was 55.4 per cent in the EU28. It was 38.4 per cent in 2002, showing some improvement. In the US, it was 61.8 per cent in 2016.

The employment ratio does not say much about work intensity, namely the number of hours of work in a year. In 2016, Germany, followed by Denmark, the Netherlands, France, and Luxembourg were leading in terms of the lowest number of hours per capita and per year. The annual number of hours ranged from 1,363 hours per capita in Germany to 1,842 in Portugal and 1,922 in Poland. This figure results from two main effects: the employment ratio effect just seen and the number of hours per worker. The case of the Netherlands is interesting: it has a high employment ratio and at the same time one of the lowest number of hours per worker in the EU, which leads to quite a low number of hours per capita. As shown in the OECD (2004), there is a negative cross-country correlation between the employment ratio and average annual hours per worker implying that each country reacts differently, intensively or extensively, to improvements in productivity and living standards. As we are going to see below, the European labour market is changing towards increasing part-time work.

13.3. Unemployment Insurance

In all European countries, protection against unemployment predominantly takes the form of cash benefits from the unemployment insurance system. The nature of the system may change according to economic, social, and institutional factors but, in general, contributions paid in work generate entitlement to unemployment insurance benefits. These benefits tend to be income-related in Bismarckian countries or they can be flat-rate in Beveridgean ones. For unemployed individuals whose employment record does not entitle them to unemployment benefits, or who have exhausted their entitlement, a social assistance or minimum safety-net benefit is available in all European countries. This benefit is generally means-tested and unlimited in duration, although additional criteria may be attached.

It is however important to note that the majority of the unemployed in the EU do not receive unemployment benefits. On average in the EU only less than 40 per cent of the short-term unemployed receive unemployment benefits (European Commission 2013). Whereas this share varies widely across countries, it may represent more than 50 per cent and 80 per cent of unemployed in France and Germany respectively. The reasons for this low figure vary. While some workers are not covered or not entitled because they did not work long enough, some simply do not claim the benefit.

Unemployment benefit systems differ considerably across European countries in terms of entitlement criteria and duration of benefit payments. Table 13.2 shows unemployment benefits as a share of GDP for the EU as well as public expenditure on active labour market measures. Unemployment compensation as well as early retirement programs for labour market reasons are passive benefits. They do not contribute to fostering employment as opposed to active spending aimed at training, subsidizing employment or financing public employment. The active measures correspond to temporary support that aims at activating the unemployed, helping people to move from inactivity into unemployment and to maintain the jobs of those threatened

Table 13.2. Labour market policy in the EU: 2015

Country	Total	Active measures	Unemployment compensation	Unemployment benefit net replacement rate
Austria	2.25	0.75	1.50	55
Belgium	2.44	0.72	1.72	63
Bulgaria	0.58	0.17	0.41	37
Croatia	0.77	0.43	0.33	37
Cyprus	0.93	0.16	0.77	n.a.
Czech R.	0.63	0.44	0.19	52
Denmark	3.28	1.98	1.30	68
Estonia	0.64	0.21	0.42	41
Finland	2.93	0.97	1.96	66
France	2.98	1.01	1.98	57
Germany	1.52	0.63	0.88	53
Greece	0.74	0.26	0.49	22
Hungary	1.16	0.91	0.25	31
Ireland	2.13	0.65	1.49	73
Italy	1.76	0.47	1.30	23
Latvia	0.56	0.14	0.41	46
Lithuania	0.54	0.31	0.23	38
Luxembourg	1.25	0.57	0.68	64
Malta	0.50	0.20	0.31	49
Netherlands	2.59	0.77	1.82	66
Poland	0.73	0.46	0.28	44
Portugal	1.54	0.53	1.01	51
Romania	0.18	0.08	0.11	31
Slovakia	0.54	0.20	0.34	39
Slovenia	0.76	0.24	0.53	53
Spain	2.50	0.59	1.91	48
Sweden	1.80	1.24	0.55	60
United Kingdom	0.69	0.39	0.29	49

Notes: Unemployment compensations also include early retirement schemes. Net replacement rates are for the year 2013 and are obtained as an average of various income level and household situations and for 60 months of unemployment

Source: OECD (2017b) and European Commission (2017a)

by unemployment. The figures in Table 13.2 are then much comprehensive than those presented in Chapter 3 where only unemployment spending was concerned.

Total public expenditure on labour market policy is in a range from a low 0.2 per cent in Romania to 3.3 per cent of GDP in Denmark. The expenditures vary between countries reflecting differences not only in the relative generosity of the systems but also in the level of duration of benefits, the way they are targeted, and of course the size of unemployment. The generosity of unemployment benefits is then reflected by their net replacement rate. Table 13.2 presents OECD estimations of average net replacement rates for different household composition and household earnings after 60 months of unemployment. The rate goes from 22 per cent in Greece to 68 per cent in Denmark. Few countries have a net replacement rate above 50 per cent.

The differences between countries reflect not only the economic situation but also the strategies adopted in terms of labour market policy. In recent decades, labour market policies in the EU have evolved towards more and more activation of employment. Denmark is a good example of the gradually increase of active labour market policies in the fight against unemployment. At a time when other countries were experiencing high unemployment, Denmark managed to reduce its unemployment to a level which is among the lowest in Europe. The Danish model, which was briefly presented in Chapter 5 and is called 'flexicurity', has achieved outstanding labour market performance and has been praised as an example. The model combines flexible hiring and firing with a generous unemployment insurance system and an extensive system of activation policies. This comes at a price and Denmark is the country in Europe that spends the most in percentage of GDP for its labour market policy as shown in Table 13.2. The Danish success has inspired labour market policy reforms in other European countries and in recent years, one observes a certain tendency towards more and more activation of employment.

13.4. Flexibility and Protection

One of the major changes in labour market programs in the last two decades has been the particular attention dedicated to the institutional factors that determine the structural level of unemployment. It has entailed a change in the tools to fight unemployment. The passive labour market programs that compensate the unemployed for their loss of income, without controlling their job-seeking behaviour, are more and more supplemented by strong employment-focused programs. The goal is to reduce barriers to employment but also to facilitate matching with employers. This means that aside from unemployment benefits, labour market policies comprises a range of financial, regulatory, and practical interventions that aim to bring the unemployed and the inactive into employment or to help workers on-the-job to find better opportunities.

Thus unemployment insurance and active labour market programs are only one of the components of policies dedicated to employment. In addition, one can cite two main regulatory tools that are widely debated: the legal minimum wage policy and employment regulations. They are often seen as a serious impediment to flexibility in the labour market.

The minimum wage is the lowest wage rate (or a minimum weekly wage for full-time workers) that employers can legally pay to employees irrespective of

Table 13.3. Minimum wage and employment protection: 2014

	Minimum wage relative to average wages of full-time workers	Employment protection	
		Protection of permanent workers against individual and collective dismissals	Regulation on temporary forms of employment
Belgium	0.42	2.99	2.42
Estonia	0.34	2.07	3.04
France	0.49	2.82	3.75
Germany	0.43	2.84	1.75
Greece	0.32	2.41	2.92
Hungary	0.40	2.07	2.00
Ireland	0.37	2.07	1.21
Latvia	0.39	2.91	1.79
Luxembourg	0.45	2.74	3.83
Netherlands	0.39	2.94	1.17
Poland	0.41	2.39	2.33
Portugal	0.39	2.69	2.33
Slovakia	0.37	2.26	2.42
Slovenia	0.49	2.39	2.13
Spain	0.31	2.36	3.17
United Kingdom	0.40	1.59	0.54

Note: The indicator on employment protection legislation is compiled from 21 items covering three different aspects of employment protection regulations. It is the average of a scale corresponding to 0 (least restrictions) to 6 (most restrictions)

Source: OECD (2017b)

their education, skill, training or productivity. This policy typically applies to all workers, including school dropouts without work experience, and recipients of unemployment and disability benefits should they decide to return to work. Some countries achieve an effective minimum wage arrangement through more or less comprehensive collective bargaining agreements which can lead to different minimum wage laws for specific sectors of activity. In a few countries some groups of workers are not covered by minimum wage laws; in others (e.g., the Netherlands) the minimum wage can vary according to age.

Employment protection usually refers to the rules and procedures governing the dismissal of individuals or groups of workers or the hiring of workers on fixed-term or temporary work agency contracts (Martin and Scarpetta 2012). These regulations constrain the ability of employers to alter the size of their work force in response to changes in the demand for their output; hence, an employment contract becomes a fixed cost to the employer generating caution in the addition of permanent workers to the enterprise. Such regulations also lead to disguised unemployment in periods of slack demand, as employers are constrained from firing workers.

Table 13.3 presents recent indicators on the level of the minimum wages and employment regulations for a series of European countries. In the EU, the level of the minimum wage compared to the average wage of a full-time worker varies markedly across countries. It ranges from 49 per cent in France and Slovenia to 31 per cent in Spain. Both protection of permanent workers and regulation of temporary employment also vary widely across European countries. Belgium, Latvia, and the Netherlands offer the strictest employment protection and the UK has the lightest. Overall, strict regulation for temporary contracts tends to go hand-in-hand with strict regulation for permanent contracts. There are some notable exceptions such as the Netherlands. There are few or no restrictions on the use of temporary contracts in the UK.

The minimum wage regulation and the substantial protection of employees can have both positive and negative economic impact on the level of employment and economic growth. For a long time only the positive impact was emphasized: reduction of poverty and income disparity; protection against severe income losses; quality of employer–employee relationships; efficient job search and employment match. However, in recent decades and particularly after the recent economic crisis of 2007, the negative effects have become increasingly apparent: reduction in the labour demand for low wage, low-skilled individuals; substitution of temporary employees for permanent workers; increase in part-time employment, reduction in the willingness to work and in the incentive to engage in job search; increase in the costs of enterprises; mounting rigidities in the labour market. Particularly, the falling demand for low-skilled workers, the lack of work incentives, and the increase of the labour cost have been often highlighted. These adverse effects of generous and accessible income protection policies are even more serious when income protection policies are loosely structured, poorly integrated or ill managed.

The European example is often contrasted with the United States where the package consists of low minimum wage, modest social protection and few barriers to hiring and firing. Particularly over the last decades, the United States has experienced rapid employment growth and modest wage increases. However, this good performance is contrasted with high levels of poverty among the populations of workers while the high and accessible level of income protection benefits and high minimum wages in Europe have successfully maintained a relative low level of inequality. Figures presented in Chapter 2 for the year 2015 indicate the Gini coefficient for the USA at 39.4 while it is only 25.2 in Sweden and Finland, 26.2 in Belgium, and 29.2 in France. The same holds for poverty rates. They are lower in Europe than in the US.

Since the early 2000s, in Europe, the idea that one cannot avoid the trade-off between the level of minimum income guarantee and the severity of work disincentives has spread. Labour market policy is turning to programs that aim at both making work pay and 'activate' unemployed people to facilitate their professional integration. The aim is to increase the employment opportunities for job seekers and to improve matching between jobs and workers. In a lot of European countries, benefits claiming is now conditioned on employment and targeted at low-income families; this to avoid the unemployment trap. The amount of benefits is decreasing as income is increasing and is conditional on a minimum level of activity. Even countries that were initially reluctant to check whether beneficiaries of unemployment insurance are willing to work, like Belgium or France, have now introduced sanctions for insufficient willingness to work.

Most European countries have gradually developed (or are in the process of developing) activation programs coupled with high work incentives with the stated objective of finding the right mix of labour market flexibility and employment protection. The leading example, which we have mentioned earlier, is the Danish flexicurity model which over recent years has been successful in terms of low unemployment and low poverty. The European Commission has strongly promoted flexicurity in the mid-2000s, even if a series of countries slowed implementation in recent years (mainly because of an increase in inequality and social tensions due to the 2007 crisis). Active labour market policies are now one of the major tools for tackling long-term unemployment.

In addition to activation and the protection of unemployed workers, recent reforms have engaged in reinforcing flexibility to stimulate employment and boost the economy. The question of employment protection is thus becoming central since regulations are thought by many to be a key factor in generating labour market rigidity. However, the net impact of employment protection legislation on aggregate unemployment is theoretically ambiguous. Empirically, minimum wage and employment protection has been shown to be responsible in some cases for high unemployment and joblessness. They can also hurt the employment of youth and prime-age women and contribute to long-term unemployment.

A clear tendency towards reducing the strictness of employment protection is observable and this is also the result of a steady decline in trade union density among European countries. The choice should not be between a high level of employment protection relative to unemployment benefits or vice versa. Those two policies are tightly linked and one cannot discuss them in isolation. Blanchard and Tirole (2004), looking at the French case, recommend adopting a global view where both unemployment insurance and employment protection are considered jointly. They studied employment protection in France where employment regulation is particularly strict and unemployment high. They observed an increasingly dual and unequal labour market with two classes of workers, those on permanent contracts and those on temporary ones. They look for a reform that would allow firms to lay off a worker but make them make a redundancy payment. How does this compare

Unemployment and Poverty

to the way employment protection is currently designed in France? In France, as in a number of other continental European countries, unemployment contributions are collected through a payroll tax, not a lay-off tax. This means that firms that lay off more workers do not pay more. At the same time, the judicial system may prevent firms from laying off workers. Blanchard and Tirole thus suggest a shift from a payroll tax to a lay-off tax, and, in exchange, a reduction in the role of judges. How could it be done? The answer comes from the system of experience rating in the US. The employers' social security contributions are calculated partly on the basis of the lay-off activity of the firm: a firm's tax rate is determined by individual status based on the unemployment insurance benefit paid to workers it has recently laid off. The main motivation of experience rating is to prevent firms from using unemployment insurance as a subsidy for temporary lay-offs and to avoid dual labour markets. Ideally these contributions could go towards the financing of the unemployment insurance system. It has the big advantage holding employers accountable for their decisions.

13.5. The Changing Nature of Employment

One important aspect of the recent evolution of employment in Europe is the dramatic changes in how people work. In addition to the increase of the number of part-time and temporary jobs, two major phenomena increase: the posting of workers and the 'uberization' of employment.

13.5.1. *Posted Workers*

Since the onset of the economic crisis of 2007, there has been an increase in the number of part-time jobs as well as a growth in temporary jobs. Although this form of employment provides more flexibility to employers, it increases job insecurity for workers. Furthermore, these forms of employment may not necessarily give entitlement to social benefits and protection in the same way as do more standard jobs. This may result in a labour market segmentation where some workers, given a more atypical career, increase their risk with regards to social protection and contributions.

As seen above, posted workers are different from regular mobile workers in that they remain in the host country temporarily and do not integrate into its labour market and its social security system. Their status is directly defined by a directive of the European Union that guarantees rights and working conditions throughout the EU and the system has provoked accusations of social dumping. The number of posted workers has increased tremendously in Europe and in 2015 there were around two million workers posted in the

EU. This number indicates the number of social security 'portable documents' that were issued and that indicate that a worker pays social security contributions in another European country. Although this number may appear to be small, the posting of workers has been steadily increasing. On average the number of posted workers has grown by 10 per cent each year since 2010 (De Wispelaere and Pacolet 2015).

Initially, in addition to stimulating intra-European labour mobility, the aim of posting workers was to increase the economic situation of households in economically less-favoured countries. The rules guaranteed an equal or, most of the time, higher income for posted workers compared to what they would be paid in their country of origin. Also, since posted workers pay taxes in their home country, the posting mechanism has become a form of fiscal transfer that may serve as a stabilization tool when the home country experiences economic troubles. However, the mechanism can sometimes be seen as social dumping, which harms social conditions in the host country due to increased competition with countries with lower social protection. Such a risk is likely to be overestimated because the effect on the host country's labour market is limited by the short duration of most postings (which last on average around ninety days).

The main issue with posting workers is that it discriminates among workers in the same country. First, in theory, the posted worker is paid according to the host country's regulations. This means that the worker must be paid at least the host country's minimum wage, which might be lower than the actual wage paid in the relevant sector of activity. Second, the posted worker is not entitled to the same social protection and advantages as resident workers. It means that for exactly the same job, two workers are paid and socially protected differently. In addition to social dumping, this question has been highly debated and has forced the European Union to introduce amendments to the directive that regulates the conditions of posted workers. In 2017, discussions started among European countries to promote equal status for posted workers to improve the ability of employers to compete on an equal basis.

13.5.2. *Uberization and Automation*

Another aspect of today's employment is the growing number of jobs that are related to the use of new technologies and are based on new collaborative economy models. Europe, but also the US, are witnessing a trend towards a new way of producing services. The most visible examples are the companies Airbnb and Uber, which provide platforms to rent apartments and share cars respectively. The last example, gives its name to the term 'uberization', which characterizes this new operational model where people exchange the under-utilized capacity of existing assets or resources while incurring very low transaction costs due to the internet. The cost of finding someone to drive you, cook for you, or accommodate you has fallen dramatically. The advantages for workers are potentially high financial gains due to the lack of regulatory constraints, the instantaneity of the transaction, and the absence of fixed costs.

The effects on employment of this new digital labour market are for now difficult to estimate. Some analysts are pleased with the new opportunities that are created, especially for low-skilled and unskilled workers, while others warn about the insecurity of working conditions. These new technologies are changing the way professional services are delivered and the way employment relationships are organized. They are also changing the relationship between workers and the welfare state and could have enormous consequences for workers' wellbeing and the future of the welfare state as we know it. One of the main problems from a social point of view is the absence of adapted legislation which ensures equal treatment among workers whatever the contractual agreement. Jobs in this new economy are often characterized by insecurity, low pay, and longer work hours. Furthermore, given the totally dematerialized nature of the relationship between employers and employees, it is difficult to assert rights to social security, training or protection. Furthermore, the companies behind the digital platforms can be located in other countries such that profit and the employees' income can easily be hidden from the local tax authorities.

Finally the emergence of these digital labour markets has revived concerns about automation and digitalization and the fact that they might be the death sentence of a large part of current jobs. A recent study based on a series of OECD countries finds that about 9 per cent of jobs are automatable (Arntz et al. 2016). The threat thus seems to be low and it is unlikely that automation will destroy large number of jobs in the future. Although jobs will not entirely disappear, it is likely that low-skilled workers will have to bear the burden of the adjustment cost since their jobs are more automatable than high skilled workers. For the rest, jobs will probably be redefined and news skills will emerge.

13.5.3. *The Universal Basic Income*

Facing the danger of automation and the rise of unemployment, some have brought up to date the idea of a Universal Basic Income. The concept is simple and would consist, in its more extreme form, of a fixed sum of money given to all citizens over the age of 18, free from the necessity of having a paid job. Both those who work and do not work would be entitled to it, whatever their social or family situation. The basic income could replace all, or most, existing benefits by a single payment made unconditionally. Those who support this program point out that the technological development related to automation and digitalization implies that the number of jobs will be significantly reduced, depriving many people of the prospect of paid jobs. Thus it has also been pointed that the program could be at least partially financed through taxation on automated and digitalized activities.

A massive argument in favour of a universal basic income is that such a program could achieve the objectives of the social protection schemes more effectively and at a much reduced administrative cost. Social programs have become very complex and they are often criticized for failing to erase poverty. The universality behind the benefit would be such that even those who work would receive it and all means-tested programs for those who cannot support themselves through paid work would be abolished. The measure would release people from the necessity of having a job and would force employers to revise job quality and working conditions.

Although the idea is appealing, it is far from being economically and politically sustainable. First of all, the choice of the level of the benefit is debatable and it is difficult to correctly assess what amount of money would be appropriate for a basic income. Furthermore, the provision of a universal basic income at a level that would suffice to erase poverty or at least to provide a serious alternative to low-paid jobs is dramatically expensive. Kay (2017) tries to give a simple arithmetic estimation of the cost of a basic income for six countries which have been at the forefront of the basic income debate (see Table 13.4). The level of the basic income comes from a variety of sources that reflect the figures that could prevail in case of adoption of the measure. For example, in France, a benefit of 750 Euros has been proposed by presidential candidate Benoit Hamon. The Swiss figure is that which was put forward for the 2016 referendum. The UK figure is based on the Green Party's 2015 election manifesto. The Finnish figure is that used in the country's current experiment and the US proposal was suggested by a former chief economist at the US Department of Commerce.

The proposals are different between countries and the lowest figures are those from the UK and Finland, where the level of basic income is below

Table 13.4. Basic income estimations

	France	Germany	UK	US	Finland	Switzerland
Proposed basic income (in Euros)	750	664–1500	430	1307	560	2059
Proposed basic income as a % of the median full-time earnings	34	43	18	49	20	43
Proposed basic income as a % of GDP per head	27	32	14	37	17	37
Minimum wage as a % of the median full-time earnings	66	61	56	34	n.a.	n.a.

Source: Kay (2017)

20 per cent of median full-time earnings. In Germany, the US, and Switzerland, the basic income would represent more than 40 per cent of median earnings. Table 13.4 shows also that in terms of the percentage of GDP per head, the basic income proposals represent a rather high fraction of the national income per capital. These figures are also far from the levels of income that are provided by low-paid employment. The provision of income at the same level as the minimum wage would be impossibly expensive. Besides the cost of a basic income scheme that leads to a decent living standard, there is the risk that it would disconnect large chunks of the population from the positive aspects of working for a living.

13.6. In-Work Poverty

On Continental Europe it has been typical to think of the poor as non-working people, such as the unemployed, pensioners, and children—or at least as people whose ability to work is restricted, such as single parents. However, in Europe, a substantial share of the poor work, and a majority of the poor live in households with at least one member working. By 2014, 10 per cent of European workers were considered poor. Having a job is not a sufficient condition to make a living and employment does not always protect from poverty.

Table 13.5 presents some data for the European countries for the year 2015. In the EU28, 9.5 per cent of workers are considered poor but we can see how the prevalence of in-work poverty varies across countries. The extent of poverty among workers ranges from a low 4–5 per cent in Czechia, Belgium, Ireland, and the Netherlands up to 13 per cent in Spain or Greece and almost 19 per cent in Romania.

One clearly sees that employment status (full time or not) is important. Yet even full-time workers can be poor. Does that mean that their wage is insufficient? In part, yes. But the main reason is that they do not live alone. A wage may be quite sufficient for a single individual, but much too low for four-person households even with the appropriate equivalence scale. Most in-work poverty is related to household size and structure. Particularly, in a lot of cases the presence of children increases the risk of poverty even after accounting for child allowances. McKnight et al. (2016) show that the highest in-work poverty is observed for single-parent households. Two main forces explain the higher poverty rates in households with children than households without. One is simply the additional demands on resources in these households. The second is the lower paid work intensity in households with children.

In Table 13.5 we see how poverty is also related to the intensity of work such that the likelihood of a part-time worker being poor is twice as great as a

Table 13.5. In-work poverty in the EU: 2015

Country	Total	According to contract Permanent	According to contract Temporary	According to work time Part-time	According to work time Full-time
Austria	7.9	6.8	12.3	11.1	5.9
Belgium	4.6	2.6	10.4	6.4	3.7
Bulgaria	7.7	5.5	24.7	30.3	6.7
Croatia	5.9	4.2	8.3	20.4	5.4
Cyprus	9.1	6.6	27.3	17.0	7.6
Czech R.	4.0	2.5	7.9	6.3	3.8
Denmark	5.5	3.6	9.8	7.6	4.0
Estonia	10.0	7.1	25.7	18.1	8.9
Finland	3.5	1.8	5.3	9.0	2.9
France	7.5	4.7	13.2	13.2	6.0
Germany	9.7	7.5	18.1	14.5	7.1
Greece	13.4	4.7	15.8	28.2	11.6
Hungary	9.3	6.4	32.0	18.2	8.4
Ireland	4.8	3.1	11.9	9.7	2.9
Italy	11.5	7.8	19.1	18.5	9.8
Latvia	9.2	7.3	26.7	18.4	8.2
Lithuania	9.9	7.6	20.6	28.1	8.6
Luxembourg	11.6	9.5	23.1	16.5	10.0
Malta	5.4	4.6	3.2	14.9	4.7
Netherlands	5.0	3.3	9.9	4.5	4.4
Poland	11.2	5.6	10.8	18.3	10.7
Portugal	10.9	6.5	13.3	29.5	9.6
Romania	18.8	5.1	12.1	59.4	14.7
Slovakia	6.0	2.6	7.6	19.0	5.4
Slovenia	6.7	4.5	12.5	14.6	5.9
Spain	13.1	5.9	23.3	27.1	10.3
Sweden	7.1	5.3	15.9	11.1	6.7
United Kingdom	8.1	5.1	7.3	13.0	5.6
EU 28	9.1	5.7	15.6	15.3	7.7

Notes: poverty is measured as disposable income below 60% of the median income
Source: Eurostat (2017a)

full-time worker, on average in the EU. This picture is true for all countries with poverty rates higher for part-time workers than full-time workers. Unsurprisingly, the poverty rate among part-time workers is much higher in countries where part-time workers are more likely to be primary earners. Frazer and Marlier (2010) point to the link between part-time work and low pay as an explanation for this difference.

Table 13.5 also shows that workers on temporary contracts have a much higher risk of poverty (15.6 per cent in the EU28) than those on permanent contracts (5.7 per cent). This disparity can be largely explained by the difference in wages between temporary and permanent workers, rather than by the individual and household characteristics of those in temporary work. The factors leading temporary workers to poverty are the same as those for workers in general, namely being young, low skilled, and living in a household with greater needs.

Thus low-pay jobs are the main driver of in-work poverty but the different figures indicate also that work intensity, the type of contract, and household structure are also crucial. These three drivers are likely to be associated to each other, and it is the interaction between them that will leave households most vulnerable. This is also why the increase of temporary and part-time jobs is worrying. The huge increase in the use of zero-hours contracts for workers in the UK or the mini job in Germany have attracted a lot of attention.

13.7. Conclusion

We have seen that labour market policies are not just about unemployment insurance. Employment protection and programs that activate workers and ensure their social protection are also important in fighting unemployment. The European figures show big disparities. Some countries have experienced relatively high levels of unemployment while others have been successful in preventing long-term unemployment. One of the main challenges for future policies is to maintain the labour market attachment of those who lose their jobs by preventing the persistence of unemployment. It is crucial to avoid situations in which those losing their jobs find it hard to get back into work. Examples of activation and job search assistance programs have been shown to be effective in that respect.

In this chapter we have also seen that being employed does not mean being out of poverty. Some groups are more vulnerable than others, i.e., the young, women, and the unskilled. The causes can be found in low pay, low work intensity and household composition. It is then important to keep in mind that policies that are designed to improve work incentives will not necessarily address in-work poverty.

Finally, the nature of employment is changing. The 'job for life' as well as the regular full-time job is less and less the norm on the labour market. Social and economic changes have given rise to new forms of working and while some may appear to offer flexibility and security, others may lead to precarity. Collaborative employment, job sharing, new-technology-based employment, among others, are transforming the traditional relationship between employers and employees but they are also changing the way workers are entitled or not to social protection.

14

Family Policy

> **KEY CONCEPTS**
> early child development
> childcare
> family allowance
> parental leave
> child poverty
> horizontal and vertical redistribution
> tax breaks

14.1. Introduction

In this chapter, we study the effect of family allowances on poverty in Europe. While there appears to be a remarkably redistributive effect, family allowances are only one component of child policies. Further their objective is not just poverty alleviation; they also aim to foster female employment and fertility. Sharp differences exist in the level and pattern of child policies across European countries, the Nordic countries leading the pack in terms of generosity. We then move to the issue of early child development, which is considered to be crucial for achieving a successful life. Finally, we address the issue of reconciling parenthood and employment.

14.2. Evolution and Structure of Child Benefits

Family allowances are available in all European countries, although their generosity and their rules of entitlement vary across countries. The share of expenditure on family allowances is far from being as big as that of the big two components of social spending, health and retirement. Yet, as this chapter

Family Policy

shows, its impact on income inequality and poverty is quite impressive. In that respect, family allowances are likely to be one of the most efficient social programs in terms of Euros spent.

In 2014, family/child benefits represented 8.6 per cent of total social benefits in the EU28, placing the function 'Family and children' in third position after 'Old age and survivors' (45.9 per cent) and 'Sickness, healthcare and disability' (36.5 per cent). This share has decreased over the last decades, following variations in the fertility rate and the relative size of the youth population. The relative level of benefits for the family and children varied between countries. It accounted for about 12 per cent or more of total social benefits in Luxembourg (15.6 per cent), Ireland (13.1 per cent) and Hungary (11.9 per cent), but for less than 5 per cent in the Netherlands (3.1 per cent), Greece (4.4 per cent) and Portugal (4.6 per cent). Expenditure above 1,000 euros per inhabitant was registered in Denmark (1,668€), Sweden (1,368€), Finland (1,212€), Germany (1,132€), Austria (1,071€) and Ireland (1,060€). At the opposite end of the scale, expenditure stood below 200 euros per inhabitant in several other poorer countries such as Romania (91€), Bulgaria (112€) and Lithuania (135€). On average in the EU28, expenditure on family/child benefits amounted to 651€ per inhabitant.

Though the data used in international comparisons covers not only family allowances, but also other transfers, such as maternity benefits, but, in this chapter, we focus on family allowances *sensu stricto*, that is, the universal benefit paid to the parents (often the mother) or the guardian of dependent children. Within this narrower definition, Ireland, Luxembourg, Austria, the UK and Germany are the biggest spenders (in per cent of GDP), and Spain, the smallest, as shown in Table 14.1.

In most countries, child allowances are universal; most often benefits increase with the number of children and with the age of the child. There are few cases of means-tested benefits. Even though, today, everyone agrees that the main function of family allowances is to help families with children—that is to avoid child poverty and to implement some horizontal redistribution between families with and without children—it was introduced in some countries as a way of encouraging fertility. France is typical of such a dual approach; family allowances only start after the second child.

What the ideal pattern of family allowances in relation to age, family size, and income should be is not clear. Public finance is astonishingly silent on this matter. The main lesson that emerges from the existing scanty work is that family allowances cannot just be restricted to horizontal equity; they also affect vertical redistribution in a world where redistributive taxation is heavily constrained. Political science and political economy have emphasized the key role of universal family allowances in terms of political support for the welfare state. Indeed, flat-rate family allowances represent one of the few programs

Table 14.1. Family allowances and tax breaks in 2014

	Family allowances (% of GDP)		Tax breaks for families (% of GDP)
	Sensu largo	Sensu stricto	
Austria	2.8	2.0	0.04
Belgium	2.2	1.8	0.52
Bulgaria	1.9	1.2	–
Croatia	1.5	1.2	–
Cyprus	1.4	1.2	–
Czechia	1.7	1.5	0.94
Denmark	3.5	1.4	0.00
Estonia	1.6	1.6	0.16
Finland	3.2	1.5	0.00
France	2.5	1.6	0.78
Germany	3.1	2.0	0.94
Greece	1.1	1.0	–
Hungary	2.3	1.8	0.69
Ireland	2.5	2.2	0.10
Italy	1.6	1.3	0.55
Latvia	1.3	1.0	–
Lithuania	1.1	0.8	–
Luxembourg	3.5	2.6	0.00
Malta	1.2	1.0	–
Netherlands	0.9	0.6	0.47
Poland	1.5	0.8	0.48
Portugal	1.2	0.7	0.22
Romania	1.2	0.8	–
Slovakia	1.7	1.5	0.00
Slovenia	1.9	1.3	0.00
Spain	1.3	0.5	0.12
Sweden	3.1	1.4	0.00
United Kingdom	2.8	2.2	0.17
United States	1.2	0.1	0.50

Source: Eurostat (2017c) and OECD (2016c)

that reach a wide range of social groups. This holds in particular for the middle-aged and well-to-do healthy households that do not draw any benefits from unemployment, health care, social security, or welfare programs. This positive and non-normative argument explains, in part, why the French government decided a decade ago to drop the means-tested benefit rule and revert to universalism.

Family allowances are also to be contrasted with the use of children's allowances as part of the direct tax system. Table 14.1 presents those tax advantages as a percentage of GDP. They are nil in Nordic countries and relatively high in Germany, Czechia, and France. Family allowances are more egalitarian than these tax advantages, as the poorest parents may lack sufficient income to benefit from them. At the same time, family allowances, being tax-exempt, are criticized as favouring the top income brackets subject to high marginal tax rates. There is an interesting comparison[1] between Germany and France, which takes into account both tax privileges and family allowances, and shows how they differ between the two countries for different family size and different earnings structure. The reference income is the average income in both countries.

Child allowances represent a large part of benefit spending. Given that in France they are only awarded for 2 children and more, the largest marginal advantage is for having one child in Germany and three in France. Benefits are also relatively higher for couples with one earner than for couples with two earners. This raises a key question. If one believes that family benefits hardly affect fertility and have mainly a redistributive impact, why is there discrimination against one-child families? At the same time, the low fertility rate observed in Germany relative to France seems to indicate that family allowances might have an enhancing effect.

14.3. Child Poverty

Children are generally at a higher risk of poverty than the population as a whole. In addition, child poverty trends have for the most part not been favourable over the past decade. The latest 2015 EU-SILC data shows that between 2005 and 2015 the at-risk-of child poverty rate increased in 16 out of 25 countries (EU28 minus Croatia, Bulgaria and Romania). Child poverty rates rose particularly in Sweden, France, Greece, and Spain.

Poverty gaps (the gap between net income and the poverty threshold) for children have also risen between 2005 and 2015 in most European countries. This deteriorating situation is of course the result of rising unemployment, even though a sizeable minority of poor children live in households with all working age members in employment. Table 14.3 provides the poverty rates of children. They range from 32 in Romania to 7.6 in Denmark. Finland also has a rate below 10 (9.3). And Bulgaria, Croatia, Greece, Hungary, Italy, Latvia, Lithuania, Luxembourg, Malta, Poland, Portugal, Romania, and Spain have rates above 20 per cent. These are countries from the South and from the East.

We are interested in the impact of family allowances on poverty. We distinguish the effect of family allowances on the poverty rate for the whole population and for the children. Clearly, the incidence of family allowances depends on three factors: the generosity of the program, the rules of entitlement, and the correlation between income and family size.

Table 14.2 gives the actual poverty rates in EU28 and the hypothetical rates, assuming that there were no family allowances. The difference is an indicator of

---

[1] Meister and Ochel (2003).

Table 14.2. Family allowances and poverty: 2014

Country	With allowances	Without allowances	Efficiency score
Austria	14.4	22.2	7.8
Belgium	15.0	19.5	4.5
Bulgaria	21.0	23.2	2.2
Croatia	19.5	25.1	5.6
Cyprus	15.3	19.6	4.3
Czechia	8.6	13.5	4.9
Denmark	11.7	13.3	1.7
Estonia	18.5	20.1	1.7
Finland	11.8	18.8	7.0
France	13.7	19.3	5.6
Germany	15.9	20.6	4.7
Greece	22.7	23.7	1.0
Hungary	14.3	24.7	10.4
Ireland	14.1	26.8	12.7
Italy	19.0	21.8	2.8
Latvia	19.3	21.0	1.7
Lithuania	20.5	23.7	3.2
Luxembourg	15.7	26.5	10.9
Malta	15.7	19.6	3.9
Netherlands	10.2	13.9	3.6
Norway	10.8	16.0	5.1
Poland	17.3	21.4	4.1
Portugal	18.7	20.1	1.4
Romania	22.4	26.3	4.0
Slovakia.	12.8	17.9	5.1
Slovenia	14.5	20.6	6.1
Spain	20.2	20.5	0.2
Sweden	14.6	18.6	4.0
UK	15.7	24.8	9.1

Source: Authors' calculations from EU-SILC data

the efficiency of family allowances at reducing poverty. That efficiency score varies a lot, ranging from 12.7 in Ireland to 0.2 in Spain. More specifically, we can distinguish a group of countries with high efficiency: Ireland, Belgium, Luxembourg, France and the UK, and countries with low efficiency: Sweden, Denmark, Finland, Germany and the Netherlands. Note that the efficiency of family allowances is not closely correlated with the before-allowance poverty rates nor with the generosity of the system. The benefit structure plays an important role.

Table 14.3 focuses on the poverty rate among children. One notes that these poverty rates are generally higher than those observed in the whole population. As to the efficiency scores, they are consistently higher for children than for the whole population, as expected. Those scores are particularly high in Austria, Belgium, Croatia, Finland, Germany, Hungary, Ireland, Luxembourg, and the UK. They are low in the Scandinavian countries, Germany, and the Netherlands. Spain has again an extremely low score. In fact, we have the same clustering as observed for the whole population, but the differences here are sharper.

Family Policy

Table 14.3. Family allowances and poverty among children: 2014

Country	With allowances	Without allowances	Efficiency score
Austria	19.1	44.5	25.4
Belgium	17.2	33.9	16.7
Bulgaria	28.6	37.9	9.3
Croatia	21.9	38.8	16.8
Cyprus	15.6	27.1	11.5
Czechia	10.9	25.1	14.2
Denmark	7.6	16.5	8.9
Estonia	17.9	32.8	14.9
Finland	9.3	35.3	26.0
France	17.9	34.5	16.6
Germany	14.4	36.1	21.6
Greece	28.4	34.6	6.2
Hungary	23.3	53.6	30.4
Ireland	15.8	40.6	24.8
Italy	24.7	33.0	8.4
Latvia	22.6	31.9	9.3
Lithuania	26.8	39.5	12.7
Luxembourg	23.6	51.1	27.5
Malta	24.1	33.9	9.8
Netherlands	12.6	24.2	11.6
Norway	10.2	25.0	14.8
Poland	22.9	32.1	9.2
Portugal	24.1	28.7	4.6
Romania	32.0	42.9	10.9
Slovakia	19.9	35.1	15.1
Slovenia	14.8	34.0	19.3
Spain	26.9	27.7	0.8
Sweden	15.1	31.6	16.6
UK	18.7	44.0	25.4

Source: Autors' calculations from EU-SILC data

Caution is needed in interpreting those numbers. First, as already seen, there are other ways of helping children: tax credits, maternity leave, housing subsidies, day care, which are not studied here. These other benefits, which are important in Scandinavian countries, explain why in these countries the rate of poverty of children is low even before introducing family allowances (*sensu stricto*). Secondly, efficiency depends on the generosity of the program; in other words one has to take into account the expenditure per child. In that respect, one can contrast Denmark with an efficiency score of 8.9 and generous family allowances with Ireland, that spends much less and yet exhibits an efficiency score of 24.8.

14.4. Early Child Development Policies

To a large extent, the focus on child poverty can be misleading. Most importantly, the way child poverty is measured is questionable. Typically, one takes the income of the household to which the child belongs and if that income, adjusted for the size of the family, is below the poverty line, then the child is considered to be poor. This implies that the parents are loving parents who will devote a fair amount of resources to their children. There are many cases of children who are not statistically poor but that do not receive proper care from lack of love or information. Take the example of increasing child obesity that affects kids from the middle class. By contrast, some families that are considered as poor can provide their children appropriate care and values that lay the foundations for later success in life, both in terms of well-being and social integration.

Recent research has pointed out the importance of early child development. The emotional, social and physical development of young children has a direct effect on their overall development and on the adult they will become. That is why investing in very young children is so important, so as to maximize their future well-being. James Heckman, Nobel Laureate in Economics, in his ground-breaking work with a consortium of economists, psychologists, statisticians, and neuroscientists shows that early childhood development directly influences economic, health and social outcomes for individuals and society. Adverse early environments create deficits in skills and abilities that drive down productivity and increase social costs—thereby adding to financial deficits borne by the public. As a result, he advocates proactive policies to enhance child development observing that the 'short-term costs (such policies involve) are more than offset by the immediate and long-term benefits through reduction in the need for special education and remediation, better health outcomes, reduced need for social services, lower criminal justice costs and increased self-sufficiency and productivity among families.[2]

Such policies should cater to children from disadvantaged backgrounds but not just them. It is thus important to analyse the education and care systems for young children (from birth to compulsory school age) in different countries. It is interesting to observe wide discrepancies in the way these countries are cooperating to develop high-quality and accessible provision across Europe. A recent study by the European Commission (2014) analyses the extent of formal programs providing early childhood education and care. On average participation among children under 3 is very low. Only a minority of countries has reached the target of 33 per cent. Denmark stands out with 74 per cent. The Netherlands and Sweden have a participation rate slightly above 50 per cent. They are followed by Belgium, Spain, France, Luxembourg, Iceland and Norway with rates around 40 per cent. The majority of countries are below the rate of 33 per cent of children under 3, which was chosen as a target.

---

[2] Heckmann (2012).

14.5. Types of Child Care Policies

Although policies and instruments in support of families may seem wide-ranging, their main goal, regardless of the country in question, can be summarized as creating favourable framework conditions for families through financial support, facilitating a work–family balance, and providing access to childcare.[3] Public support for families is designed as an essential tool to counter the adverse consequences of demographic changes to labour markets and social security systems in developed countries. Thus, policy instruments aim to increase fertility and female labour market participation. The type of support that is available for families varies greatly across countries. Key instruments include, for example, child-related leave entitlements, childcare services and direct or indirect subsidies for families (such as childcare benefits, tax benefits) or flexible working measures for working parents.

Childcare policies are often viewed as the most efficient way to encourage both fertility and female employment. They usually take three forms: publicly funded child care, replacement income for parents who temporarily quit their job in order to take care of their infant (parental leave), and financial support to help parents deal with child expenses (family allowances and tax benefits). In a quite original paper, de Henau et al. (2005) assess the relative generosity of child policies in EU15 and they also evaluate to what extent these policies are what they call 'dual-earner-family-friendly'.

Their research is based on an in-depth collection and aggregation of data. They provide a ranking of countries based on the three fields of child policy. It allows for some interesting comparisons. The Nordic countries are the most generous as regards childcare. Considering that their generosity scores regarding parental leave and, above all, cash and tax benefits are rather low, we can conclude that they have clearly chosen to support working families with children by focusing on public child care systems. When looking at the combined index, these Nordic countries ranked well.

At the other extreme, in the bottom ranks of the combined index, one finds the Southern countries (Portugal, Spain and Greece) and the two Anglo-Saxon countries. These also are the 'usual suspects'. Italy can be distinguished from the other countries of the South of Europe, particularly as regards child-care programs. France and Belgium are ranked at the top. France leads for its generosity towards parental leave, but surprisingly is not well ranked for cash and tax benefits. The reason is that France grants no cash benefits for the first child in the family.

---

[3] Gornick and Meyers (2003).

Table 14.4. Index of family-related policies

Country	Index
Denmark	96
Sweden	92
Finland	79
Belgium	75
France	69
Netherlands	69
Luxembourg	69
Germany	63
UK	45
US	29

Source: Gornick and Meyers (2003)

These numbers show sharp differences in the level and in the type of generosity of European family policies and these differences reflect the complexity of the issue. The policies pursue different objectives: poverty alleviation, horizontal equity, female employment, and fertility. Regarding the latter, the conventional wisdom is that public child-care facilities are a more efficient tool than family allowances. One clear objective of family-related policies is to ensure a balance between work and family. Gornick and Meyers (2003) have constructed an index of the relative performance of such policies in different countries. They consider policies in two groups: those potentially affecting families with children from birth to the age of five and those affecting families with school-age children. For the first group they consider public early childhood education and care, family leave policy and working time. For the second group the variables are school schedules, relevant leave policies and working-time regulation. The ranking that is presented on Table 14.4 is not surprising. Denmark, Sweden, and Norway rank the highest. Most of the continental European countries cluster together at a lower rank, despite strong working-time regulations, primarily. The English-speaking countries, particularly the US and Canada lag behind the European countries.

14.6. Conclusion

In this chapter we have studied the effect of family allowances on poverty in a number of European countries. The first conclusion is that their effect is quite remarkable in some countries, particularly when focusing on poverty among children.

The second conclusion is that a large part of this effect is merely due to the amount of money that is spent. At the same time, we observe that after controlling for spending, alternative benefit applied to the same income distribution yield about the same scores. This implies that what really matters are not the differences in benefit rules, but the differences in the relative position of families with children with respect to the poverty line. In other words, family allowances are particularly efficient in countries where a number of families have their income slightly below the poverty level. As to benefits per se, they have a different incidence when they do treat all children equally, and family patterns vary.

15

Conclusion

15.1. Two Views

As often mentioned, there are as many welfare states as there are states. However, it might be interesting to contrast two canonical welfare states: the British and the French one. In the UK, the Conservative governments of Margaret Thatcher, first, and of John Major, later, have introduced drastic and painful reforms into the British welfare state. The power of the unions was broken and a number of social programs were abandoned, or tendered out to the private sector. As a result, one has the feeling that compared not only to France but also to a number of other European countries, the UK is today quite different in its attitude towards entitlements, assistance, and labour participation.

In the UK, a number of pressure groups with entrenched interests have lost ground. Entitlements have been restricted. The idea that income support ought to be limited in time is becoming prevalent. The perspective of welfare recipients has changed, particularly with regard to the vision of what recipients need to do for themselves, relative to what the state will do for them. More persistent job-search activities are in evidence. There is a wider acceptance of a labour market that generates high-variance wage and earnings distributions. In that respect, Tony Blair's 'New Contract for Welfare' was typical. It placed much of the responsibility for income support for families with low earnings capacity on their own efforts in the private labour market.

This apparent change in attitude and perspective is unthinkable in France. Since the start of the Fifth Republic, either conservative or socialist governments have ruled France. Right or left were equally conservative towards their social institutions and neither one has been able to modernize French society, particularly in terms of breaking their 'dependency' on public transfers and a number of privileges. There have been several attempts to reform some aspects of social protection by making it more sustainable and equitable. But most often governments had to back down after several weeks of strikes for the vested interests were too powerful at blocking reforms. The current president, Emmanuel Macron, might succeed where his as predecessors have failed but it much too early to say.

We do not want to suggest that everything is fine in the UK and bad in France. Hopefully, so far, France has been able to avoid tragic situations *à la* David Blake[1], who was denied employment and support allowance despite his doctor finding him unfit to work. He ended as a consequence suffering from a deadly heart attack. The HDI, the UNDP indicator of welfare still puts France at the top of its ranking. Our indicator of performance, presented in Chapter 8, also puts France ahead of the UK. We are merely conveying the idea, often heard in the UK, that the Labour Party is grateful to the Conservatives for having done the dirty job for them, and that some French socialists would have liked their political opponents to have done the same.

We firmly believe that most European countries need to go through a painful process of reform. And that basically amounts to breaking some vicious circles caused by entrenched interests, acquired rights, entitlements, and persistent assistance. We believe that a drastic purge, such as the one experienced by the British, could be avoided, and that the same effects could be obtained more smoothly. Yet, unfortunately, it is not impossible that some countries will be forced to 'lose weight' through a severe and harsh medical treatment, rather than through a progressive and reasonable diet.

15.2. The Acquired Rights Issue

There is a wide consensus that the main difficulty facing the welfare state is within itself. Clearly, the issues of ageing, declining growth, globalization, family splits, increasing dependence, and disincentives are real ones. But they can be solved with an appropriate reform of social protection. In other words, they can be solved if the welfare state can evolve and move away from sectors or people who are no longer in need.

Unfortunately, we live in a world where people feel entitled to benefits even when they have not contributed to them, and when they have enough resources to do without them. Examples of what is often called acquired rights are numerous. To recap, these are rights which at one time were given to a category of people in order to meet particular and legitimate needs, but which have lost that legitimacy because those needs have disappeared, or have been eclipsed by other priorities. Such illegitimate entitlements might be, for example, rent control regulations when most of the beneficiaries are middle- and upper-middle class,

---

[1] Daniel Blake is a 2016 drama film directed by Ken Loach.

pension regimes that involve benefits well above the young age earnings, agricultural policy that benefits well-to-do farmers.

The removal of such entitlements is essential in order to bring fairness into the working of the welfare state, and above all, to provide it with additional resources. But caution is needed. Before assessing that an entitlement is illegitimate, one has to make sure that it is not the outcome of a commitment made behind the veil of ignorance to protect individuals against a reversal of fortune. What makes an entitlement illegitimate is that the law of probabilities, or the economic setting on which it was initially based, has changed significantly. Such changes could be an unexpected increase in longevity, a new medical technology, or an economic depression, which makes former commitments difficult or impossible to meet. This argument leads us to have reserves towards grandfathering in case of reforms. To take the example of pension policy reform, the grandfather clause implies that the old rule continues to apply to the current pensioners while the new rule will apply to all future pensioners. Those exempt from the new rule are said to have been grandfathered in and this delays the effects of the reform.

15.3. Towards a European Social Protection

We have observed a limited tendency towards convergence in spending levels, and in the broad structure of provision. Mediterranean countries with Social-Democratic governments have increased their level of spending, while at least some Northern governments have put a cap on it. There is also some narrowing of the gap between Bismarckian and Beveridgean social insurance systems.

It is unclear how far this trend will go towards eroding the disparity between welfare and social insurance systems. As long as standards of living are different across European countries—and they should remain so for some time—it is not realistic to expect complete convergence in the near future. Some people advocate a voluntarist policy of harmonization, if not uniformization, of social protection systems. In so doing, they cannot expect low-income countries to afford the same generous programs as the high-income countries. Consequently, to be implemented, harmonizing social protection in the EU requires some important revenue sharing, but this is unlikely to be affordable, both politically and financially. This observation holds true even were the demand for harmonization to be cast in relative, rather than in absolute terms, that is to say, if social benefits vary across countries according to national median income.

It is clear that with increasing mobility, schemes providing benefits on the basis of work records are less exposed to erosion than schemes granting uniform or means-tested benefits. There is thus a case for organizing welfare programs at the European level so that we avoid the undeniable inflow of welfare recipients into the most generous countries, and ultimately a race to the bottom resulting in the death of welfare programs. Indeed, one likely outcome of economic integration and mobility, in the absence of supranational intervention or international cooperation, is the generalization of Bismarckian systems, that is, systems that provide earnings-related benefits.

If national governments really come under pressure, particularly through the electoral process, to reduce that part of social spending that is essentially redistributive, there may arise a demand for a European safety net, that is, a minimum standard for social protection.

15.4. Looking Ahead: Two Challenges

Looking ahead, we see two big challenges for the welfare state: fighting the social divide and coping with the digital revolution.

15.4.1. *Digital Revolution*

For the welfare state, the current digital revolution is like Aesop's tongue, the best and the worst thing. The best because through digitalization governments can potentially conduct current policies more effectively and perhaps before too long, design policy in new ways.[2] They can have better information, build better systems, and design and implement better policies. Hopefully tax evasion and avoidance will decrease. On the spending side, one can hope to expand benefit coverage. Attempts to fight poverty through redistribution are often thwarted by the failure of many eligible citizens to register for benefits. Non-take-up rates can be high. If information about individuals is synchronized across public agencies and employers, changes in individual circumstances automatically captured in these data could immediately trigger coverage and benefit payment without requiring lengthy and possibly stigmatizing procedures for proving eligibility.

So far we have evoked the rosy side of the digital revolution, including in that concept artificial intelligence and robots. Its dark side pertains to its expected effects on income distribution and on compliance with social regulations. The question is what happens in an economy in which suddenly you introduce this capital (robots) that is productive enough to compete with humans. The clear-cut effect is that productivity increases, but at the same

---

[2] Gupta et al. (2017).

time, one can expect a fall in wages and a rise of inequality as the owners of robots will cash most of those productivity gains[3].

Europe has seen dramatic changes in how people work. Many more people have part-time or temporary jobs, or are self-employed. These shifts that mainly come from the digital economy provide a hint of the 'future of work,' and have enormous consequences for people's wellbeing, as well as for the survival of the welfare system. These new workers do not have any job security or much coverage from the social welfare system. The digital economy, including the sharing economy (Uber, AirBnb, etc), generates a blurring of job types and categories that makes enforcement of labour laws very difficult. A number of studies have found widespread abuse, with businesses treating many types of workers as self-employed in order to avoid paying social security contributions and providing them job security. Further to make matters more complicated, the digital economy makes it much easier to locate and temporarily hire self-employed freelancers instead of permanent workers. That further reduces economic stability.

15.4.2. *The Social Divide*

The greatest problem our societies are facing is undoubtedly its growing social divide, namely the widening gap between more-and less-educated individuals, as evidenced by indicators of social well-being, including marriage, parenting, employment, crime, civic engagement and basic trust. It threatens to permanently split societies into groups of haves and have-nots, the latter lacking strong families and tightly knit communities that endow the former. Because this gap in welfare correlates with a gap in income, the two are often seen as the same problem. Policymakers focus on increasing economic resources for low-income households, hoping to close the divide. But that amalgamation is a mistake and leads to sterile proposals. Social divide and income inequality are simply not the same thing. As a number of studies have indicated, the social divide is multi-causal. Lack of financial resources can explain the feeling of rejection but this is not the only cause. One can also cite the feeling, real or not, of being deprived of medical facilities, good schools, internet access, the right connections, a gratifying occupation, and good health. Further, there is a dynamic dimension: people compare their current status with the one they or their parents had before.[4]

Working conditions are particularly important. Money cannot replace the social stigma and economic consequences associated with not working or having a precarious job. Ensuring that even those with very low human

---

[3] Berg et al. (2016).   [4] Chauvel (2016).

capital enter and remain in the workforce offers one of the best leverage points for breaking the cycle of social decay. A job provides not just a wage, but also structure, skills, and social engagement. New policies should aim to make work pay, not paying regardless of work. The proponents of the basic income often forget this point. Also it is important that none feels rejected because of his location, gender, or origin. Quite clearly, to address the social divide, one needs to renew the toolbox of the social planner. Fighting poverty and inequality remains important. Ensuring full employment with gratifying jobs is essential. But this is not enough. It is also crucial to reconcile those who feel abandoned with their political and social leaders and give them adequate empowerment to find room in society.

15.5. Wrapping Up

It is now time to wrap up the main ideas of this book. We view the welfare state as an institution aimed at reducing poverty and providing protection to all. Yet the welfare state is not the only institution doing that. The market and the family can do it but with their own limitations: the market does not redistribute; the family lacks universality. The action of the welfare state is not restricted to one of spending; it operates also through laws and regulations that affect market and family decisions (minimum wage, parental duties). So far, the welfare state has been working quite well. It has reduced uncertainty and poverty. It has had positive effects on growth. At the same time the setting in which it now operates is different from what it was fifty years ago when it was initiated. Now it operates within a context of:

- family break-ups;
- tax competition and globalization;
- evolving labour markets;
- various sources of social divide.

The actors of the welfare state behave according to their own incentive structure, and that leads to productive and distributive inefficiencies. Funds are not always allocated to those who should benefit from them, and more and better services could be produced with fewer resources. All these factors, including new settings and inefficient behaviour patterns, lead one to wonder whether the welfare state has not evolved like a dinosaur, increasingly ill adjusted to the surrounding world. Yet there is a difference: a world without dinosaurs happens to be quite habitable. On the other hand without a welfare state, our society might well change for the worse. In any case, without going that far, these factors do put a heavy pressure on the welfare state, calling for reforms ranging from complete dismantlement to shallow plastic changes.

From the viewpoint of public economics, the reforms should include playing on the complementariness of the market and of the informal sector, changing the benefit rule so as to avoid costly Bismarckian schemes or means-tested programs. This viewpoint is sometimes perceived as naive or technocratic because it neglects the political dimension. More specifically, it is important to ensure political support to sustain a program, and to take into account political resistance from entrenched interests to any reform.

In theory, one can design a means-tested program that takes into account the problems raised by people who try to abuse the system on the grounds that the government cannot screen those who need assistance and those who do not. Yet in practice, because of a lack of political support, such a program will be progressively dismantled. In the final analysis, the poor will get less from it than from a program yielding uniform benefits to all.

In designing a viable program, it is crucial to incorporate those political constraints. It is just as important to be watchful so as not to end up with a program that is politically resistant, but does nothing or very little to help the needy. It is our view that there is always a cost in keeping social programs alive that don't effectively fulfil their basic objectives. Indeed, if the private sector does as well; these social programs had better be dropped.

Another equally important consideration is that of the implications for the future. When designing a program, with the understanding that some of its benefits go to the non-needy, one has to control for the possibility of demographic or social changes that enable vested interests to divert the program from its original purpose. The reform of the welfare state is not an easy task. It consists of delicate choices. The first concern is the adding of non-needy beneficiaries for the purpose of ensuring political support, and not for their own sake. It is important to check that the program does not lose its impact.

The second delicate choice concerns commitment. It is essential that the welfare state be committed to fulfilling some tasks. Individuals want to count on social protection programs in the future, but at the same time they need to accept that some of them are contingent on demographic, economic, or technological changes. In other words, 'yes' to commitment to principles but 'no' to specific spending. How can one reasonably promise a constant 75 per cent replacement ratio to retirees or full coverage of heart transplants in an evolving world? Fulfilling these promises can turn out to be socially inefficient because of other more pressing priorities.

Let us finally dare to make three recommendations. First, let us conduct a relentless fight against inefficiency. Secondly, let us retarget the priorities of the welfare state towards redistribution and poverty alleviation through programs offering uniform benefits to all. Access to supplementary schemes should be facilitated to allow reasonable replacement ratios to those who can afford them. Finally, let us avoid commitments that lead to unaffordable entitlements by making benefits contingent.

These reforms are urgent. Unfortunately, they do not look that way to the individual citizen. Nor do they look urgent to politicians who keep having a short run accounting view instead of a long run generational view of financial balances. Indeed, waiting for a crisis to force people to accept a long overdue reform is a mistake—not necessarily a deadly mistake, but at least a costly one. The welfare state is not a dinosaur, but it might become a Titanic. The icebergs are gleaming threateningly ahead. There is still time to avoid them.

Glossary

Active welfare state Social policy aiming for an active and responsible society while maintaining the objective of adequate social protection. The objective is a stronger integration between social, fiscal and employment policies.

Actuarial principle Applied to social protection finance, it means that the contribution (premium) is determined by the size of the expected benefit to be received.

Adverse selection The situation that occurs when the people most likely to receive benefits from a certain type of insurance are the most likely ones to purchase it. The problem can be overcome by making insurance mandatory, if possible. And if not, by policies targeted toward specific risk groups.

Altruism Concern for the well-being of others, as opposed to self-interest.

Annuity A payment that lasts until recipient's death.

Basic income It is a form of social scheme in which all citizens or residents of a country receive a regular, unconditional sum of money, either from a government or some other public institution, independent of any other income.

Best practice frontier The curve showing the maximum amount of production that can be achieved with given resources. It is constructed on the basis of a sample of production units.

Beveridgean A Beveridgean system of social protection provides flat rate benefits that are funded from general government revenues and cover the entire population.

Bismarckian A Bismarckian system of social protection provides benefits that are earnings related. It is based on compulsory funding by employers and employees. The benefit rights are associated with labour status and are not universal.

Capitation-based reimbursement A system in which medical care is provided to a set of individuals for a fixed monthly fee.

Categorical benefits These benefits are provided to individuals who belong to a specific category, or who meet specific eligibility criteria.

Child care Care provided for children by someone other than the parents of those children.

Co-insurance rate The proportion of costs above the deductible for which an insured individual is liable.

Glossary

Convergence Convergence (also sometimes known as the catching-up effect) is the hypothesis that per capita incomes tend to grow at faster rates in poorer economies than in richer economies.

Copayment It is a form of cost sharing for health services or prescription drugs between insurance companies and the insured. It is a flat fee payment unlike coinsurance that is a percentage of the cost for a health service or prescription drug paid by a member after they have reached their deductible.

Cost-based reimbursement A system in which health care providers report their costs to the government and receive payment in that amount.

Commitment The capacity of policymakers to announce policy in advance and to stick to it regardless of changes in the economic environment, or in individual expectations.

Constitutional approach A two-stage collective decision process. In the first stage, the 'rules of game', namely the constitution, are chosen behind the veil of ignorance, so to speak. In the second stage decisions are made through the political process.

Consumer's surplus It refers to the area under an individual's demand curve that measures the benefit derived from buying a commodity at a particular price.

Deadweight loss Also called excess-burden, it refers to the loss in revenue brought about by a distortionary tax relative to a lump-sum tax for the same reduction in utility.

Decommodification Applied to social protection, it means that benefits and services provided by the welfare state are given as a right, not in exchange for past contributions.

Defined benefit A provision of a pension scheme by which the benefits to be received by the pensioner do not depend on the financial performance of the pension scheme.

Defined contribution A provision of a pension scheme by which the rules fix the contributions to the scheme; the benefit depends on the contribution plus the investment return.

Dependency ratio The ratio of people aged 65+ over to those aged between 20 and 64.

Distortionary tax A tax that affects the individual's economic behaviour and causes a deadweight loss.

Early child development It encompasses physical, socio emotional, cognitive, and motor development between 0–8 years of age. These early years are critical, because this is the period in life when the brain develops most rapidly and has a high capacity for change, and the foundation is laid for health and wellbeing throughout life.

Early retirement age Earliest age at which a public pension recipient can receive reduced benefits.

Earning income tax credit The EITC is essentially a subsidy to the earnings of low-income families which enables the working poor to escape poverty while it improves their work incentives. However, because of the need to phase out this subsidy when earnings are high enough, the EITC creates disincentives to work for people in the phase-out range.

Earnings-related benefits Applied to a social insurance program, this means that the amount of benefits or services is related to the level of contributions, themselves linked to earnings. (Also called Bismarckian.)

Effective retirement age The actual retirement age taking into account early retirement and special regimes.

Efficiency or Pareto efficiency An allocation of resources is (Pareto) efficient if no person can be made better off, without making some else being worse off.

Entitlement principle A principle which holds that individuals are to be regarded as entitled to the rights of benefits or property so long as these are obtained by legitimate means. The adoption of such a principle can severely limit the capacity of government when the circumstances in which the rights were granted change 'unexpectedly.'

Entitlement programs Programs whose expenditures are determined by the number of people who qualify, rather than by preset budget allocations.

Equity Also called distributive equity, it implies an idea of fairness or justice regarding the manner in which the economy's resources are distributed among individuals.

Equity-efficiency trade-off The choice society must make between the total size of the economic pie and its distribution among individuals.

Equity premium paradox This refers to the long-term historical regularity that the equity market has significantly outperformed the bond market, even after adjusting for risk.

Equivalence scale A weighting factor applied to the income of households of different sizes; it allows for a comparison of income that one calls adjusted or standardized income.

Experience rating Calculation of contributions based on the lay-off activity of the firm. More generally, making the price of an insurance a function of realized outcomes.

Exchange motive It is a motive provided to justify the phenomenon of intergenerational transfers of wealth. Potential beneficiaries must render a (non-marketable) service in exchange for the promise of inherited wealth.

Family allowance The benefit paid to the parents (sometimes the mother) or guardian of dependent children. They are a universal benefit in contrast with the US AFDC (Aid to Families with Dependant Children), which is a means-tested program targeted on needier families.

Family norm These are informal understandings that govern the behaviour of members of a family.

Fiscalization A movement of social protection financing from (earmarked) payroll taxation to general taxation.

Glossary

Flat rate benefits All who qualify receive the same amount of benefits or the same services, thus not related to earnings or contributions. (Also called universalistic or Beveridgean).

Flexicurity It is an integrated strategy for enhancing, at the same time, flexibility and security in the labour market. It attempts to reconcile employers' need for a flexible workforce with workers' need for security—confidence that they will not face long periods of unemployment.

Fully-funded scheme A scheme in which individuals contribute a portion of their salaries into a fund that accumulates interest over time. In retirement, pension benefits are financed by the principal and accrued interest.

Gini coefficient A measure of inequality that ranges from 0 to 1, and is equal to twice the area between the 45 degree line and Lorenz curve.

HDI The Human Development Index (HDI) is a composite index of life expectancy, education, and per capita income indicators, which is used to assess the level of human development of a country.

Health Maintenance Organization (HMO) Health care organization that integrates insurance and delivery of care by, for example, paying its own doctors and hospitals a salary independent of the amount of care they deliver.

Informal care It involves any person, such as a family member, friend or neighbour, who is giving regular, ongoing assistance to another person without payment for the care given.

In kind transfers In-kind benefits, unlike cash transfers, are not paid directly in cash, but in the form of goods or services for free or at a reduced rate. In-kind programs are deemed 'paternalistic' because they dictate that people spend assistance money on things governments deem most necessary.

In-work poverty It concerns individuals living in households where the household income is below the poverty threshold despite one member of the household working either full or part time.

Involuntary unemployment The unemployment, which is not desired by the unemployed person (contrasted with voluntary unemployment).

Leaky bucket Metaphor introduced by Arthur Okun illustrating the loss of efficiency inherent in the redistribution process.

Long-term care insurance puzzle In almost every country, very few people are insured against the risk of old-age dependence costs, and yet, as for the purchase of annuities, it would seem so rational to purchase an insurance against LTC, on the grounds that this is a protection against a risk that is sizeable and increasing.

Lorenz curve A curve that shows the cumulative proportion of income that goes to each cumulative proportion of the population, starting with the lowest income group.

Lump of labour fallacy This concerns the statement that the quantity of labour required in an overall economy is fixed. It is regarded as fallacious, as the consensus view is that the quantity of labour demanded varies with respect to many factors.

Glossary

Lump-sum tax A tax that has no effect on the individual's behaviour on, e.g., the labour or the capital market. Its amount is thus independent of a person's income, consumption of goods and services, or wealth. A typical lump-sum tax is the head or the poll tax.

Managed competition A system that bands people into large organizations that purchase insurance on their behalf.

Marginal tax rate The proportion of the last euro of income taxed by the government.

Market failure A situation that refers to the inability of market forces to attain efficiency. It generally arises because of externalities, market imperfections, asymmetric information, etc.

Matthew effect The perverse effect of redistributive programs that end up benefiting the non-needy, rather than the needy.

Means-tested benefits These benefits are paid to individuals only if income and wealth are below a certain level.

Merit good A good or a service the consumption of which is deemed to be intrinsically desirable, even though individuals are unwilling to purchase an adequate quantity of it.

Minimum wage This is a price floor meant to ensure that those who work earn enough to support a family. It is generally fixed above the full employment equilibrium wage, and it does create some unemployment.

Moral hazard When an individual's behaviour is affected by the fact of being insured. It is *ex ante* if insurance increases the probability of the insured event; it is *ex post* if insurance increases the consumption of services following the occurrence of the insured event.

Net social spending To get from a 'gross' to a 'net' concept of social spending, adjustments to raw data are needed. They mainly consist in taking out taxes levied on benefits and adding private but mandatory spending.

New social question This is the questioning of redistribution (through taxation or social insurance) decided behind the veil of ignorance. For one can increasingly foresee a wide range of individual risks mortality, disease, unemployment, etc.

Notional accounts Notional defined contribution accounts are designed to mimic a defined contribution plan, where the pension depends on contributions and investment returns. Pension contributions are tracked in accounts which earn a rate of notional return, set by the government, different from the investment returns in the markets.

OMC (Open Method of Coordination) The process whereby common goals are laid down and progress is measured against jointly agreed indicators, while best practice is identified and compared.

Paradox of redistribution It is the proposition that a targeted benefit system ends up achieving less redistribution than a more universal one.

Parental leave Compensation given to either mothers or fathers who temporarily quit their job to take care of their infant.

Glossary

Pay-as-you-go A pension system under which benefits paid to current retirees come from payments made by current workers.

Payroll tax Also called social insurance contribution, it refers to a tax based on the wages and salaries paid by an employer and used to finance social insurance.

Pension points In a pension points system workers earn pension points based on their individual earnings for each year of contributions and at retirement, the sum of pension points is multiplied by a pension-point value to convert them into a regular pension payment.

Political economy This is an approach to economics that focuses on the practical aspects of political action. It is a positive as opposed to a normative approach.

Populism It is an ideology or a political movement that mobilizes the population (often, but not always, the lower classes) against an institution or government, usually in the defence of the underdog or the wronged. It seeks to unite the uncorrupted and the unsophisticated citizens against the corrupt dominant elites and their followers (usually the rich and the intellectuals).

Poverty gap The relative amount of money required to raise the income of all poor households to the poverty line.

Poverty line A fixed level of income considered enough to provide a minimally adequate standard of living. A poverty line often used is half the median income.

Poverty rate The percentage of households with adjusted income below the poverty line.

Poverty trap The situation wherein a family loses from working, because its earnings plus net transfers are inferior to net transfers when not working.

Prisoner's dilemma This term arises from the case of two arrested criminals who are subject to separate interrogations. Rationally, each should not hoping that the other one will not do so. But as both will be motivated to act in their own perceived interest, they will both end up worse than if they had been able to agree between themselves not to confess. This model shows that rational behaviour at the micro-level leads to an apparently irrational macro-outcome.

Productive inefficiency Also called efficiency slack, it occurs when the performance of a production unit lies below the efficiency (best practice) frontier.

QUALYS (quality adjusted life expectancy) This indicator gives the number of years left to an individual, e.g., after a surgical operation, but weighted to reflect the physical and psychological capacity that this individual might lose.

Race to the bottom If location decisions are influenced by the available tax–welfare package, national governments acting non-cooperatively are induced to adopt a less generous social policy than they would do in autarky.

Regression An analysis that involves the fitting of a (linear) equation to a set of data points for establishing quantitative economic relationships.

Regressive Used for a tax system under which an individual's average tax rate decreases with income.

Glossary

Replacement rate The social insurance benefit an individual receives as a proportion of income earned when working.

Social divide The social divide is the boundary in society that separates communities whose social economic structures, opportunities for success, access to medical and educational facilities, use of information and communication technologies are so different that they have substantially different political values.

Social dumping Imposing lower social contributions and taxes in export markets than are imposed in home markets, with the consequence that the generosity of social protection declines.

Self-insurance This happens when an individual, instead of using an outside insurance device, relies on his own risk diversification or on his own wealth (saving for retirement).

Single provider A system that provides all citizens, regardless of income and health status, with a set of health care services at no direct cost to the insured.

Targeting Targeting implies the use of various mechanisms to identify, and distribute the bulk of benefits to, the vulnerable segments of the population.

Tax competition Imposing lower taxes on factors of production that could unfavourably move out of the country.

Tax expenditure A loss of tax revenue because some item is excluded from the tax base.

Tax shifting The difference between statutory incidence and economic incidence.

Third-party payment Payment for services by someone other than the provider or consumer.

Veil of ignorance The notion of 'being behind the veil of ignorance', or in the original position, refers to an imaginary situation in which people have no knowledge of their place in society.

Workfare It is a controversial way of giving money to otherwise unemployed or underemployed people, who are applying for social benefits. To receive their welfare benefits, recipients have to meet certain participation requirements intended to improve their job prospects or to prevent long-term unemployment. It also prevents undeserving individuals from getting these benefits.

Yardstick competition Applied to a federation or a confederation, it is the process whereby voters can exert their political rights by making meaningful comparisons between jurisdictions on the basis of their respective performance.

Bibliography

Aaberge, R., A. Bjrklund, M. Jantti, M. Palme, P. Pedersen, N. Smith, and T. Wennemo (2002). Income inequality and income mobility in the Scandinavian countries compared to the United States, *Review of Income and Wealth*, 48, 443–69.

Abott, M. and C. Doucouliagos (2003). The efficiency of Australian universities: a data envelopment analysis, *Economics of Education Review*, 22, 89–97.

Adema, W. (1999). Net social expenditure, *Labor Market and Social Policy, Occasional Papers* n° 52, OECD, Paris.

Adema, W. (2001). Net social expenditure, second edition, *Labor Market and Social Policy, Occasional Papers* n° 39, OECD, Paris.

Adema, W., P. Fron, and M. Ladaique (2011). Is the European welfare state really more expensive? Indicators on social spending, 1980–2012; and a manual to the OECD Social Expenditure Database (SOCX), *OECD Social, Employment and Migration Working Papers*, n° 124, OECD, Paris.

Agenor, P.-R. (2002). Does globalization hurt the poor? *Policy Research Working Paper 2922*, The World Bank.

Alesina, A. and G. M. Angeletos (2002). Fairness and redistribution: US versus Europe, Harvard University, mimeo.

Alesina, A., E. Glaeser, and B. Sacerdote (2001). Why doesn't the US have a European type welfare state?, *Brooking Papers on Economic Activity*, Issue 2, 187–277.

Algan, Y., E. Beasley, M. Foucault, and P. Vertie (2017). Bien-être et vote, Observatoire du Bien-être du CEPREMAAP, n° 2017-02.

Anthon, E., Klein, C. and R. Kyle (2012). Identifying the Best Buys in U.S. Higher Education, *Research in Higher Education*, 53(8). 860-87.

Arnott, R. and J. Stiglitz (1991). Moral hazard and non-market institutions: dysfunctional crowding out or pure monitoring? *American Economic Review*, 81, 179–90.

Arntz, M., T. Gregory, and U. Zierahn (2016). The risk of automation for jobs in OECD countries: a comparative analysis, *OECD Social, Employment and Migration Working Papers*, n° 189, OECD, Paris.

Arrow, K. (1963). Uncertainty and the welfare economics of medical care, *American Economic Review*, 53, 941–73.

Atkinson, A. (2015). *Inequality. What can be done?* Harvard University Press, Cambridge, MA.

Atkinson, A. B. (1991). Social insurance, *The Geneva Papers on Risk and Insurance Theory*, 16, 113–32.

Atkinson, A. B. (1995). The welfare state and economic performance, *National Tax Journal*, vol. 48, 171–98.

Bibliography

Atkinson, A. B. (2000). *The Economic Consequences of Rolling Back the Welfare-State*, MIT Press, Cambridge, MA.

Autor, D., D. Don, G. Hanson and K. Majlesi (2016). Importing political polarization? The electoral consequences of rising trade exposure, *NBER Working Paper* n° 22637.

Bambra, C. (2006). Decommodification and the worlds of welfare revisited, *Journal of European Social Policy*, 16, 73–80.

Bambra, C. (2007). Going beyond the three worlds of welfare capitalism: regime theory and public health research, *Journal of Epidemiology Community Health*, 61, 1098–102.

Banker, R. D., S. Janakiraman, and R. Natarajan (2004). Analysis of trends in technical and allocative efficiency: an application to Texas public school districts, *European Journal of Operational Research*, 154, 477–91.

Barr, N. (1992). Economic theory and the welfare state: a survey and interpretations, *Journal of Economic Literature*, 30, 741–803.

Barr, N. (1998). *The Economics of the Welfare State* (3rd edn), Oxford University Press, London.

Barra, C., Lagravinese, R., and Zotti, R. (2015). Explaining (in)efficiency in higher education: a comparison of parametric and non-parametric analyses to rank universities, *MPRA Paper* n° 67119, Ludwig-Maximilian University, Munich.

Becker, G. S. (1991). *A Treatise on the Family*, (Enlarged Edition), Harvard University Press, Cambridge, MA.

Becker, S., T. Fetzer, and D. Novy (2017). Who voted for Brexit? *CESIfo Discussion Paper* n° 1480.

Beckerman, W. and S. Clark (1982). *Poverty and Social Security in Britain since 1961*, Oxford University Press, Oxford.

Beland, O. (2005). Insecurity, citizenship and globalization. The multiple faces of state protection, *Sociological Theory*, 23, 25–41.

Bellettini, G. and C. Berti Ceroni (1989). Is social security really bad for growth? *Review of Economic Dynamics*, 2(4), 796–819.

Benabou, R. and J. Tirole (2002). Beliefs in a just world and redistributive politics, Princeton University, mimeo.

Berg, A., Buffie, E.F. and Zanna, L.-F. (2016) Robots, growth and inequality, *Finance & Development* 53(3), 10–13.

Beveridge, W. H. (1942). Social Insurance and Allied Services, Cmd 6404, London, HMSO.

Bisin, A. and T. Verdier (2004). Work ethic and redistribution: a cultural transmission model of the welfare state, NYU and Delta, mimeo.

Biorn, E., Hagen, T.P., Iverson, T., and Magnussen, J. (2003). The effect of activity-based financing on hospital efficiency: a panel data analysis of DEA efficiency scores 1992–2000, *Health Care Management Science*, 6(2), 271–83.

Bjorkgren, M., Hakkinen, U. and M. Linna (2001). Measuring Efficiency of Long-Term Care Units in Finland, *Health Care Management Science*, 4, 193–200.

Bjorklund, A., T. Eriksson, M. Jantti, O. Raaum, and E. Sterbacka (2002). Brother correlations in earnings in Denmark, Finland, Norway and Sweden compared to the United States, *Journal of Population Economics*, 15, 757–72.

Bibliography

Blanchard, O. and J. Tirole (2004). The optimal design of unemployment insurance and employment protection, *NBER Working Paper*.

Boadway, R. and M. Marchand (1995). The use of public expenditures for redistribution purpose, *Oxford Economic Papers*, 47, 45–59.

Boadway, R., M. Marchand, M. Leite Monteiro, and P. Pestieau (2003). Social insurance and redistribution, in S. Cnossen and H-W Sinn (ed.), *Public Finance and Public Policy in the New Century*, MIT Press, Cambridge, MA, 333–58.

Breen, R. and P. Moisis (2003). Poverty dynamics for measurement error, *ISER Working Papers*, 2003-17.

Brown, P. and R. Crampton (1994). *Economic restructuring and social exclusion: a new Europe?* Routledge, London.

Brown, J. and A. Finkelstein (2007). Why is the market for long-term care insurance so small? *NBER Working Paper* n° 43567.

Burkhauser, R. V. and J. G. Poupore (1997). A cross- national comparison of permanent inequality in the United States and Germany, *Review of Economic and Statistics*, 79, 10–17.

Burkhauser, R. V., D. Holtz-Eakin and S. E. Rhody (1997). Mobility and inequality in the 1980s: a cross-national comparison of the United States and Germany, in *The Distribution of Welfare and Households Production*, S. P. Jenkins, A. Kapteyn, and B. van Praag (eds), Cambridge University Press, Cambridge, MA, 111–75.

Burton, L., Zdaniuk, B., Schultz, R., Jackson, S., and Hirsch, C. (2003). Transitions in spousal caregiving, *Gerontologist*, 43(2), 230–41.

Cantillon, B. and K. van den Bosch (2002). Back to the basics: the case for an adequate minimum guaranteed income in the active welfare state, in J. Pacolet and E. Claessens (eds), *Trade, Competitiveness and Social Protection*, AFP Press, 73–94.

Casamatta, G., Cremer, H., and P. Pestieau (2000). Political sustainability and the design of social insurance, *Journal of Public Economics*, 75 (3), 341–364.

Castel, R. (2003). The roads to disaffiliation: insecure work and vulnerable relationships, *International Journal of Urban and Regional Research*, 29, 519–35.

Castells, M. (2000). Material for an exploratory theory of the network society, *British Journal of Sociology*, 51, 5–24.

Chauvel, L. (2016). *La Spirale du déclassement. Essai sur la société des illusions*, Le Seuil, Paris.

Cherchye, L., W. Moesen, and T. Van Puyenbroeck (2004). Legitimately diverse, yet comparable: on synthesizing social inclusion performance in the EU, *Journal of Common Market Studies*, 42(1), 919–55.

Cherchye, L., K. De Witte, E. Ooghe, and I. Nicaise (2010). Efficiency and equity in private and public education: a nonparametric comparison, *European Journal of Operational Research*, 202(2), 563–73.

Coelli, T. J., M. Lefebvre, and P. Pestieau (2010). On the convergence of social protection performance in the European Union, *CESIfo Economic studies*, 56(2), 300–22.

Cremer, H. and F. Gahvari (1997). In-kind transfers, self-selection and optimal tax policy, *European Economic Review*, 41, 97–114.

Cremer, H. and P. Pestieau (1996). Redistributive taxation and social insurance, *International Taxation and Public Finance*, 3, 259–80.

Bibliography

Cremer, H. and P. Pestieau (2004). Factor mobility and redistribution, in V. Smith and J. Thisse (eds), *Handbook in Urban Economics* III, North Holland, Amsterdam, 2529–61.

Cremer, H., P. Pestieau, and G. Ponthiere (2012). The economics of long-term care: a survey. *Nordic Economic Policy Review*, 2, 108–48.

Cremer, H., V. Fourgeaud, M. Leite-Monteiro, M. Marchand, and P. Pestieau (1997). Mobility and redistribution. A survey of the literature, *Public Finance*, 51, 325–52.

De Graeve, D. and T. Van Ourti (2003). The distributional impact of health financing in Europe: a review, in *The World Economy*, Blackwell, London, 23, 1459–79.

de Henau, J., D. Meulders, and S. O'Dorchai (2005). The childcare triad? Indicators assessing three fields towards dual-earner families in the EU15, unpublished, ULB, Brussels.

De Lathouwer, L. (2004). Reforming the passive welfare state: Belgium's new income arrangements to make work pay in international perspectives, in P. Sounders (ed.), *Social Security and the Welfare to Work Transition*, vol. 10, International Studies on Social Security, Ashgate, Aldershot.

Deleeck, H. (1979). L'effet Matthieu, *Droit Social*, 11, 375–84.

Devaux, M. and M. de Looper (2012). Income-related inequalities in health service utilisation in 19 OECD countries, 2008–09, *OECD Health Working Paper* No. 58. OECD, Paris.

De Wispelaere, F. and J. Pacolet (2015). *An Ad-Hoc Statistical Analysis on Short Term Mobility—Economic Value of Posting of Workers*, HIVA Research Institute for Work and Society, Leuven.

Diamond, P. (1992). Organizing the health insurance market, *Econometrica*, 60, 1233–54.

Dilnot, A. (2011). *Fairer Care Funding: The Report of the Commission on Funding of Care and Support*, London: Commission on Funding of Care and Support.

Disney, R. (2004). Are contributions to public pension programmes a tax on employment? *Economic Policy*, 19, 267–311.

Dulal (2017). Technical efficiency of nursing homes: do five-star quality ratings matter? *Health Care Management Science*, 20(78), 1–8.

European Commission (2014). *Key Data on Early Childhood Education and Care in Europe*. 2014 Edition. Eurydice and Eurostat Report. Luxembourg: Publications Office of the European Union.

European Commission (2015). *The 2015 Ageing Report*, European Commission, Brussels.

Edwards, J. and M. Keen (1996). *Tax competition and the Leviathan*, European Economic Review, 40, 113–34.

Erlandsen, E. and Forsund, F. R. (2002). Efficiency in the provision of municipal nursing and home care services: the Norwegian experience, in *Efficiency in the Public Sector*, Kevin Fox (ed.), Kluwer Academia Publishers, Amsterdam.

Esping-Andersen, G. (1990). *The Three Worlds of Welfare Capitalism*, Princeton University Press, Princeton.

Eurobarometer (2011), Eurobarometer 74.1, European Commission, Brussels.

Eurofound (2017). *Income Inequalities and Employment Patterns in Europe Before and After The Great Recession*, Publications Office of the European Union, Luxembourg.

Bibliography

European Commission (2000). Taxation trends in the European Union. Data for the EU Member States, Iceland and Norway—2007. European Union.

European Commission (2009). Taxation trends in the European Union. Data for the EU Member States, Iceland and Norway—2007. European Union.

European Commission (2012). The 2012 Ageing Report: Economic and budgetary projections for the 28 EU Member States, (2010-2060). European Union.

European Commission (2013). Unemployment benefits in EU member States. European Union.

European Commission (2015). The 2015 Ageing Report: Economic and budgetary projections for the 28 EU Member States, (2013-2060). European Union.

European Commission (2016). Taxation trends in the European Union. Data for the EU Member States, Iceland and Norway—2016. European Union.

European Commission (2017a). Directorate general for employment, social affairs and inclusion, (DG EMPL).

European Commission (2017b). Taxation trends in the European Union. Data for the EU Member States, Iceland and Norway—2017. European Union.

Eurostat (2017a). Welfare and living conditions database.

Eurostat (2017b). National accounts database.

Eurostat (2017c). European Social Protection Expenditures and Receipts database.

Eurostat (2017d). Labour Force Database.

Eurostat (2017e). Social protection database.

Eurostat (2017f). Health database.

Eurostat (2017e). Population database.

Ewald, F. (1986). *L'Etat-Providence*, Grasset, Paris.

Ferrera, J., E. Crespo, F. Chaparro, D. Santín (2011). Exploring educational efficiency divergences across Spanish regions, *Revista de Economia Aplicada*, Pisa 2006, vol. 19(3), 117-45.

Fields, G. S. and O. S. Mitchell (1993). Reforming social security and social safety notes program in developing countries in *Developing Issues, Development Committee*, Washington, DC, 32, 113-19.

Fleurbaey, M. and E. Schokkaert (2009). Unfair inequalities in health and health care, *Journal of Health Economics*, 28(1), 73-90.

Garavglia, G., E. Lettierie, T. Agasisti, and S. Lopez (2011). Efficiency and quality of care in nursing homes: an Italian case study, *Health Care Management Science*, 14, 22-35.

Garnero, A., A. Hijzen, and S. Martin (2016). Earnings inequality and earnings mobility: new evidence from OECD nations, VOX, March 2016.

Geishecker, I. and T. Siedler (2012). Job loss fears and (extremist) party identification: first evidence from panel data, *IZA Discussion Paper* n° 6996.

Giddens, A. (1998). *The Third Way. The Renewal of Social Democracy*, Cambridge University Press, Cambridge.

Gill, I. S., T. T. Packard, and J. Yermo (2004). *Keeping the Promise of Social Security in Latin America*, The World Bank, Stanford University Press, Washington DC.

Gok, S. and B. Sezen (2011). Analyzing the efficiencies of hospitals: an application of data envelopment analysis, *Journal of Global Strategic Management,* 5(2). 137-46.

Bibliography

Gornick, J. C. and M. Meyer (2003). *Families That Work: Policies for Reconciling Parenthood and Employment*, Russel Sage Foundation, NewYork.

Gruber, J. and D. Wise (1999). Introduction and summary, in *Social Security and Tax on Work around the World*, NBER, Chicago University Press, Chicago.

Gruber, J. and Wise, D. A. (2010). *Social Security Programs and Retirement around the World: The Relationship to Youth Employment*, NBER Book series, University of Chicago Press.

Gupta, S., S. Keen, S. Shah, and G. Verdier (2017*), Digital revolutions in public finance*, International Monetary Fund, Washington DC.

Haelemands, C., K. De Witte and J. Blank (2012). On the allocation of resources for secondary schools, *Economics of Education Review*, 31(5), 575–86.

Hassler, J., J. Rodriguez Mora, K. Storesletten, and F. Zilibotti (2003). The survival of the welfare state, *American Economic Review*, 93, 87–112.

Heckman, J. (2012). Invest in early childhood development: reduce benefits, strengthen the economy. *The Heckman Equation,* December 2012.

Herr, A. (2008). Cost and technical efficiency of German hospitals: does ownership matter? *Health Economics,* 17(9), 1057–71.

Hirst, M. (2005). Carer distress: a prospective, population-based study, *Social Science & Medicine*, 61(3), 697–708.

Illich, I. (1976). *Medical Nemesis. The Expropriation of Health*, New York, Random House, Pantheon Books.

Johnes, J. (2006). Data envelopment analysis and its application to the measurement of efficiency in higher education, *Economics of Education Review*, 25(3), 273–88.

Johnes, J., S. Bradley and A. Little (2012). Efficiency in the further education sector in England, *Open Journal of Statistics*, 2, 131–40.

Kaldor, N. (1956). Alternative theories of distribution, *Review of Economic Studies*, 23, 83–100.

Kay, J. (2017). The basics of basic income, *Intereconomics*, 52, 2, 69–74.

Kirkegaard, J. (2009). *Europe and the US: Whose Health Care is More Socialist?* Peterson Institute for International Economics, Washington, DC.

Kittelsen, S., B. Winsnes, K. Anthun, F. Goude, O. Hope, U. Häkkinen, B. Kalseth, J. Kilsmark, E. Medin, C. Rehnberg and A. Ratto (2015). Decomposing the productivity differences between hospitals in the Nordic countries, *Journal of Productivity Analysis*, 43(3), 281–93.

Klimaviciute, J. and P. Pestieau (2017). Long-term care social insurance. How to avoid big losses? *International Tax and Public Finance*, forthcoming.

Klimaviciute, J., S. Perelman, P. Pestieau, and J. Schoenmaeckers (2017). Caring for dependent parents: altruism, exchange or family norm? *Journal of Population Economics*, 30, 835–73.

Korpi, W. and J. Palme (1998). The paradox of redistribution and strategies of equality: welfare institutions, inequality, and poverty in the western countries, *American Sociological Review*, 63(5), 661–87.

Korpi, W. and J. Palme (2003). New politics and class politics in the context of austerity and globalization: welfare states regress in 18 countries, 1975–95, *American Political Science Review*, 97, 425–46.

Bibliography

Kotlikoff, L. J. and A. Spivak (1981). The Family as an incomplete annuities market, *Journal of Political Economy*, 89, 372–91.

Krugman, P. (1995). Growing world trade: causes and consequences, *Brookings Papers on Economic Activity*, 1, 327–62.

Krugman, P. (1996). The causes of high unemployment. The inequality or unemployment trade-off, *Policy Options*, 17, n° 6, 20–4.

Kunreuther, H. (1978). *Disaster Insurance Protection. Public Policy Lessons*, John Wiley, New York.

Kuznets, S. (1955). Economic growth and income inequality, *American Economic Review*, 45, 1–28.

Layard, R., Nickel, S. and R. Jackman (2005), *Unemployment: macroeconomic performance and the labour market,* MIT Press, Cambridge.

Lefebvre (2013). Social Security and Retirement: the Relationship between Workers, Firms and Governments, *Annals of Public and Cooperative Economics*, 84(1), 43–61.

Lefebvre, M. and P. Pestieau (2015). *L'Etat-providence en Europe: performance et dumping social*, Collection du CEPREMAP, Editions Rue d'Ulm, Paris.

Lefebvre, M., S. Perelman, and P. Pestieau (2017). Productivity and performance in the public sector, in E. Grifell-Tatjé, C. A. K. Lovell and R. C. Sickles, eds, *The Oxford Handbook of Productivity Analysis*, Oxford University Press, Oxford.

Le Grand, J. (1982). *The Strategy of Equality Redistribution and the Social Services*, George Allen & Unwin, London.

Leonard, H. B. and R. J. Zeckhauser (1983). Public insurance provision and non-market failures, *The Geneva Papers*, 8, 147–57.

Lindbeck, A. (1995a), Welfare states disincentives with endogenous habits and norms, *Scandinavian Journal of Economics*, 97, 477–94.

Lindbeck, A. (1995b), Hazardous welfare-state dynamics, *American Economic Review*, 85, Papers and Proceedings, 85(2), 9–15.

Lindbeck, A., S. Nyberg and J. Weibull (1999). Social norms and economic incentives in the welfare state, *Quarterly Journal of Economics*, 114, 1–35.

Lindert, P. (2004). *Growing Public: Social Spending and Economic Growth since the Eighteenth Century*, Cambridge University Press, Cambridge.

Lipszyc, B., Sail, E. and A. Xavier (2012). Long-term care: need, use and expenditure in the EU27, *Economic paper* 469.

Lucas, R. (2005). *The Industrial Revolution: Past and Future*, Annual Report Essay, Federal Reserve Bank of Minneapolis.

Martin, J. and S. Scarpetta (2012). Setting It Right: Employment Protection, Labour Reallocation and Productivity, *De Economist*, 160(2), 89–116.

Marx, I., Nolan, B and J. Olivera (2015). The welfare state and antipoverty policy in rich countries, in A.B. Atkinson and F. Bourguignon (eds) *Handbook of Economic Distribution*, vol. 2, Elsevier.

Marx, I. and D. Vandelanoote (2014). Matthew runs amok. The Belgian service voucher scheme, IZZA working paper n°87–17.

Masson, A. (2004). Les pouvoirs publics et la famille, *Cahiers Français*, 322, 81–7.

Masson, A. (2009). *Des liens et des transferts entre générations*, Éditions EHESS, collection En temps & lieux, Paris.

Bibliography

McKnight, A., K. Stewart, S. Mohun Himmelweit, and M. Palillo (2016). Low pay and in-work poverty: preventive measures and preventive approaches, *Evidence Review*, European Commission, Brussels.

Meister, W. and W. Ochel (2003). Tax privileges for families in an international comparison, *CESifo Dice Report*, 1, 42–5.

Merton, R. (1968). The Matthew effect in science, *Science*, 159, 56–63.

Meyers, M. (2004). A devolution revolution? Change and continuity in US state social policies in the 1990s, Eleventh International Research Seminar on Issues in Social Security, Sigtuna, Sweden.

Mitchell, O. (1997). Administrative costs in public and private retirement systems, in *Privatizing Social Security*, M. Feldstein (ed.), Chicago University Press, Chicago.

Moene, K. and M. Wallerstein (2001). Inequality, social insurance and redistribution, *American Political Science Review*, 95 (4), 859–874.

Mukherjee, K., R. Santerre, and N.J. Zhang (2010). Explaining the efficiency of local health departments in the U.S.: an exploratory analysis, *Health Care Management Science*, 13, 378–87.

Ni Luasa S., D. Dineen, and M. Zieba (2017). Technical efficiency of nursing homes: do five-star quality ratings matter? *Health Care Management Science*, forthcoming.

Nolan, B. and I. Marx (2000). Low pay and household poverty, in G. Salverda and S. Bazen, *Laborer Market Inequalities: Problems and Policies in International Perspective*, Oxford University Press, Oxford.

OECD (2004). OECD employment outlook 2004, OECD, Paris.

OECD (2014). Focus on top incomes and taxation in OECD Countries: Was the crisis a game changer? Directorate for Employment, Labor and Social Affairs, OECD, Paris.

OECD (2015). Health at a glance, OECD, Paris.

OECD (2016a). Poverty rate, (indicator). doi: 10.1787/0fe1315d-en, OECD, Paris.

OECD (2016b). Income inequality, (indicator). doi: 10.1787/459aa7f1-en, OECD, Paris.

OECD (2016c). Social expenditure database, OECD, Paris.

OECD (2016d). Insurance indicators database, OECD, Paris.

OECD (2017a). OECD health statistics 2017, OECD, Paris.

OECD (2017b). OECD employment and labour market statistics, OECD, Paris.

OECD (2017c). Modèles impôts-prestations de l'OCDE, OECD, Paris.

OECD (2017). Pension markets in focus, OECD, Paris.

Okun, A. M. (1974). *Equality and Efficiency*, The Brookings Institution, Washington.

Olivera, J. (2015). Preferences for redistribution, *IZA European Labour Studies*, 4, 1–18.

Ooghe, E., E. Schokkaert and J. Fléchet (2003). The incidence of social security contributions: an empirical analysis, *Empirica*, 30(2), 81–106.

O'Rourke, K., B. Eichengreen, and A. de Broomhead (2012). Right wing political extremism in the great depression, *CEPR Discussion Paper* n° 8876, London.

Osterkamp, R. (2004). Measuring efficiency of health-care provision: intercountry comparison and changes over time, unpublished.

Pauly, M. V. (1990). The rational non-purchase of long term care insurance, *Journal of Political Economy*, 98, 153–68.

Persson, T. and G. Tabellini (1994). Is inequality harmful for growth? *American Economic Review*, 84, 600–21.

Bibliography

Pestieau, P. (1994). Social protection and private insurance. Reassessing the role of public versus private sector in insurance, *The Geneva Papers on Risk and Insurance Theory*, 19, 81–92.

Pestieau, P. (2004). Globalization and redistribution, unpublished.

Pestieau, P. and H. Tulkens (1993). Assessing and explaining the performance of public sector activities, *FinanzArchiv*, 50, 293–323.

Pestieau, P. and G. Ponthière (2017). The public economics of long term care, in M. Guzman, ed., *Economic Theory and Public Policies: Joseph Stiglitz and the Teaching of Economics*, Columbia University Press, New York.

Pierson, P. (1997). *Dismantling the Welfare State? Reagan, Thatcher and the Politics of Retrenchment*, Cambridge University Press, Cambridge.

Pierson, P. (2001). Coping with permanent austerity: welfare state restructuring in affluent democracies, in P. Pierson (ed.), *The New Politics of the Welfare State*, Oxford University Press, Oxford.

Poterba, J. (1996). Government intervention in the markets for education and healthcare: how and why? in V. Fuchs (ed.), *Individual and Social Responsibility*, Chicago University Press, Chicago, 277–304.

Ravallion, M. (2003). The debate on globalization, poverty and inequality: why measurement matters, *International Affairs*, 79, 739–53.

Razin, A. and E. Sadka (2005). The Decline of the Welfare State: Demographics and Globalization, MIT Press, Cambridge, MA.

Rochet, J-Ch., (1991). Incentives, redistribution and social insurance, *The Geneva Papers on Risk and Insurance Theory*, 16, 143–66.

Rodrik, D. (2017). *Populism and the economics of globalization*, Harvard University Press, Cambridge MA.

Rosenvallon, P. (1995). *La Nouvelle Question Sociale*, Seuil, Paris.

Sandel, M. (2017). Lessons from the populist revolt in our world, *New Europe*, n° 1193.

Sandmo, A. (1991). Economists and the welfare state, *European Economic Review*, 35, 213–39.

Sandmo, A. (1995). Introduction. The welfare economics of the welfare state, *Scandinavian Journal of Economics*, 97, 469–76.

Schulz, R. and Sherwood, P.R. (2008). Physical and mental health effects of family caregiving, *Journal of Social Work Education*, 44 (3), 105–13.

Sinn, H.-W. (1990). Tax harmonization and tax competition in Europe, *European Economic Review*, 34, 489–504.

Sologon, D. and C. O'Donoghue (2012). Earnings Mobility, Earnings Inequality, and Labor Market Institutions in Europe, in J. A. Bishop and R. Salas (eds), *Inequality, Mobility and Segregation: Essays in Honor of Jacques Silber* (Research on Economic Inequality, Volume 20), 237–83, Emerald Group Publishing, Bongley (UK).

Stigler, G. (1965). The tenable range of functions of local government, in E. Phelps (eds), *Private Wants and Public Needs*, Norton, New York City, 167–76.

Stiglitz, J. (1983), On the social insurance. Comments on 'The State and the demand for security in contemporary societies', *The Geneva Papers*, 8, 105–10.

Stiglitz, J. (2015). *The Great Divide*, Allen Lane.

Bibliography

Storms, B. (1995). L'effet Matthieu dans le domaine de l'accueil des enfants, Centrum voor Social Beleid, UFSIA, Antwerpen.

Storto (2013). Evaluating technical efficiency of Italian major municipalities: a data envelopment analysis model, *Social and Behavioral Sciences*, 81(28), 346–50.

Struk, M. and M. Matulova (2016). The application of two-stage data envelopment analysis on municipal solid waste management in the Czech Republic. Unpublished.

Svallfors, S. (1997). World of welfare and attitudes to redistribution: a comparison of eight Western nations, *European Sociological Review*, 13, 283–304.

Summers, L., J. Gruber and R. Vergara (1993). Taxation and the structure of labor markets: the case of corporatism, *Quarterly Journal of Economics*, 107, 385–411.

Taylor-Gooby, P. and S. Svallfors (1999). *The End of the Welfare State? Responses to State Retrenchment*, Routledge, London.

Townsend, P. (1979). *Poverty in the United Kingdom*, Penguin Harmondsworth, London.

Vaalavuo, M. (2015). Poverty Dynamics in Europe: From What to Why—DG Employment Working Paper 03–2015, Luxembourg.

Valdes-Prieto, S. (1998). Administrative costs in a privatized pension system. Paper presented at the Pensions Systems Reform in Central America Conference, Cambridge, MA.

Van Houtven, C., N. Coe, and M. Skira (2013). The effect of informal care on work and wages, *Journal of Health Economics*, 32 (1), 240–52.

Vandenbroucke, F. (2001). The active welfare state: a social democratic ambition for Europe, *The Policy Network Journal*, issue 1.

van Ineveld, M., J. van Oostrum, R., Vermeulen, A. Steenhoek and J. van de Klundert (2016). Productivity and quality of Dutch hospitals during system reform, *Health Care Management Science*, 19, 279–90.

Varabyova, Y. and Schreyogg, J. (2013). International comparisons of the technical efficiency of the hospital sector: Panel data analysis of OECD countries using parametric and non-parametric approaches, *Health Policy*, 112(1–2), 70–9.

Varian, H. (1980). Redistributive taxation as social insurance, *Journal of Public Economics*, 14, 46–68.

Waldo, S. (2007). Efficiency in Swedish public education: competition and voter monitoring, *Education Economics*, 15, 231–51.

Whelan, Ch., R. Layte and B. Maitre (2003). Persistent income poverty and depreciation in the European Union. An analysis of the first three waves of the European Community Household Panel, *International Social Policy*, 32, 1–18.

Wildasin, D. (1995). Factor mobility, risk and redistribution in the welfare state, *Scandinavian Journal of Economics*, 97, 527–46.

Wise, D. A. (2017). *Social Security Programs and Retirement Around the World: The Capacity to Work at Older Ages*, NBER Book series, University of Chicago Press.

Zuckman, G. (2015). *The Hidden Wealth of Nations. The Source of Tax Havens*, University of Chicago Press.

Name Index

Aaberge, R. et al. 22
Adema, W. et al. 34
Alesina, A. et al. 56–7
Algan, Y. et al. 24
Arnott, R. 111
Arrow, K. 155
Atkinson, A. B. 30, 86, 106, 108, 114
Autor, D. et al. 24

Bambra, C. 50n3
Barr, N. 4, 118n6
Becker, G. S. 106, 115
Becker, S. et al. 24
Beckerman, W. 51
Beland, O. 75
Bellettini, G. 86
Benabou, R. 56
Beveridge, W. H. 94
Bisin, A. 56
Blanchard, O. 166–7
Boadway, R. et al. 113
Breen, R. 22
Brown, J. 151
Brown, P. 113
Burkhauser, R. V. 22
Burton, L. et al. 152

Casamatta, G. et al. 53
Castel, R. 14
Castells, M. 75
Ceroni, C. 86
Clark, S. 51
Coelli, T. J. et al. 102
Cremer, H. 113
Crompton, R. 113

de Henau, J. et al. 181
De Wispelaere, F. 168
Deleeck, H. 91
Diamond, P. 94, 118
Dilnot, A. 155
Disney, R. 52

Esping-Andersen, G.
  The Three Worlds of Welfare Capitalism 48–50, 59

Fields, G. S. 113
Finkelstein, A. 151
Frazer, H. 172

Gahvari, F. 113
Garnero, A. et al. 22
Geishecker, I. 24
Gill, I.S. et al. 94
Gornick, J.C. 182
Gruber, J. 131, 132

Heckman, J. 180
Hirst, M. 152

Kaldor, N. 86
Kay, J. 170
Kirkegaard, J. 34
Korpi, W. 30n1, 53
Kotlikoff, L. J. 106
Krugman, P. 62, 63, 91n4
Kunreuther, H. 111
Kuznets, S. 85

Layard, R. et al. 132
Le Grand, J. 91, 92
Leonard, H. B. 112
Lindbeck, A. 56
Lindert, P. 87–8
Lipszyc, B. et al. 150
Lucas, R. 11n2

Marchand, M. 113
Marlier, E. 172
Martin, J. 164
Marx, I. 92
McKnight, A. et al. 171
Meyers, M. 182
Mitchell, O. 93, 94, 113

Name Index

Moene, K. 53
Moisis, P. 22

O'Donoghue, C. 22
O'Rourke, K. et al. 24
OECD 12, 22, 45, 161, 162
Okun, A. M. 5
Olivera, J. 55

Pacolet, J. 168
Palme, J. 30n1, 53
Pauly, M. V. 153
Persson, T. 86
Pestieau, P. 113
Pierson, P. 30
Poupore, J. G. 22

Rochet, J-Ch. 113
Rodrik, D. 63
Rosenvallon, P. 8n4

Sandel, M. 9
Sandmo, A. 4n3, 81
Scarpetta, S. 164
Schulz, R. 152
Sherwood, P. R. 152
Siedler, T. 24
Sinn, H-W. 64

Sologon, D. 22
Spivak, A. 106
Stigler, G. 64–5
Stiglitz, J. 107, 111
Summers, L. et al. 80
Svallfors, S. 30

Tabellini, G. 86
Taylor-Gooby, P. 30
Tirole, J. 56, 166–7
Townsend, P. 92
Trump, D. 9

Vaalavuo, M. 23
Valdes-Prieto, S. 94
Van Houtven, C. et al. 152
Vandelannoote, D. 92
Varian, H. 113
Verdier, T. 56

Wallerstein, M. 53
Whelan, Ch. et al. 22
Wildasin, D. 72
Wise, D. 132

Zeckhauser, R. J. 112
Zucman, G. 68

Subject Index

Note: Tables and figures are indicated by an italic *t* and *f*, respectively, following the page number.

acquired rights 125, 185–6
  see also entitlements
active policies 57–8
  child development 180
  labour market 58–9, 161, 162*t*13.2, 163, 166
administrative costs 51, 90, 170
  medical 141, 149*t*11.5
  social insurance 93–4, 98, 117*t*9.3
adverse selection 94, 112, 117*t*9.3, 137, 153
Ageing Report (2015) 139
Airbnb 69, 168, 188
altruism 11n1
  family 106, 155
  and long-term care 155
  and poverty alleviation 9
Anglo-Saxon model 49, 50, 59, 110
APA (Allocation Personalisée d'Autonomie) 156
Austria
  child benefits 175
  health care 145
  poverty rates 23, 178
  social spending 27, 29, 30, 124
automation 169–70

basic income 107–8, 169–71, 189
Belgium
  active *vs.* passive policies 58
  employment 58, 165
  fiscalization 40
  health care cost containment 143
  inequality 16, 92
  in-work poverty 171
  long-term care 155, 156
  Matthew effect in 92
  social insurance 107
  social spending 27, 30, 34
best practice frontier 73, 95, 98, 99, 100
Beveridgean system 48*t*5.1, 50, 51, 52, 161, 186
  and pension schemes 124–5, 126
Bismarckian system 50, 52, 54
  pension schemes 124
Brexit 9, 24

Bulgaria
  family allowances 175
  poverty rates 12, 16, 177
capital taxes 44
  and globalization 64–9
categorical benefits *see* flat benefits
charity 51, 110
child care
  child poverty 177–9
  family allowances 174–7
  inequality in social spending 92
  policies 174, 179–83
Chile 94
class interest 9
co-insurance 143
competition 7, 24
  fiscal, and globalization 64–7, 68, 189
  fiscal, and insurance 114, 117–18
  managed, in health care 142–3
  and payroll taxes 41–3
  and performance 89, 97–8, 103
confiscatory taxation 82, 83
constitutional approach 9
consumer's surplus 79, 80
consumption taxes 41, 44, 114
Continental model 49–50, 60
convergence
  future trends 186
  of health care spending 138
  of social spending 32–6
  of welfare state performance 91, 101–2
corporatist economies 19–20, 45, 49, 60, 80
cost-based reimbursements 141, 142–3
Croatia
  pension trends 135
  performance indicators 99
Cyprus, poverty rates 17, 23
Czech Republic
  employment rates 159
  health care spending 139
  inequality 16
  in-work poverty 171
  poverty rates 12

Subject Index

DEA (data development analysis) 95, 99–102
deadweight loss 80, 82
decommodification 49–50
defined benefit (DB) scheme 126
defined contribution (DC) scheme 126
Denmark
  child policies 180
  child poverty 177
  family allowances 175
  'flexicurity' model 58–9, 163, 166
  health care spending 138, 139
  income inequality 22
  labour market policy spending 162
  payroll tax 39
  social insurance 107
digitalization 169–70, 187–8
disability 4, 157, 164, 175
  benefits, individual behaviour 80, 83
  disincentive effect 52
  and early retirement 131
  and public spending on LTC 153–4
  and social insurance redistribution 116
disincentives 6, 40
  and employment 6, 52, 80–1
  means-tested benefit 51
  social spending 78
disposable income 12, 17, 82, 88, 92, 104
  of elderly people 127
distortionary taxation 82–3
distributive inefficiency 90, 189
  Matthew effect 91–3
dual income tax system 64n3

earnings-related benefits 48, 51, 94, 124, 187
  disincentives 52
  efficacy debates 53
education 13, 24–5, 54, 65
  and efficiency 8, 97t8.2
  performance indicators 100t8.3
  public spending 92
efficiency 88–91, 103
  economic 78, 80, 82, 87–8
  vs. equity 5–7, 52, 53–4
  of family allowances 178–9
  productive 94–8
  of social insurance 93–4
  of social spending 87–8, 91–3
  vertical expenditure 51
EITC (Earned Income Tax Credit) 52
elderly population
  and long-term spending 153
  pensions 123–36
  resources 106, 107t9.1
employment 157–8
  active and passive policies 57–8
  automation and digitalization 169–70, 187–8

disincentives 6, 52, 80–1
  of elderly, and pensions 129–32
  experience rating contributions 167
  and fears of job loss 24
  flexibility of 58–9, 163, 166
  and globalization 62–3, 69
  in-work poverty 171–3
  Matthew effect 92
  payroll tax 38–45
  posted workers 69, 167–8
  protection and minimum wage 163–6
  rates 158–61
  uberization 168–9
  universal basic income 169–71
entitlements 36, 49, 72, 185–6
  child-related benefits 174, 177, 181
  illegitimate 185–6
  labour market 125–6, 161, 167, 168
  programmes 36–7
equity-efficiency trade-off 5–7, 52, 53–4
equivalence scale 12, 59, 171
ethics 11, 65
  beliefs 56
  inequalities in health care 145
  norms 8
  welfare-induced migration 72
Eurobarometer survey (2011) 54
European Community Household Panel 22
European Social survey 55
EU-SILC 145, 177
excess burden (wage taxation) 79–83
expenditure 26
  administrative costs 93–4
  convergence 32–3
  data adjustments 33–4
  disincentives 78
  efficiency 87–8
  entitlement programmes 36–7
  evolution of 30, 31f3.2
  family allowances 174–7
  by functions 29
  and GDP 26–8, 30, 31f3.2, 35f3.4, 35t3.4, 85–6, 138
  and globalization 70
  gross to net convergence 35–6
  on health care 138–42
  and inequality 19–20
  on labour market policy 162
  level 26–7
  on long-term care 150–1, 153–4
  Matthew effect 91–3
  and openness 70
  out-of-pocket-spending 34, 118, 143, 144, 146
  and pensions 124–5
  and poverty 18–19

214

Subject Index

on social and private insurance 108–10
and universal basic income 170–1
experience rating 167

family 4–5, 59–60, 111, 189
   allowances 5, 29t3.2, 37, 45, 48, 174–9
   child care policies 174, 179–83
   and long-term care provision 152–3, 154, 155–6
   as form of insurance 106, 107t9.1
Finland
   basic income estimation 170
   family allowances 175
   poverty 12, 23, 177, 178
fiscalization 40
Flanders 58
flat benefits (universalistic) 34, 40, 48, 50
   advantages 51
   disincentives 52
   efficacy debates 53
   family allowances 175–6
flexibility, 'flexicurity' 58–9, 163, 166
France
   basic income estimation 170
   child care policies 181
   elections, and populism 9, 24–5
   employment protection 165, 166–7
   family allowances 175
   health care spending 138, 144
   inequality 16
   long-term care 151n1, 156
   social spending 26
   vs. UK model 184–5
Front National (FN) 9, 24–5
fully funded schemes (pensions) 126, 128

GAFA (Google, Apple, Facebook, Amazon) 68
GDP
   per capita 13t2.1
   and social expenditure 26–8, 30, 31f3.2, 35f3.4, 35t3.4, 85–6, 138
   impact of taxation on 83
generosity vs. redistribution 50, 72
Germany
   basic income estimation 171
   employment 159, 160, 173
   family allowances 175, 177
   government responsibility 54
   health care expenditure 138
   inequality 16, 22
   long-term care 156
   pension system 126, 134
   poverty 14
Gini coefficient 13t2.1, 15–17, 19t2.3, 20f2.5, 70, 165
globalization 61
   and employment 62–3

impact on private insurance 115
and information networks 75
and populism 63
and redistribution 69–72, 75–6
and tax competition 64–7
Greece
   employment 159, 163
   family allowances 175
   health care expenditure 139, 142, 144, 145
   in-work poverty 171
   poverty 12
   social spending 29, 124

HDI (Human Development Index) 73–4, 75n7, 185
health care 9, 137–8
   access to 142, 146t11.3, 147f11.2–11.3
   cost containment 142–4
   efficiency studies 97t8.2
   expenditure 138–42
   inequality 144–8
   insurance 107, 111, 113, 115, 118, 142
   and life expectancy 142
   performance indicators 99
   private vs. public 148, 149t11.5
   and social spending 29, 34, 48, 92
   see also long-term care (LTC)
Health Maintenance Organizations (HMO) 141
households
   and cost containment 143
   and expenditure on labour market policy 162
   in-work poverty 171–3
   Matthew effect on 91–2
   poverty measurement 12–13, 15, 17–18, 22
housing expenditures 29, 89, 92
Hungary
   family allowances 175
   poverty 17, 128
   social burden 30

income inequality 22–3, 50, 73, 87, 188
   impact of social spending 19–20
   measurement 12–13, 15–17
   at old age 127
   and redistribution 51, 55
   role of the family 106
Income Support 48
individual behaviour
   effect of taxes and benefits on 79–81
individualization 59
inequality 70
   and economic growth 85–7
   in health care 144–8
   performance indicators 99, 100t8.3

215

Subject Index

inequality (*cont.*)
  and poverty 12–13, 15–17, 25, 127–8
  and social expenditure 91–3
  see also equity-efficiency trade-off; social divide
informal care *see* long-term care
information networks 75
in kind transfers 48t5.1, 116, 119
insecurity 14, 91
  of working conditions 167, 169
in-work poverty 171–3
Ireland
  ageing in 153
  family allowances 175, 178, 179
  insurance expenditure 108
  in-work poverty 171
  social spending 29, 39
  wage tax 42, 46, 63

labour
  mobility 58, 64, 65, 67, 69, 114, 167–8
  taxation 40–4
labour market
  policy expenditures 161–2
  and social insurance 114
  social protection 29t3.2, 39
Latvia
  employment protection 165
  health care expenditure 138, 139
  poverty 17, 128
  social spending 26
lay-off tax 167
'leaky bucket' 5
life expectancy 8, 23, 73, 99, 104tA.8.4
  ageing trends 128, 132, 136
  indicators 142
  social insurance redistribution 107
life insurance 44, 107, 115
Lithuania
  family allowances 175
  health care spending 138, 139
  inequality 16
long-term care (LTC) 150
  expenditure 150–1, 153–4
  insurance puzzle 153
  programme designs 154–6
  role of the family 152–3, 155–6
Lorenz curve 15
lump-of-output fallacy 132
lump-sum tax 82–3
Luxembourg
  employment 130, 160
  family allowances 175, 178
  government responsibility 54
  health care expenditure 138, 139
  insurance expenditure 108
  tax competition 67

mandatory schemes 33, 34, 36, 98, 125, 131
marginal tax 40, 51, 88, 177
market, and social protection 4–5
market failure 8, 11
  and government intervention 7
  in social insurance 111–12, 117
Marxism 9
maternity 29, 175, 179
Matthew effect 53–4, 91–3, 103
means-tested programmes 2, 48–9, 50, 190
  for child allowances 175
  disadvantages 51, 84
  efficacy debates 53
  in health care 153
  inefficiency 90
  in long-term care 156
  for unemployment 161
merit goods 8n5, 107
mobility 2, 10, 71–2, 76, 186–7
  and income equality 22, 23
  labour 58, 64, 65, 67, 69, 114, 167–8
moral hazard 111–12, 115, 117t9.3, 143, 149t11.5

Netherlands
  child policies 180
  disability compensation 52, 131
  employment protection 164, 165
  employment ratio 161
  family allowances 175
  health care 138, 139, 144, 145
  inequality 16
  in-work poverty 171
  long-term care spending 154
  poverty 12, 18, 22, 23, 70, 128
  social spending 27, 30
net social spending 35–6
'New Contract for Welfare' 184
'new social question' 8n4
non-profit sector 4–5, 96
Nordic Dual Income Tax 64n3
Norway 22, 180
notional defined contribution (NDC) principle 126, 134

OMC (Open Method of Coordination) 72–3, 74t6.3, 77tA.6.2, 101
openness
  and poverty alleviation 69, 71f6.5
  and redistribution 67, 69, 71f6.4, 76tA.6.1
  and social spending 70
opportunistic behaviour 3–4
Oregon (USA) 143–4
out-of-pocket-spending 34, 118, 143, 144, 146, 148

216

Subject Index

paradox of redistribution 43
Pareto optimality 7
paternalistic altruism 9
pay-as-you-go (PAYG) 81, 126, 128, 129, 131, 133, 134
payroll tax 38–40, 45
  alternatives to 44–5
  on earnings-related schemes 52
  and employment protection 167
  impact on competition 41–3
  as regressive 40–1
  shrinking tax base 43–4
  and social insurance 44–5, 114–15
pensions 123
  expenditures 29, 124–5
  financing regimes 126
  future trends 133–6
  old-age dependency ratio 128–9
  and old-age employment 129–32
  and poverty alleviation 126–8
  sustainability of 124, 133
performance of the welfare state 3, 4, 11, 73, 75, 86–7, 98–103, 182, 185
point system (PS) schemes 126, 134
Poland 30, 138, 144, 160
political economy 9, 86, 175
populism
  and globalization 61, 63
  and social divides 9–10, 23–5
Portugal
  employment 160
  family allowances 175
  health care expenditure 29, 138, 139
  performance 101
  poverty 22, 23
posted workers 69, 167–8
poverty
  child 177–9
  family allowances 174–7
  increases in 14
  and inequality 5–6, 12–13, 15–17, 25, 92
  in-work 171–3
  and life-cycle income 21
  performance indicators 99, 100t8.3
  persistent 22–3
  poverty trap 52, 80–1
  regression analyses 18, 19t2.3, 20
  and social spending 18–19
poverty alleviation 15
  and altruism 9
  and charity 110
  and economic growth 86, 87
  effects of 17–18
  efficacy 53
  and openness 69, 71f6.5
  and pensions 126–8

poverty line 12
prisoner's dilemma 76
private insurance 106
  credibility and commitment 115–16
  expenditure 108–10
  and globalization 115
  and the labour market 114
  in long-term care 152–3, 155
  vs. public 117–18, 148, 149t11.5
  redistribution 107
productive efficiency 89, 103
  measurement 94–8
profit shifting 68
PSD (Prestation Spécifique Dépendance) 156

QUALIS (quality-adjusted life years) 142

race to the bottom 62, 64–7, 69, 72, 187
Rawlsian maximin 9
redistribution 4–5, 75–6, 88
  and economic growth 86–7
  effects on social protection 17–23
  ethical issues 56, 72
  vs. generosity 50
  and health care financing 146, 148t11.4
  inefficiency of 90–3, 189
  market 4–5
  Matthew effect 53–4, 91–3
  and openness 69, 71f6.4, 76tA.6.1
  paradox 53
  and poverty alleviation 9, 17–18
  and social insurance 107, 112–13, 116–22
  survey on 55
regime cluster states 49
regressiveness
  of health spending 146
  of payroll tax 40–1
replacement income 40, 44, 181
responsibilization 54, 56–7, 59, 106
retirement homes 95, 96, 97t8.2
retirement insurance 94, 115
RMI (Revenu Minimum d'Insertion) 48
Romania
  family allowances 175
  health care 138, 145
  inequality 16
  in-work poverty 171
  labour market policy expenditure 162
  poverty 12, 23, 177

savings 81, 115
Scandinavian model 49, 59
self-employment tax 44
self-insurance 106n2, 112
self-interest 8, 90
sharing economy 68–9, 158, 188
single provision 117t9.3, 141, 143

217

Subject Index

Slovakia
  ageing in 153
  health spending 139
  poverty of the elderly 128
Slovenia
  employment protection 165
  inequality 16
  poverty 23
social burden 30, 32–3, 36, 86
social cohesion 1, 9–10, 86
social contracts *see* 'veil of ignorance'
social-democratic states 49
social divide 188–9
  and populism 9–10, 23–5
social dumping 4, 41, 62, 69, 76, 114, 117t9.3, 167, 168
social insurance 4, 105–6, 141
  administrative costs 93–4
  contributions 45–6
  credibility and commitment 115–16
  defining features 106–8
  expenditure 108–10
  and the labour market 114
  long-term care 151–6
  market failures 111–12
  vs. private insurance 117–18
  and redistribution 107, 112–13, 116–22
  role of the family 106
social protection 4, 5f1.1
  charity 110
  effects of redistribution 17–23
  expenditure and private insurance 109t9.2
  and political economy 9
  taxonomy of 48–60
social risks 14, 110n4, 111, 112
social security 3, 34, 53, 58
  and GDP 86
  and individual behaviour 80, 81
  and social spending 29, 33, 93–4
solidarity contributions 38, 40, 52
Spain
  employment protection 165
  and inequality 16
  in-work poverty 171
  long-term care spending 154
  poverty 12, 14, 18
SPI (Sum of Partial Indicators) 73, 99, 100, 101f8.2
Sweden
  basic income estimate 170
  child policies 180
  elderly employment 130, 160
  family allowances 175
  health care expenditure 138, 139
  inequality 16, 22
  performance indicators 99
  poverty 14

  social spending 70
  tax wedge 42
Switzerland
  basic income estimate 171

tagging (redistribution) 120–1
taxation
  and charities 110
  confiscatory 82, 83
  distortionary 82
  efficiency *vs.* equity 6
  and family allowances 176–7
  lump-sum tax 82–3
  see also payroll tax
tax competition
  and globalization 64–8
  payroll tax 41–3
tax havens 68
tax shifting 41
tax wedge 41–3, 45
transport, public spending 92
trickle-down theory 6

Uber, uberization 69, 168–9
UK
  basic income estimate 170
  employment protection 165
  vs. French model 184–5
  health care spending 138, 141
  inequality 92
  long-term care 155
  poverty 14, 23
unemployment
  active and passive 57–8
  disincentives 80–1
  and flexibility 59
  and globalization 62
  insurance 161–3
  performance indicators 99, 100t8.3
  and poverty 13–14
  rates 158–60
  and social spending 29, 33, 37
universalistic benefits *see* flat benefits
US
  basic income estimate 171
  debates on welfare regimes 52–3
  Earned Income Tax Credit (EITC) 52
  elections, and populism 9, 24
  employment protection 165
  employment rate 160
  health care spending 138, 142, 143–4
  health insurance costs 94
  income inequality 22
  populism 63
  poverty 12
  social spending 27, 30, 34, 48

Subject Index

'veil of ignorance,' social contracts 8, 113, 186

wages
 distribution of 19–20
 and globalization 63
 minimum 163–6
wage tax 79–83
welfare state
 British *vs.* French 184–5
 definition 4n3
 development 7–9
 digitalization 187–8
 efficiency 88–103
 financing 38–46
 future reforms 189–91
 models 47–60
 performance 98–102
 questioning 1–2
 trends 186–7
work *see* employment
workfare 58
 and social insurance redistribution 117, 121–2
workforce *see* labour
World Value Survey 57

yardstick competition 73

219